Praise f
Homest

D0000360

"*Homestead* is one of my all-time favorite works of nonfiction. It literally makes me laugh and cry. Jane's experiences amaze me, her gift of writing inspires me, and the way she lives her life gives me real courage to face the challenges in my own. *Homestead* is a must-read for anyone who wants to embrace the realities and rewards of a well-lived life. Well done, Jane!"

—MELODY CARLSON, author of *Crystal Lies* and *Finding Alice*

"*Homestead* is a moving adventure story of modern pioneers, full of courage, hard work, tender moments, and life-changing experiences."

—BARBARA JENKINS, co-author of *The Walk West* and
The Road Unseen

"*Homestead* is a rich, compelling story that combines the spirit of adventure with the warmth and humor of a James Herriot tale."

—*Oregon Historical Quarterly*

HOMESTEAD

OTHER BOOKS BY JANE KIRKPATRICK

NOVELS

A Land of Sheltered Promise

Tender Ties Historical Series
A Name of Her Own
(Oregon Book Award finalist, Ken Kesey Award for the Novel)
Every Fixed Star
Hold Tight the Thread

Kinship and Courage Historical Series
All Together in One Place
(finalist, Best Inspirational Novel, Affair de Coeur)
No Eye Can See
What Once We Loved

Dreamcatcher Collection
A Sweetness to the Soul
(winner of the Western Heritage Wrangler Award for Outstanding
Western Novel of 1995; named by Oregon Heritage Commission
as one of Oregon's Best 100 Books published in past two hundred years)
Love to Water My Soul
A Gathering of Finches
Mystic Sweet Communion

NONFICTION

A Simple Gift of Comfort
(formerly *A Burden Shared*)
inclusion in anthologies: *Crazy Woman Creek*
and *The Storytellers' Collection Book 2*
Daily Guideposts, 1992

Modern Pioneers Pursuing the Edge of Possibility

HOMESTEAD

JANE KIRKPATRICK

A MEMOIR BY THE AWARD-WINNING AUTHOR OF *ALL TOGETHER IN ONE PLACE*

WATERBROOK
PRESS

HOMESTEAD
PUBLISHED BY WATERBROOK PRESS
12265 Oracle Boulevard, Suite 200
Colorado Springs, Colorado 80921
A division of Random House Inc.

Portions of this story have been published in *Northwest Magazine* of the Sunday *Oregonian,* *Ruralite* magazine, *Western Flyer* magazine, *Small Farmer's Journal,* Willamette Writers' Kay Snow Contest winners, and "Jane's Monthly Memos" at www.jkbooks.com.

Scripture quotations are taken from the the following: *New King James Version.* Copyright © 1982 by Thomas Nelson Inc. Used by permission. All rights reserved. *King James Version. New American Standard Bible®.* © Copyright The Lockman Foundation 1960, 1962, 1963, 1968, 1971, 1972, 1973, 1975, 1977, 1995. Used by permission. (www.Lock man.org). *Holy Bible, New International Version®.* NIV®. Copyright © 1973, 1978, 1984 by International Bible Society. Used by permission of Zondervan Publishing House. All rights reserved.

ISBN 1-4000-7061-9

Cover photo by Jerry Kirkpatrick: the landscape of the homestead on a winter morning.

Library of Congress Cataloging-in-Publication Data
Kirkpatrick, Jane, 1946–
    Homestead : a memoir of modern pioneers pursuing the edge of possibility / Jane Kirkpatrick.— 1st ed.
        p. cm.
    ISBN 1-4000-7061-9
    1. Frontier and pioneer life—Oregon—John Day River Valley. 2. Pioneers—Oregon—John Day River Valley—Biography. 3. Kirkpatrick, Jane, 1946—Family. 4. Kirkpatrick family. 5. John Day River Valley (Or.)—Social life and customs. 6. John Day River Valley (Or.)—Biography. I. Title.
    F882.J76K57 2005
    979.5'78—dc22

                                                            2005016963

Printed in the United States of America
2005—First Edition

10 9 8 7 6 5 4 3 2 1

To Jerry,
who kept his faith in God,
the dream,
and me

Desire accomplished is sweet to the soul.
PROVERBS 13:19

Moses' hands became heavy…[so] Aaron and
Hur supported his hands.
EXODUS 17:12

Prologue

LIKE STEPPINGSTONES ALONG a meandering stream, dirty puddles of water dotted the dusty road. Nothing more than a trail, really, the remote old road cut a wagon-width path through rolling acres of Oregon wheat fields. Barbed cheat grass and weeds growing between the tire tracks scratched against the bottom of the almost-new Datsun station wagon.

A tail of dust billowed up behind us, which seemed odd, with water standing in the road.

"Must have been a rain shower shortly before we got here," I noted. I shifted down, slowing the car as we hit the first puddle, spattering mud against the bright red paint. The slower pace helped us maneuver the ruts, already hardened, which another vehicle had carved into the road some time before us. Slowing down didn't relieve my anxiety about being on that isolated trail, however.

Slick, tarry mud pulled against the tires, forcing a fishtail swerve. The men wouldn't be happy if they knew we were driving here without anyone knowing. Traffic was so scarce that no one would find us for days if we had trouble. The wind blew untethered across the wheat stubble, pushing at the little car as we bounced across the old, hard ruts and swerved through the puddles.

Years later, that trail would become the symbol of our conquered fears, of plans made and shifted, of the fickleness of nature and the constancy of faith, and of the kindness and complexity of the people who changed with us because we all drove down that old rutted road to carve a new one.

But on that day in 1982, I drove on that road for the first time.

"Jerry has always driven when we've come here before," I said to the somber passenger beside me. "But I'm sure this is the right way. I just didn't pay that much attention to the distance, so I'm not sure how far the dirt road goes before we reach the river." My friend, Kay Krall, nodded, her white knuckles grasping the door handle.

We traveled a few more miles in silence.

Pungent puppy breath steamed the edges of the windows. Too young to leave behind, two eight-week-old puppies accompanied us. Occasionally, we tried to drown out the squeals of the roly-poly pups by turning up Vivaldi's *Four Seasons* playing in the tape deck.

I adjusted the rearview mirror to deflect the sun's glare as it began its descent behind Mount Hood. Dusk would settle in soon. It would be unwise to stay out here until dark.

A massive power line stretched across the road in front of us, cutting a slice through the fields. The power company had replaced several of the huge steel structures and, like a giant deserting his Erector Set, tossed the old ones in a graveyard heap next to the road.

Beyond the power line lay vast miles of wheat land and prairie, with neither buildings nor trees to break the view. Wheat stubble glowed dark gold on either side of us, a sign that harvest—and the afternoon—was completed.

Fortunately, no snow yet slicked the narrow dirt road of Sherman County—Oregon's smallest—or dusted the fields like powdered sugar over fork-pressed peanut-butter cookies.

Purples and deep oranges on the rimrocks broke the dusky shadows in the distance above the John Day River—the river that would change my life, Jerry's, and the lives of others in ways we couldn't have imagined then.

As Kay and I rode in the Datsun, we couldn't see the river yet; but I pointed, directing Kay's eyes to the top of the dry ravines that broke steeply to the stream below.

An occasional chukar, a game partridge, ran down the road in front of us before lifting and setting its striped wings to soar down one of the deep ravines. A mule deer popped its head above the sagebrush, then, seemingly unconcerned with our presence, lowered its head to resume grazing.

The puddles disappeared from the center of the road as we rolled down a steep incline. The Datsun straddled more deep ruts before we reached flatter ground. We crossed one cattle guard and then another. Finally, Kay said cautiously, "Just how far away *was* the last farmhouse?"

"There was a ranch about six miles back," I answered with my most positive voice, "but no one lives there. The nearest real person, I think, lives just before we left the pavement, nearly eleven miles back."

Kay nodded again, and I loved her for not saying aloud what she must have been thinking.

The road now wound through native bunch grass and pale sage. "It *is* beautiful," Kay said, though her voice was still strained. "I've never seen so much open space with nothing to break it up. We can see for fifty miles. Sure different from Wisconsin." She was referring to our shared native state, the one I'd left eight years earlier.

As I concentrated on avoiding the larger rocks that seemed to be growing in the road, our pace slowed even more. I hoped the tires were good and that we wouldn't have a breakdown.

Eventually, we dropped down another steep descent on what resembled a cattle path. On Kay's side, the road hugged a hill as steep as a cow's face; on my side, deep ravines cut away from the road's edge. A rock knocked loose by the Datsun bounced like a basketball over the close edge, dropping nearly nine hundred feet to the bottom. I longed for guardrails and reflectors.

We crept around the hairpin turn, the needle not even registering on the speedometer. My foot hovered over the brake. I stayed as close to the inside edge as I could, remembering a time when my mother had driven us on a steep dirt road after a rain in Wisconsin, and the side of the road had fallen away.

And then we saw it: a panoramic view of massive canyon walls topped by ancient lava flows, signatures of river breaks. They'd been carved by ages of wind, occasional rains, and the perpetual flow of our destination, the John Day River.

The river still meandered as it had a century ago, when thousands of pioneers had crossed it six miles downstream, nearing the end of the Oregon Trail. It meandered twenty-nine more miles before flowing into the Columbia River, separating Oregon from its northern neighbor, the state of Washington. It meandered right through the ranch. *Our* ranch, the one we now owned. There were no buildings, no electricity, no phone; only this precipitous, rutted dirt road to bring us to our 160 acres bordering that wild and scenic river.

I stopped the car, set the brake, and we got out to get a better view. The air was clean and clear. October air. Crisp, but not cold as it was 160 miles south, against the mountains near Bend, Oregon, where Jerry and I had been living during our six years of marriage. I inhaled the aroma of sage and listened to the quiet, which was broken only by the piercing call of a red-tailed hawk and the low chattering of Canada geese settling in along the river for the night.

Kay surveyed the view. I heard her catch her breath at the winding road before us. It had been simply bladed out of the side of the ridge and wound down like a potato peel past a tipped-over car deserted long ago. Other more vertical and now abandoned trails scarred the hills above it.

"The road goes all the way to the river, but I don't think we'll go any farther," I said. I wanted to reassure my friend that we would head back out before dark. "Our driveway turns off in another mile or so. It's pretty steep there." I remembered a sharp 16 percent incline with deep ruts that would swallow a truck tire. "When we're ready to leave, I think I can turn around right here," I said, "unless you *want* to go all the way down." I knew I didn't.

Kay hastily shook her head no.

She hadn't spoken. Either she was awed by the canyon, the river, and the road, or she was struggling to find something encouraging to say.

"You can't see the spot where we plan to build," I said, stepping to the edge and pointing. "It's sort of under this ridge, up on a bench, above the river flat, so if the river ever floods, as it did back in '64, the house won't be threatened. And we plan to have grapes on the bench above the river, and an airstrip someplace. We'll need to clear the sagebrush. It hasn't been farmed since the flood, but they raised hay on it then. We'll probably do that, too."

Kay was still silent, so I continued, filling the void. "I know the road is pretty bad, but it is a county road, even this part we're on…"

I didn't really want to know what my dearest and oldest friend thought about our plan to sell everything, leave secure jobs and family, and move here, twenty-five miles from the nearest town and eleven miles from a paved road. Most of the time, I could hardly describe our reasons to myself, let alone to someone else.

"Sometimes I think it's just insane, this plan to come here, grow grapes, and get out of our old ruts; but we both feel so strongly that it's what we're supposed to do. I don't know. Most people dropped out in the sixties. I guess we're just late bloomers," I added lamely.

We had shared our plans with few people, and had brought only my parents and two other friends to actually see the land, fearing the horror in their eyes as they contemplated the road and our "crazy scheme."

Jerry and Kay's husband, Don, were together elk hunting in the mountains, and she and I had toured Oregon for a week, sharing our vacations with the puppies. In two days, she and Don would be returning to Wisconsin, to jobs and routines and normal living. We would be temporarily returning to our normal life too, but with a difference: we had sold our house and were preparing to leave jobs and routines to come here, to homestead.

Kay turned. A tall woman, she looked down at me as she spoke, putting her arm around my shoulder, hugging me as only a great friend can do, and said, "I have a lump in my throat for you."

She squeezed my shoulder into hers as we stood staring out across the canyon that spread before us. I swallowed back my tears, not knowing I was rehearsing for a future that would take us beyond the old ruts of our relationships, expand our spiritual beliefs, push our bodies to their limits, test our skills and ingenuity, and force us to face our fears of failure, disappointments, and even death.

We couldn't see, then, what lay ahead. We couldn't see the agony, difficulties, and physical pain of harnessing a spring for drinking water, of securing electricity, of building a barn without electrical power, of living in a home so far from supplies, of laying miles of phone wire—twice—in 100-degree heat, of losing acres of crops to wind and days of work to floods. We couldn't see the shell of the plane, the fuselage bent, its wing destroyed, its seats becoming a house for a striped cat.

Nor could we know then of the miracles, large and small, and the people whom we would come to know and care about, who would help us, heal us, bring humor to our lives, share our tears and laughter, and take us closer to each other and to God.

"Pretty awesome, huh?" I asked, swallowing away the tears, trying to laugh. "I'm gonna be a rancher, writer, and rattlesnake fighter!"

"It isn't anything Don or I would want to do or *could* do," Kay said. "But I have no doubt that you and Jerry can make it happen."

I didn't feel safe enough then to tell her that it was our belief that our stepping out onto a cloud of faith, believing we wouldn't fall through, was what enabled us to take this risk.

We lingered a few minutes longer. I had felt peaceful once we had gotten to the land, but thinking of the road back created prickles on the back of my neck. "It could be dark before we hit the gravel again," I said, moving toward the car.

As we climbed back into the Datsun, I wondered just how far our new house *would* be from the pavement.

Gingerly, I turned the car around in the narrow rocky road, and we started climbing back up, then out across the open prairie. As we approached the wheat-stubbled fields, the road reverted from rock to dirt, the puddles reappeared, and we splashed through the ones I couldn't avoid. We both exhaled together as we plunged through the last mudhole and felt the tire grab the firmer gravel road. I laughed. "It's nice to be back on solid footing."

Kay smiled, patting my hand on the gearshift that separated our seats. "You guys are just incredible. How did you ever find this place?" she asked.

"Divine intervention!" I said. "There's just no other explanation!"

We chuckled together, then, as I began to tell her of this "intervention," not knowing that our faith in that explanation would be well tested. I also could not know then how that faith would carry us through the years as we bounced over the old ruts and onto the new roads we never dreamed were there.

Part I

SEEKING STARVATION POINT

God speaks to each of us:
You, sent out beyond your recall,
Go, to the limits of your longing.
Embody me.

—RAINER MARIA RILKE,
The Book of Hours, Love Poems to God

The reptile road.

1

The Burden of a Great Potential

I WAS THIRTY-THREE YEARS OLD in 1979 when we began our grand adventure with the land. Jerry had just turned forty-nine. We were old enough to understand the warning label some people put on life: Be careful what you wish for, because you just might get it. But we were still young enough to wish and hopeful enough to dream.

That's what the land was in the beginning, just something we dreamed about, a vision of "someday," when we would have enough acreage for some cattle. The land needed a year-round water supply and a several-month growing season suitable for nurturing grapes. Room for an airstrip was important too, although neither of us knew how to fly, and we didn't own a plane. But we had completed the aviation ground school and were optimistic.

We also shared a belief that the land needed to support more than just ourselves. In the beginning, we thought of this as physical support, like having enough room for a large garden whose bounty we would share, or for water and space for more than one family.

Later we would consider spiritual or emotional support as a function of the land. We didn't talk about that part much, because there was nothing logical about it.

Our vision was clearest when it was prompted by a news report on the wars and famine in the world or by a sermon on hunger and poverty. Then we'd both think of the land as a kind of refuge, where we imagined we could survive if things got rough in the outside world.

At other times, we felt the pull of the land without reason, often in the early morning, when each of us would discover the other was awake and we'd lie talking in the cool, predawn darkness.

"I can't explain it," Jerry would whisper quietly. "It's just that I think we might need to care for others, maybe in the family. Maybe my parents or yours, and we need the land to do that."

I understood the feeling without knowing why.

So we had begun looking at property just two years into our marriage, taking weekend trips to faraway places with names like Cove and Spray. We always stayed within Oregon, Jerry's native state.

If it all worked, we thought, when we found the perfect property, I'd quit my job as director of the local mental health center. We'd move there, wherever "there" was, living on the proceeds from the sale of our home and fifteen acres near Bend until the first grape harvest. Or something like that.

Our vision turned vague when we got into finances, or the reality of Jerry's physical limitations, his disability and back pain since falling from a scaffolding, or the fact that neither of us was a farmer, or that I seemed to need a lot of friends and enjoyed my job and liked carrying a briefcase and having my nails siliconed and manicured twice a month, or that we had never lived in an isolated area, or that we didn't know anything about grapes or... on and on and on.

And that's when I'd get scared.

But then the whole idea would seem as elusive as fireflies on a summer night—just another dream, like nighttime dreams that disappear with daylight.

On a June day in 1979, though, the dream was bright, and I was impatient to see the land.

My husband's former wife sat across from me, daintily picking at the plate of pastel scrambled eggs the waitress placed before her.

Looking through the restaurant window, I could see the Cascade Mountains shimmering white against a clear blue sky. A fresh snowfall on the Three Sisters Mountains the night before kept its promise of a cool morning in the foothills where Bend nestles. But by noon I'd be shedding my designer jeans and jacket for shorts and sunscreen.

The more than 270 days of sunshine and the dry alpine air were two of the reasons Jerry had returned to his hometown of Bend, leaving behind places like Ohio and Arizona where he'd made his living designing and building houses and small commercial buildings such as veterinary clinics and machine shops.

In 1973 the accident had left him with four broken vertebrae, two inches less height on his once five-foot-eleven-inch frame, and a changed life.

Jerry had a married daughter, Kathleen, who lived out of state. His only surviving son, Matt, lived with us during the school year. But in a few minutes, Matt would be leaving with Lelah, his mother, the woman picking at her scrambled eggs.

I thought of her as the pastel lady. She always looked so calm and cool, so perfect in pink, so consummately coiffured.

Their oldest son, Kevin, had been killed two years earlier, in 1977, while on a job interview in the Southwest. His body had been found on the Arizona desert, a victim of a gunshot wound. Since his brother's death, Matt had not done well, and the strings that held us all together were pulled tight, ready to snap. Eager for a relief, I was looking forward to being alone with Jerry for the next three months and happily looking together for land.

Jerry had found a listing for some property we'd be seeing later that day after Matt, Lelah, and her husband had left. The listing in the *Nickel Ads Magazine* was sandwiched between "used washing machines" and "used cars."

The acreage sat 160 miles north of Bend, almost on the Oregon-Washington border, in Sherman County. The ad described "320 acres along the John Day River surrounded by BLM [Bureau of Land Management] land. $95,000 cash."

"We don't have ninety-five thousand dollars, Jerry," I pointed out. But such realities never bothered my husband much, which was why he managed to accomplish so many things, refusing to be limited by the facts.

"There isn't much land available along the John Day," he said. "I haven't heard of any being sold for years, except to the Rajneeshees. If this is real, it would be too good to pass up."

"We don't need 320 acres, do we?" I persisted, thinking of my fantasy garden of a few peas and carrots.

But on that day in June 1979, Jerry wanted to see that acreage, so we hugged Matt, shook his stepdad's hand, waved good-bye to Lelah, and headed north.

The pictures we took that day show us beaming happily, Jerry and I waving from inside our green Chevy pickup truck.

My short mousy brown hair stood out against Jerry's prematurely white hair and closely trimmed beard. His face was already tanned to a handsome bronze, thanks to his Choctaw heritage. My sturdy German stock kept me pale. We wore jeans, the casual wear of a Central Oregon Saturday, topped with a western shirt for Jerry and a blue, bare-midriff sun top for me. I planned to sunbathe beside the John Day River.

We left behind the hardy juniper trees and pines of Bend, driving north on Highway 97, passing through the fragrant scents of mint and anise near Madras, then on through towns that became increasingly smaller: the ghost town of Shaniko, then Kent, population 28. A population surge in Grass Valley, 165, was followed by another in Moro, 302.

Few trees dotted the landscape during our morning trip, except in towns where they'd been tended lovingly for years.

Near Kent, where Sherman County began, the fields turned to the greens of winter wheat, or the gold of stubble, or to dark, plowed ground lying fallow and collecting moisture before being seeded in the fall. Rainfall, not irrigation, fed the thirsty soil.

The landscape seemed monotonous, broken only by an occasional grain elevator or ranch. I hoped the piece of property we were driving to didn't look as barren as this.

"No trees," I said.

"Only eight inches of rainfall," Jerry said; then we both went back inside our thoughts.

We drove into Moro, the county seat, one town short of where we were to meet the real-estate agent. We stopped at the lush city park, then walked briefly around the town. We sauntered past a general store, the Branding Iron Bar and Restaurant, and the newspaper office with its double-facade front. Later we learned that the paper came out whenever it wanted to. A white church steeple sliced through leafy trees of a street beyond. Dogs barked in the distance.

Past a little office that turned out to be the library, the flavor of this rural county of twenty-two hundred people was captured in a list on the library window that announced overdue books and their tardy readers. Two titles were checked out to the same person. The first was *Everything You Ever Wanted to Know About Sex but Were Afraid to Ask.* I wondered, would I want everyone in the community to know that I had that book out? And that it was overdue? The second title, checked out to the same person, was *What to Name the Baby.*

We left Moro, drove ten miles farther, dipped into a dimple within the rolling wheat fields, and found Wasco, a town of three hundred, where we waited for the agent under the shade of a huge locust tree. An old depot building burned hot in the sun, a remnant of bygone years when Wasco had been a booming town with railroads and families following workers who were constructing the big hydroelectric dams on the Columbia River just a few miles north.

Now men in caps and blue coveralls visited in preharvest leisure beside pickups parked in the Sherman County Grain Growers' parking lot. Nearby, children laughed, eating ice-cream cones as they walked the quiet sidewalks past the little drugstore, a barber shop, a restaurant, and Dale's Clothing and Liquor Store.

Bart, the agent, arrived, and we headed east, following him out of town, driving through more wheat country, and finally turning north onto a gravel road.

When the road made a sharp turn to the left, Bart's truck slowed and pulled onto a dirt road that seemed to disappear into a green field.

This can't be a driveway, I thought.

Bart climbed into our truck with us, and we drove through the field along the faintly visible trail. "It's seven miles ahead," Bart said calmly. "If you buy this place, you'll have to give me rights to fish for steelhead." He smiled. "It has one of the best native runs in the state."

Bart and Jerry chatted about the terrain and the population of the chukar, a favorite game bird of Jerry's, and of the deer herds in the area, while I wondered what a steelhead looked like.

I don't remember many details of our trip that day as we rumbled down the canyon with Bart. But I do remember the first breathtaking view of the river and the 220 acres he showed us first. He was a good salesman, show-ing us what the land *could* look like—with a lot of work.

Grass rose belly-high to the cattle that grazed lazily along the river. Blue sky reflected in the clear water. A few Canada geese stood sentry along the gravel bars, either early returnees from the south or year-round nesters. Tall, lichen-licked rocks rubbed the river's edge. Bees flitted from wildflower to wildflower as the blossoms' sweet, warm fragrance filled our heads.

Jerry and I walked hand in hand along the river, one of the most peace-ful places I'd ever been. We ignored, temporarily, how far we were from civi-lization and the difficulties we had had in getting there.

"You can grow anything here," Bart said, waving his hand to take in the wide expanse of river bottom. "See those fruit trees there, and the walnut tree? This piece wasn't affected by the flood of '64. Those trees survived." He paused to admire them. "The growing season goes at least a month longer down here in the canyon than on top. Hard freezes won't come until late October usually," he continued.

"There was a homestead there once." He pointed to a cluster of old farm buildings and trees. "But the house burned."

Burned?

Later I would remember that.

Bart said a family had lived in the house, once, in modern times; they had kids who went to school, traveling the steep, winding road year-round. At least I *thought* that's what he said.

Bart also told us about rattlesnakes and black widow spiders. But I quickly forgot his warnings, proving that we hear what we choose to hear.

We returned along the same road, passing through two gates, still following the meandering river, until we came to the other section of land that was for sale, about 160 acres, ten of it across the river.

We didn't actually drive onto this land. We started up the switchback road, crossed a fake cattle guard, stopped at the top, and looked down over the edge toward the river below. Since we didn't have the money anyway, since the owners wanted cash, and since the only *reasonable* piece of land— if either was reasonable at all—was the first one, which had power running to it and buildings that resembled civilization, and where the land was already under cultivation, I just discounted this undeveloped 160 acres.

I returned my attention to the book I'd brought along.

Bart and Jerry discussed how Bob and Marion Boynton, the owners, had once farmed the piece; and they talked about when the steelhead ran.

An old homesteader's cabin sat on a bench above the river. "Old Con Davis lived there for years," Bart reminisced, taking me from my book. "He had a spring down there somewhere. That could be your domestic water supply. It wasn't hurt in the flood of '64." This last statement was spoken in Bart's softest voice. "Still," he added, as only a grand salesman can, "it's got great potential."

Great potential.

I remembered a poster I'd once had on my office door showing a cartoon character philosophizing that one of life's heaviest burdens is "a great potential."

On the drive back into Wasco together, Jerry asked Bart if the owners would take any less money for the acreage, or break it up, or finance any part of it, since we didn't have $95,000 in cash.

Bart said we were the first people he'd shown the land to, and if we were interested, he'd see what he could do.

I don't remember being interested. In fact, I had a headache, and we stopped at the Wasco Drugstore for aspirin. The white-haired pharmacist took my money, then, surprisingly, handed me a glass of water.

"Anyone buying aspirin on a nice day like this," he said, "must be wanting to take some right away."

Driving home, Jerry and I discussed the land's "potential." To me, it didn't seem to have any. It had a northern exposure, no electricity, no running water, and no buildings other than the weathered cabin. A terrible road wound down to it, and it was covered with twelve-foot-tall sagebrush.

True, it had room for an airstrip. ("But we don't own a plane!")

And while the size was right, the growing season perfect, and the water supply supposedly sufficient, the thought of building a home and living there, deep down in the canyon, so far from anything, sobered me. I enjoyed *reading* diaries of homesteaders, admiring their stamina and grit, but I knew I didn't want to endure the same kinds of hardships myself.

A few weeks went by before Jerry informed me that the owners would only sell the 160-acre section, the plot with no buildings but bountiful sagebrush, though at terms we could manage over the next ten years.

I had secretly hoped they wouldn't sell. It was such a very long way from my manicurist.

The day we actually wrote the check purchasing our "potential," we looked at a detailed map of the region. Our property bordered the John Day

River for a half-mile; it was part of a federal waterfowl refuge. Eight thousand acres of mostly public lands surrounded it. A state scenic waterway, the John Day River, ran through it, and it was reachable on a long, winding, rutted—but public—dirt road. On the map, our property was labeled "Starvation Point," announcing to all the world that we were purchasing "poverty property."

That should have been a sign.

But the most significant piece of paper we carried away that day described the water rights. There was something solemn about the passing on of words written seventy years earlier. The thin, parchmentlike paper brown with age offered barely readable words, but it was the umbilical cord from the past to the present, the key to our survival. If we were to truly live on the land, we needed the river and the water.

Thirty-seven acre-feet of river water went with the property. We hoped it would be enough to irrigate the flat and the bench that paralleled the river, where the grapes would grow. The water was our lifeline, so the assurance of its presence, written there on old brown paper, remains what I remember most of the day we purchased our great potential and began our grand adventure with the land.

2

Intruders on Starvation Point

ELSIE DRINKARD RODE IN AND OUT of our lives one day in a cloud of dust, teaching us in minutes what some folks never learn, that newcomers are intruders who must accommodate and compromise in order to survive.

It was early October 1979—hunting season in Oregon. We decided to camp while Jerry hunted on our land. Wanting peace and quiet, we headed for our hidden valley, where we were unlikely to encounter intruders.

It was my first time actually setting foot on our soil and not just looking down on it from the top of the ridge-hugging road.

The winding, twisting portion of the road seemed bad enough, but I could taste fear in my mouth as I looked at the incline leading off the public dirt road and onto our private dirt driveway. My stomach churned precariously as Jerry aimed the truck (filled with tent, gear, and dog) down the steep grade that resembled the screaming side of a roller coaster.

I braced myself, sure we would break an axle in the deep washes, or worse, tip the truck over. By the time we reached the bottom, where hard rains had sliced an open wound in the dirt, I was hyperventilating and wishing I'd taken a double dose of my stomach-acid medicine.

Jerry stopped the truck and turned to me.

"You're being silly, you know," he said. "It's just dirt. Nothing bad is going to happen here."

"I'm just not used to it!" I said, my voice shaking.

"We'll grade the road, smooth it out when we move, and it'll be just fine," he assured me, patting my knee. I had little time to argue as Jerry hit the accelerator to gain enough speed to climb the steep hill up the other side of the roller-coaster grade. With large eyes I saw we were headed straight toward the river. But as my scream escaped, the truck turned quickly, and we spun around a corner resembling the arc on the padlock guarding the gate a few yards farther up the last steep incline.

I caught my breath while Jerry opened the wire gate.

To our right, benches of sagebrush-sprinkled land reached out like fat fingers toward the river. Between the benches sank jagged ravines crisscrossed with deer trails. Like a blue-satin ribbon circling a gift wrapped in hazy greens and browns, the river wound its way along the entire edge of the property on the right. A spear of land formed an island at the gate end of the river. Downstream, the water made a bend back toward the ridge we'd just wound down and then turned north in a sweeping arc that disappeared out of sight.

To our left, the bunch grass moved up a hill nearly as steep as a cow's face. Farther along, old rocks dribbled their way down the ravines to the river. A lava-rock wall hugged the river on the other side, too, right to the bend, where a row of trees separated the river from a neighbor's field. There, the hills reached nine hundred feet or more to the top.

I rolled down the truck window. The air felt sultry but sweet with the scent of blooming sage. Jerry drove on slowly, trying to engage me in his vision. "We'll plant grapes on the bench," he said. His arm swept across the windshield toward the river. "And we'll clear the flat and put the alfalfa in there, next to the river. Of course, we'll have to move some dirt back from when the flood hit. Look! Up there! That's the top of the road we just came down."

My eyes followed his, searching upward along a ravine that reached easily nine hundred feet above us. Had we really just come from there, that point so far away?

"I figure the barn and hangar can go near that shack." He pointed to a lower bench almost straight ahead. We were approaching the bottom of another steep grade, only slightly less frightening than the previous roller-coaster section.

He parked next to the weathered cabin. Rusty engine parts and bolts, bent tin cans, and broken glass littered the area like aphid dust around a rosebush. Uneven rocks served as the cabin's foundation. A lean-to kitchen off the back kept it from being perfectly square. Two windows faced us; one window and a door faced the river. Another small window looked out at us from under the roofline.

Inside, a homemade ladder of sagebrush roots led up to the loft; old pots and pans lay scattered about. The floor had holes and mouse remains. Tumbleweeds clustered in the corners.

I wondered if Jerry would suggest we live here.

"Con Davis used to salvage junked cars," Jerry said, wise from his visits with Bob and Marion Boynton, who had bought the land from Con and later sold it to us. "They say he was quite a character. He used to bring home people who were down and out and help 'em out through the winter. He sure picked a good spot to live."

Jerry took in a deep breath, looking out the empty window toward the river. "The view is perfect—lots of sun, and well above the flat if the river should flood again. We could fix it up to live in while we build."

He didn't see my eyes enlarge as he continued.

"Con's water supply came from over there somewhere, I guess." He pointed to a grassy area to our right, below the bench where the road seemed to disappear beneath the gnarled green growth of sagebrush and slick weed.

We set up camp in the grassy area, where six-foot-high sagebrush soon filtered shade onto our tent.

After unloading the cooking and reading supplies, we set up two lawn chairs and drifted slowly into the evening, talking around a small fire and patting Ricky, our English setter, as he lay at our feet in the dust. I could see the cabin from where I sat. It might not be so bad to live in. For a while. We'd have to buy window glass and doors.

Though the river was almost a quarter of a mile away across the flat, we heard the water wash gently against a ripple. We slept soundly that first night on our land.

In the morning, birds of a half-dozen different varieties—meadowlarks, red-tailed hawks, nighthawks, thrushes, and geese—serenaded us. In the distance, a blue heron rose from the river's edge, dragging its slender legs against the pink morning sky, barely lifting its body above the rimrocks.

No street sounds, no machine sounds, no phones ringing. No stomach acid.

Jerry left early to go hunting, and I had the day to explore, or simply sit and read. I marveled at the distance between me and any other human being (besides Jerry, somewhere in a ravine). The nearest neighbor ranched eleven miles, three cattle guards, and a winding dirt road away. Who knew where the nearest phone rang? A trip to town was twenty-five miles from where I sat beside the river in the shade of the sage. We'd have to set our mailbox, should we ever live here, seven miles away.

A thimbleful of fear nudged at me as I sat there alone, removed from help in case of danger. I wondered about my courage should something go wrong. But contentment also visited. I knew I was truly "by myself," free to do whatever I wanted: yell, scream, dance in the sand.

I made my way through the tangle of sagebrush to the river, exploring. Between my fingers, I filtered the fine black sand, said to hold specks of gold; I filled my pockets with rainbows of agates glistening on the long stretches of beach. I listened to the distant calls of geese making seasonal stops. River fragrances carried on occasional breezes drifted by. Time vanished as I sat hugging my knees by the river.

As it neared noon, the breezes ceased. I could feel the heat of the canyon sucking my energy, even in October, and I walked slowly back to the tent, happy to gather up my reading book and Ricky for company.

My solitude was soon broken by the hum of a distant engine. I heard it, then saw it: a vehicle chased by a parachute of dust far above me on the ridge. The truck disappeared around the switchback, then materialized again along a lower ridge, then on a bench above the tent, then twisting, turning, and dropping until it stopped before me in a spray of dirt.

Intruders had arrived in a dusty, beat-up pickup truck.

The driver was a large woman who appeared to be in her late fifties (though her sunburned, weathered face could have camouflaged a younger soul). Beside her were two unsmiling teenage girls; behind her, in the truck box, sat two dust-shrouded boys.

They all appeared to be locals, but I wasn't sure if the natives were friendly.

They all wore faded western wear. One of the girls was especially attractive, with large brown eyes setting off her striking, somber face. The others I don't remember much.

The older woman shut off the truck's engine, obviously intending to stay. I stood up but kept my distance.

"The name's Elsie Drinkard," the woman said, introducing herself while she leaned out of the open truck window, one elbow perched against the frame. "You the new owners?"

"Yes," I said. "We're the Kirkpatricks."

"These are my kids," she said, shrugging her head toward the silent majority in the truck. "They's rattlesnakes 'round these parts," she said next, though I don't think she meant to mention the reptiles in the same breath as her children. "Gets pretty dangerous sometimes."

Because I had forgotten Bart's earlier warning, her words unsettled me as I recalled my day exploring, having paid scant attention to where I reached or sat.

Trying to sound nonchalant, I said, "We had rattlers in Wisconsin, too. But most of the time you never saw them."

She grunted, perhaps surprised that I hadn't been frightened by the snakes.

"Where you from, now?" she challenged next. "Portland?"

It was said with a kind of contempt, the way some Oregonians refer to visitors from California, or Wisconsinites comment on those big-city visitors from Chicago. I knew from her tone that she considered me a greenhorn who was in over my head.

"No, from Bend," I answered, hoping that town wasn't too urban for Elsie.

"You gonna live here?" she persisted.

"Maybe someday. Not for a while, though," I said.

She was thoughtful. A meadowlark warbled in the pause.

Then deciding to lay her visit on the line, she said, "Well, I own all the land that surrounds yours." She moved her thick, muscular arm expansively, to take in the land we'd been told was public land. "Graze my cattle on it," she finished, not expecting a response. I had noticed signs of cattle on our piece of property, too.

"Really?" I managed, sounding more confident than I was. "I thought the land surrounding us was public, managed by the Bureau of Land Management."

She was thoughtful again, as if calculating my knowledge level.

"Well, yeah, but I have the leases on it. So's it's almost the same as mine."

We knew that ranchers sometimes became possessive with land they leased, cared for, grazed their cattle on. They were sensitive about ownership and access. I dug my foot in the dirt in front of me, wondering. Then I looked up at her and asked, "And have your cattle grazed on our land, too?"

Elsie hesitated.

"Some," she said.

I could tell by her tone that this was the heart of the matter.

Elsie wondered whether the new owners—intruders—would give her trouble about having her cattle roam over onto these desolate, sagebrush-covered acres.

She was wondering how quickly we would change the rules, ask everyone to shift patterns, the way newcomers often do, forgetting that people like to walk old paths and only slowly move to make new and different trails.

My response would tell her how we'd be as neighbors, how flexible or how bold.

"It'll be some time before we move here or can do anything with this land," I began. "So I don't see any harm if your cows should happen to wander here. Might keep the sagebrush down some," I said, remembering Jerry's words when he'd first noticed signs of cattle next to the river.

It must have been the right gesture. Elsie nodded, then added, "That dirt road along the ridge gets pretty bad sometimes. Wait a few minutes after it rains before you drive on it—won't be so slick."

At first her comments sounded like non sequiturs, since we had been discussing cattle, land, and ownership, not dusty roads. But her warning told me I'd passed the first test of an intruder: we would be reasonable, share the space, not try to overtake it.

In return, the locals would dole out the tips that might take years of pain and strain to learn, but that ultimately permitted survival on Starvation Point.

Elsie started the engine, the kids waved, and she nodded, turned the truck around, and drove out as swiftly and dustily as she came.

Dusk crept quietly into the canyon. Ricky lay sleeping at my feet. I considered my encounter with Elsie. She no longer seemed an intruder; maybe we wouldn't be to her.

Suddenly Ricky's ears perked; he sat statue still. I turned toward the river, imagining it was Jerry coming back.

But it wasn't Jerry.

Instead, five mule deer—a large gray doe, a smaller deer, and three fawns—moved slowly between the clumps of sage, stepping gingerly, about to pass single-file behind the tent. They froze at my movement, blending into the October dusk like rocks beneath the river. Each of us stood silent, as if honoring the other's right to be there.

But I knew we were the intruders. Our tent was pitched too near the path they daily walked from ridge to water. We should have noticed earlier and moved. If we were to be good neighbors, honoring Elsie's aid, we must learn to adjust.

I held my breath. The quiet moment passed.

Ricky began to bark, pulling against his chain. The gray doe moved her head, looked me in the eye, then led her brood hurriedly up the bank, kicking out little puffs of dust behind them, disappearing much the way Elsie had.

The deer became regular visitors to our ranch, but I never saw Elsie again. She died before we moved permanently to the Point. Until then, her cattle spent a month or two each year "intruding" on our land. Their presence cost us nothing; instead, they reminded us of Elsie's first, priceless lesson of survival.

She is etched in my memory as the first of many visitors who would meander through the dust to see us, not at all certain about those people who labored to become "locals," and who chose to live at the end of a rutted dirt road.

She comes to mind especially whenever a spring downpour slickens the dirt road. It's then I remember a long-ago warning given to a newcomer willing to accommodate. And then, before driving the winding, twisting, ridge-hugging switchbacks, I wait until the moisture sinks into the thirsty soil. I wait, and I think of Elsie.

3

History and High Tech

NOW THAT WE'D FOUND the land, we needed to outline next steps. Jerry must have done that in his mind, but he said nothing to me. I was content just to possess the land—afraid, perhaps, to face the vastness of the task that confronted us if Jerry convinced me to actually live there one day.

Leaving our hunting camp that day in October did nothing to encourage me. With gear loaded in the truck bed, and Ricky and Jerry perched on either side of me in the seat, we headed out: up the first incline past the shack, along the bench, out the gate, around the padlock turn, and creeping down the next breath-holding slope. Then Jerry suddenly jammed the accelerator to the floor, and we lurched back up the gut-wrenching roller coaster.

The truck careened wildly across the hard ruts, tossing us about like three watermelons in a wheelbarrow. Our truck wasn't four-wheel drive. I wondered what we'd do if we got stuck, tipped the truck over, or were injured in our precarious departure. I screamed, "Slow down!" But Jerry yelled back he had to have speed to make the grade.

Ricky loved it.

His setter tongue hung happily out the side of his mouth. His white-and-red-splashed body bounced across me to explore out Jerry's window, then back to watch sagebrush rushing by mine, paws stomping on my stomach, body flopped against my chest. My elbows pushed against his furry body to steer him, finally, upright in the seat.

We were *all* panting when we reached the top.

"We have to do something about the driveway," Jerry said matter-of-factly to the terrorized figure beside him.

We drove several miles of twisting dirt road before I really believed we were safe. I wondered how our family and friends would take it once they experienced this road. We'd been selective about sharing the property with others. Maybe that was a sign that we knew, in the far reaches of our minds, that our idea of living in such a remote place bordered on bizarre. The raised eyebrows, shaking heads, and plethora of objections that greeted us when we told others of the land made us choosy. We learned quickly that some people share easily in the wispiness of dreams, while others are frightened, maybe threatened, by such risks.

Each time I drove the road, I became a little more anxious myself about its condition, about what would happen if we had a flat tire or a wreck, if we ran out of gas—or if we met someone coming the other way. And I wondered how we'd get out in the winter.

For the next few months we didn't talk about the land much. Jerry's back pain was increasingly debilitating, and he hadn't been able to consistently work on blueprints or construction projects for several months. He had little energy to fish and hunt, the activities he loved the most, or even to take a walk. We'd plan a weekend away but then cancel the trip because of his severe headaches or his spasms in his back.

My job was demanding, but part of me welcomed the pressure of developing and delivering human services. The work diverted me from the less rewarding pressure at home, where my worries about Jerry and our hassles with Matt caused constant stress. At least I was able to accomplish small but important tasks working with the pleasant and capable staff at the mental health clinic.

Jerry and I even began seeing a counselor to help us define what we had control over in our lives and what we didn't. The therapy gave us permission to take care of ourselves while trying to put our family and future into some kind of perspective.

During those times, if we spoke of the land or our dream of it at all, it was to consider selling it.

Our income was modest; the land payments and other expenses of a family of three were taking their toll. We forgot how peaceful we had felt next to the river. I thought of the terrible road, the difficulties of building on the land, and our inadequacies for completing an impossible dream.

When Matt decided to join the army at eighteen, I couldn't have been more relieved. He left that June without ever having seen the land except in photographs. He had only Jerry's descriptions of the deer they could have hunted together, the chukars they could have chased, the bass and steelhead they might have caught.

"He's almost as lost to us as Kevin," Jerry said sadly after we put Matt on the bus.

In July, Jerry felt up to working on a remodeling project on an out-of-the-area house. The income would help, even though it meant he would only be home occasionally, since it was a six-hour drive away. And I could join him only on weekends when I felt up to the same long drive.

For months there had been little discussion about the land. But our short-term separation and the surrounding events began the restructuring of the dream.

We ended up writing almost daily. "Reading your letters is like listening to you without being able to interrupt," Jerry wrote, much to my delight, in his large, scrawling, uphill script. He was in Elgin, Oregon, remodeling a house, while I spent a month in Annapolis, Maryland, as part of a special training for professionals working in bureaucracies.

The training turned out to be educational about the past and our future as well. It was Annapolis, with its narrow row houses snuggled together along the cobblestone streets and its restored homes and eighteenth-century gardens, that reminded me, again, of the romance of homesteading. The settlers of Annapolis must have had a vision; they must have seen, with great detail, a future perfect enough to make them cross an ocean to the wilderness by the bay. People had survived there, making changes in their lives, handling adversity, adapting. I loved reliving history in that town.

Restored homes that filled the corners of the city like jeweled cobwebs represented their homesteading battles. The pain of carving a living from a foreign land and the triumph of surviving major life changes showed up not so much in the elegantly furnished parlors of those restored homes but in the back rooms. In the kitchens, candles had been laboriously created once a year by dipping wicks over and over again in hoarded, melted wax.

The sweat of hard labor lived on in the carriage sheds, too, where the wagons were repaired and readied for trips for critical supplies down rugged, battered, rutted, dirt roads. The bedrooms hinted of cold drafts seeping through clapboard walls, and beds piled high with quilts made less for beauty than for need.

Seeing how those souls of sturdy stock had cleared ground, planned for the seasons, stored their food, purified their water, and shared their lives with travelers were the highlights of the month I spent walking around Annapolis, though the daily letters from Jerry competed for first place.

Our letters brought back memories of our first encounters. We shared the little things, the easy conversations once so easily expressed but then interrupted by grieving and struggle with work, family, and Jerry's physical pain. We missed each other.

I wrote of the storms that swept across the city and of the route I jogged each day. I described the pottery-shop owner with laughter wrinkles about his eyes who told me he had left a high-tech job to make and sell his artwork. He said he had chosen to "work only for a living and not to live for work."

Jerry wrote about his remodeling job, the construction and delays, about how Ricky lay sleeping at his feet, and about how cool the bed felt without me.

In one letter—almost in passing—Jerry told me of a trip he'd taken with his elk-hunting buddy, Dave Larson, to Red's Horse Ranch, a dude ranch in the Eagle Cap wilderness of northeastern Oregon. It is accessible only by a long horseback ride.

Or by air.

Dave flew us in and we had breakfast, he wrote. *And we ran into Mrs. Peacock, the widow of Bill Peacock, who used to own the lumber company at Alicel. You remember.* (I didn't; but he continued, always giving me more details than I needed or would store.) *They flew Bill's Rallye in. It's sure a neat little plane. It's been up for sale for over two years now, and when Dave asked her what she absolutely would take for it, cash, bottom line, she said twenty thousand, which is a steal.*

I won't do anything about it until you get back, he finished.

The next day's mail included a photograph of the four-seat, single-engine plane built in France in 1974 and designed for short-field takeoffs and canyon runways. Jerry gave me great details and added again, *I won't do anything until you see it, but I did go up with Dave and Tom Potton, the guy who is selling it for her. He'd like to buy it himself, but can't afford it.*

I wondered how Jerry thought *we* could.

My letters to him spoke of a ferry ride across the Chesapeake to the old town of Saint Michael's, where author James Michener had a home while writing his historical novel *Chesapeake.*

Jerry's letters spoke of gas mileage, cruising speed, and maneuverability.

The subjects seemed miles apart—history and the high technology of Franklin engines and variable-pitch propellers—but they weren't. Both were part of the dream that would take us to the land. History would provide precedents, motivation, and encouragement. And the plane would make homesteading in the twentieth century easier, creating an alternative route to the outside world and a way to counter the remoteness of our ranch. Or so we thought.

Jerry kept his word and didn't *do* anything about the plane until I arrived back from Annapolis. But the next weekend we flew in the Rallye from La Grande.

The sky was a calm sea floating around white porcelain islands of clouds that September day. Tom, the pilot, and our friend Dave met us at the airport situated just beyond the Blue Mountains, where pioneers once began the last great mountain climb before reaching the end of the Oregon Trail.

Tom rolled the plane out of the hangar, took off the multicolored For Sale ribbons, and walked us around it, pointing out its many features, most of which escaped me.

Eventually, we stepped up onto the low wings and down into the four-seat cockpit. Tom pulled a canopy of hard plastic over our heads and locked it, then turned to follow the preflight procedures, talking aloud as he progressed.

"Clear!" he finally yelled to any wayward souls who might be wandering near the propeller. Then he turned the key to start the engine.

I sat in the back with Dave while Tom chattered enthusiastically to Jerry in the copilot's seat. We moved easily down the taxiway. By radio, Tom announced his intentions to take off to aircraft in the area. He pushed the throttle in, advanced quickly down the runway, then lifted effortlessly into the air.

"Look at this," he yelled against the wind noise as we gained altitude. "You can turn this thing around and land if you have to, downwind." He banked the plane steeply, made a hairpin turn to the left, straightened the craft briefly, and by the time we all caught our breath, he had set it on the tarmac in the opposite direction from which we'd taken off just a minute before. The wheels squeaked to a perfect landing. "It has great maneuverability," he said.

Grinning, he pushed the throttle in as we took off once again. This time we continued gaining altitude until we soared over the Eagle Cap Mountain wilderness area, watching for mountain goats, spotting isolated snowmelt streams that glistened like tiny strips of tinsel below us. Dave pointed out their elk-hunting area.

Jerry handled the controls briefly, gently moving the stick between his knees. There was no doubt. He loved it.

The plane *was* a beauty. White, with blue stripes, its bubble-top canopy offered a 360-degree view. It was worth twice what Mrs. Peacock was asking. But I couldn't imagine how we would get the money or if we should even try, since neither of us had a pilot's license. And with Jerry's back, we weren't even sure he could pass a physical.

Beyond completing aviation ground school and passing the test, we'd made no real commitment toward owning a plane. That was something we'd set for the future, after we had a place to live in on the land.

But our dream had become something like a boat trip down a fast-moving stream. Sometimes travelers stop earlier than planned, because the perfect campsite invites them in. Jerry convinced me the plane was just an earlier campsite on our trip. It would be silly to pass it by.

In November he sold several of his guns from his prized collection, we took out a second mortgage on the house, and just like that, we owned a plane neither of us could even fly home.

Jerry took lessons twice a week from Tom. By November, when his remodeling project was finished, he was also ready to fly the plane home, solo, and continue to work on his license in Bend.

The first time we flew over our land, I could finally begin to share Jerry's vision. Circling slowly in a spring sky as blue as Jerry's eyes, I could finally imagine where the landing strip would run beside the river. I could see the hangar and the house next to the shack. The bench of fingers *did* look like good places for a vineyard; the flat, once cleared, could nourish green alfalfa and some cows.

The river shimmered beneath us.

Then, as we headed back, flying south across our canyon, I looked behind me. For the first time, flying over the massive wheat fields unbroken by trees and few roads, I realized how few houses dotted the landscape near Starvation Point, and how far apart lay the one or two that nestled under green clusters of well-tended trees.

And from two thousand feet above, I surveyed the road. It wound through the green and gold wheat like a thin black snake, slithering under the power lines, silently edging its way through sagebrush, dropping off over the side of the canyon, twisting its way to the river below.

As the engine hummed along, carrying us back to Bend, I wondered, *What would it be like to drive that road on a windy, rainy, winter's night? Would the plane prevent the wild roller-coaster rides with a bouncing man and a dog?*

A cold chill crept up my neck. We hadn't considered how the plane might change my perspective of the land. There was no way we could have known.

Neither could we have predicted how a short six years later the plane would change more than just our perspective. It would turn our dream into a nightmare.

4

Hansel

WITH THE PLANE, WE THOUGHT we were prepared for remote living, perhaps even imagining that we could pull it off with a little style. But nothing could have prepared us for how the animals would affect our lives, although we should have seen it coming.

From the beginning of our courtship, our relationship had gone to the dogs. Shortly after we began dating in late 1975, our daily ritual included Jerry's picking me up from work in his truck and driving us a few miles out of Bend to a ranch owned by his dentist friend, Bill Hurst. Parking before a small shed set in the middle of a field, we would free two energetic English setter puppies, who zipped through the rickety wooden door like water over a spillway. They raced around the field, oblivious to the cold November temperatures or the snow-encrusted ground. Like melting chocolate and strawberry sundaes, their bodies whizzed around us and then darted off through the ponderosa pines, reappearing briefly in the dusk.

Jerry and I used the dogs' running time to get to know each other during those daily trips. We watched our breath puff out before us in the cold while we waited for the dogs to tire and return to their rather expansive kennel.

That was before airplanes and homesteading, before our marriage and the move.

I informed him that I owned a large, gray, sauna-loving cat named John; he informed me that he detested cats. I informed him that horses frightened me; he advised me that mules were a better choice anyway. As the relationship progressed, the animals encountered each other and adjusted, and Jerry and I were married nine months later.

Of those first animals, only Ricky (and the mules) would eventually move with us to the land. John the cat died; the other pup moved to a family farther east. But there would be other animals. And then came Hansel.

In 1980 I wanted a guard dog. Ricky was a lovable bird dog who would invite a burglar in. Something big and protective, like a German shepherd or a Doberman, would have suited me just fine. I wanted to avoid the repetition of the terrifying incident that had faced me a week after my return from Annapolis.

I was alone in the house. Jerry was finishing the remodeling job in Elgin, six hours away, and taking flying lessons in his spare time. Ricky was with him. I'd come home from Annapolis to a bout with the flu that kept me in bed a few days. It must have looked as if no one was home.

At 3:00 a.m. something awakened me. I checked John, our wily cat, at the foot of the bed to see whether he noticed anything unusual; he slumbered on. *Bad dream, perhaps?* Then I heard it again: scratching sounds, like metal being scraped against a wooden window sill.

Someone was in the living room, or just outside.

I heard my heart pounding in my head so vigorously I wondered whether it could be heard aloud. My hands were wet and sluggish. Every sound was magnified. I could almost hear the molecules of air bumping against one another. The cat's breathing sounded like a lion's roar. *This is abject terror,* I thought. *Calm down. Maybe it's only the wind.*

I opened the bedside stand and reached for the Smith & Wesson .38 Special. It belonged to Jerry. He was comfortable with the gun, had trained police recruits in Ohio on the weapon's use, and knew its ins and outs.

Eventually, it came into the bedroom, its leather holster resting in the night-table drawer. It was difficult to understand how this lethal weapon could fit so comfortably in my gentle husband's hands.

I didn't like the revolver, but it came with the relationship. Initially, I treated it like a snake: cautiously, expecting slime instead of smooth wood and cold metal. At the practice range, I gradually learned how to place my hands, how to sight the target, and how to resist the temptation to antici-pate the recoil when the bullet left the barrel.

I gained a certain sense of pride at my increased proficiency with the .38. At Jerry's insistence, I acquired a permit for a concealed weapon and took the Special with me when I traveled, tucking it in my purse between my lipstick and coins. When I jogged along deserted country roads, the .38 rode in a leather holster beneath my left breast.

But I had never resolved my ambivalence about the weapon. I always wondered if I really could shoot it, even in self-defense. And I still wondered if such a powerful weapon could reduce potential conflict with its presence.

When my permit ran out, I failed to renew it. I stopped jogging and left the revolver in my bedside stand. That's where it was on that night in 1980 when the noises continued outside our house. Next came the sounds of the flat flesh of the prowler's hand sweeping against the Sheetrock. The intruder was reaching through the window, patting for the doorknob. He'd be inside in seconds.

Please, God, please, God, please! Make him go away. Make it be the wind, I prayed and pleaded, trying to reduce the roaring in my ears.

A fleeting thought from introductory psychology entered my mind. You *can* hold two opposing thoughts at once, because there I sat telling myself it was the wind—with the .38 Special aimed and cocked.

Then, in the middle of my greatest terror, I fell asleep.

It was years before I told Jerry of my sleeping. I knew he wouldn't have done anything so irresponsible. But one evening years later, a friend was telling us over dinner that once when he'd been camping in Appalachia, he'd miscalculated his time and didn't make it to the bear-proof cages set aside for campers. This friend, who has a doctorate in psychology, had made camp on the open trail, and in the darkness had been awakened abruptly by the snorts and grunts of a marauding bear just inches from his head. "What did you do?" I asked, fearing the worst. "I was so frightened," he said, "I fell asleep."

The memory of my own experience remained vivid in my mind.

When I awoke several hours later, I heard no more noise. Nothing was amiss in the room. The cat still slept soundly at the foot of the waterbed. Except for the revolver resting in my hand, I would have thought it all a nightmare.

When it was fully light, I ventured into the living room. There the window screen lay twisted in the middle of the floor. It had not been tossed there by the wind. The window had been pulled open.

While it appeared from the outside that anyone could slip through it, the window was an odd size and restricted entry. And the doorknob was too far, it seemed, for the prowler to reach. I went outside and tried to reach the door, duplicating the sounds I'd heard just hours before of flat flesh patting the wall.

Then I called the police, certain no wind had mauled the screen or opened windows. The lieutenant concurred. "No wind at 3:00 a.m., lady," he said as he found confirming footprints in the soft earth.

Although the window probably discouraged the intruder, it was, of course, the prayer that sent him on his way. God knew I could not live with what I might have done had someone wandered into the bedroom and met me with the revolver.

So Hansel entered our lives.

He began as another compromise.

Jerry didn't want *just* a guard dog. He wanted a dog that was versatile and could also hunt for him. A drahthaar met that criteria, even though it was a German breed I had never heard of.

Supposedly a mix of Polish water spaniel, Airedale, Russian wolfhound, and the large standard poodle, the breed had wiry hair and webbed feet. I had trouble remembering the name until I thought of the phrase "I *drahthaar* have this dog than any *othaar*."

Jerry found an ad in the classified section the day after the attempted break-in. Two evenings later, after visiting his parents, we made an out-of-the-way trip to the address listed in the paper.

We pulled into the driveway and were greeted by a very large, hairy-looking, barking dog, followed by a husky middle-aged man who had seen the last of fifty—and his hair. He scratched the dog's ears absently while telling Jerry he'd just put up the puppies for the night. "It's no trouble to let them out," he encouraged as we set out along a dark, narrow path, following him and the bouncing light from his flashlight.

Then he opened a small shed and turned on a yard light. Out bounded ten liver-and-white puppies, rolling and falling over one another and their feet, totally exuberant over their unexpected late-night reprieve.

One puppy, liver colored and a little larger than the others, came straight for me, his long ears flopping as he stumbled over his big feet. Like a short brown thumb, his stubby tail vibrated in excitement. I dropped down on one knee, and he leaped into my lap, crawled up my shoulder, and began nibbling my ear. I felt something warm dribble on my shoulder and knew he'd christened me in his excitement.

It wasn't Hansel's personality that won me, though; it was his gaze. His dark eyes stared at me, as though peering deep inside my thoughts, the way an infant does when first discovering the world. Hansel's eyes were bright, kind, and gentle—but steely, too. Years later, Blair, my friend and colleague at the clinic, watched Hansel watching me, shadowing my movements, listening to and following my directions like a devoted child, responding eagerly to "Heel" and "Stay" and searching for his sock to play with. You could tell by his eyes, she said, that Hansel was really an intelligent being held hostage in a dog's body.

Jerry tried to change my mind about my choice of the puppies, but only weakly. Perhaps he thought it was the least he could do, let me choose *which* puppy we'd take home, since he had chosen the breed.

At any rate, we paid the man his $150, and he gave us the papers, saying Hansel, born 12 July 1980, was ours. We gave him the official name of Hansel Blitz Wolfweisse in honor of his German heritage, calling him "Hunzie" (and much later "Hunzie Bunzie") for short.

He became Jerry's bird dog; but more, he was my guard dog and companion, exercising me to keep my spirits up and my stress level down. His devotion enabled me to bear bad news and offer comfort and encouragement, not only as we eased toward the land, but later, too, when the sadness and disasters sometimes seemed overwhelming—and would have been—without my Hansel.

5

Elevation in the Afternoon

HANSEL WASN'T HAPPY when I postponed our morning runs, which I began doing with some frequency in the spring of 1981, heading instead to Redmond for an hour of sweaty hands, foreign thinking, and flying lessons.

Edwin was a former Vietnam helicopter pilot and flight-instructor-turned-doctor. By day he worked for the clinic. When Jerry learned he was an instructor who wanted flying time, he declared it a perfect match. What could be more inventive, he said, than dealing with my fears of flying while learning to fly from a shrink?

Since Edwin wanted time in the air himself, he agreed to teach me for free. It seemed a good idea at the time, but one doesn't always make the best decisions when under stress.

And we did have stress. The recession was sweeping through Oregon like a night janitor with a late date waiting. At work each day, my staff and I were struggling to manage an increased demand for service from hundreds of distressed people.

At home we continued to deal with Jerry's pain, as well as with a strange gastrointestinal problem that had begun to plague me. Pain felt like an uninvited guest who had come to visit and chosen to stay.

Jerry had completed his flying license, and on his good days, he loved it. But at $1.80 a gallon for fuel, flying was an expensive hobby.

The land was never far from Jerry's mind, and ever the laser beam, he had suggested one day, "Maybe if *you* learned to fly, you'd feel less isolated… once we move. You could get out if the road got bad. You could fly to Bend to see friends or do consulting jobs you might want to do, or whatever."

Maybe flying would be a good idea, I thought, anything to avoid driving on that reptile road. My piloting would demand my total leisure-time attention, diverting me from the worry of work.

Training for my pilot's license, I told myself, had a beginning, a middle, and an end, unlike the never-ending demands of my profession.

As a child, I'd flown as a passenger in my dad's small Aeronca Sedan four-seater plane, throwing up my lunch or breakfast so dependably that an empty Folger's coffee can was kept beneath the seat. "Here," Mom would say, handing me the can as soon as the engine started and I'd smell gas fumes seeping through the plane's fabric fuselage. I'd lose my lunch, she'd dump the can, and we'd take off.

I thought it was part of the preflight procedure.

Piloting frightened me. But then most things did. I lived with *day*-mares, imagining the worst from just the slightest information. If Jerry was ten minutes later than he said he'd be, I imagined he was in a fiery crash and would greet him at the door with tears from the music played at his anticipated funeral.

To keep my imaginary fears under control, I forced myself to do things I was afraid of, putting them in perspective, preventing them from holding me hostage. I pondered Eleanor Roosevelt's wise words: "You must do the things you think you cannot do."

So if aggressive people intimidated me—and they did—I took classes on becoming assertive and even learned to teach them. The thought of supervising professionals terrified me, so I enrolled in supervision courses and applied for management jobs.

My fear of piloting something foreign and mechanical would be just another challenge, I imagined.

So, two or three days a week, I drove off to Roberts Field, a commercial-size airport in Redmond, about twelve miles from our home outside of Bend, for a 6:30 a.m. lesson. We kept the Rallye there, tied down at the end of a rainbow of planes.

After the lessons, Edwin and I drove another seventeen miles to work at the mental health clinic.

I would have been content to fly forever with an instructor. I felt safe with a real pilot in the copilot seat. I could enjoy the view and experience the exhilaration of successful takeoffs and landings without having to trust in my own competence or skill.

As instructor, Edwin nodded affirmatively if I did something right, letting me ask questions to break the gentle engine hum that filled the cockpit. He sat back and listened, rarely commenting on the gauges and needles that blinked before us, rarely posing problems I might someday face. "Flying," he said one day as we headed out over the high desert plateau toward the sunrise, "is hours and hours of boredom—followed by moments of sheer panic." He turned to me and grinned, thinking I would find that funny.

Because I had flown with Jerry, and before that with my dad, I suspect Edwin thought I knew more than I did, because with only eleven hours of flight instruction under my belt, he said: "You take it up alone and bring it down."

I wasn't ready! I was still memorizing too much. Nothing came naturally. Oh, I'd done well on the FAA ground-school exam, but I knew how to take tests. I harbored a terrible fear that if there *was* smoke in the cockpit (question #23), I would remember that the correct answer was "b" but *not* what I was supposed to do to stop the smoke!

Flying was like learning a foreign language, and I didn't want to keep translating. I wanted it to become second nature. I wanted to be dreaming in it before I went up there alone with all the things that could go wrong.

Edwin said that "natural" feeling would come later.

Edwin got out of the aircraft and walked away. I saw him standing over by the parked planes, his dark hair forming a hat around his head, his hands in his jeans, his shoulders hunched slightly inside his leather flight jacket, bracing against the March breeze. He looked like he was twenty-one. He was much too young to be instructing.

I swallowed as I sat in the Rallye at the end of the taxiway, slowly talking myself through each step on the checklist (minus the coffee can), visualizing the plane's performance, mentally seeing the procedure for takeoff.

Then the routine became real, and I felt the surge of the engine as I pushed the throttle to the engine wall, felt the power roll the plane forward, and gain airspeed. I sensed the vibration that signaled the lift-off speed and finally pulled back the stick and joyously became weightless, rising well above the sagebrush, the trees, the buildings, and the town, and climbing, ever climbing, toward the mountains, knowing I could fly above them if I chose to.

Then quickly, because I feared that if I didn't land *immediately* after takeoff I just might forget how to, I began the landing sequence. I lined up along the runway and checked wind, airspeed, fuel, and flaps. I knew there would be a sink across the sagebrush just before setting down again on runway twenty-eight, and I held steady, checking the windsock and the horizon, pulling power off, flaring, and holding wings level, until the plane settled gently down, tires rolling, slowing on the pavement. Then I grinned with a delight I could hardly wait to share with Jerry.

As I flew alone more often after that, I would still follow the routine of taking off and then immediately landing. Then—and only then—could I fly off again to play, sure that I remembered how to land, how to get safely home.

It was a joy to soar over Cline Butte toward the frosted Cascade Mountains, to fly over the house and buzz Jerry. (At two thousand feet, the plane was bug-size, and he rarely knew I was flying lazy circles above him). I'd climb to six or seven thousand feet, practice stalls and turns, turn again toward the mountains and my sister's ranch, watch the farmers moving irrigation pipe across the potato fields and alfalfa, feeling totally empowered, having conquered engine, weather, and my fears.

After my first solo flight, Edwin told me just to go out to the airport and fly, get some hours in, and then we'd reconnect for more lessons. I could even fly on weekend afternoons. Because I hadn't had much flying time in wind or changing weather conditions, I flew only when it was calm.

After several uneventful hours (on separate days) alone in the plane, I decided that I was being silly having to land *immediately* after takeoff. After all, I'd done twenty-five or thirty landings by then without incident. I'd have to venture out eventually…

The weather was calm on an April Saturday afternoon as Jerry drove me out to the airport. High, comforting clouds spread themselves like a blanket well above us, and the air was still. "I'll just take off and fly around the area, practicing maneuvers," I told him. "You go get yourself a cup of coffee and come back in an hour."

I took off—and I didn't land immediately.

After about twenty minutes of circling the local area, lulled into confidence by the steady droning of the engine and the plane's responsiveness to my gentle movements on the stick, I decided to try landing at a new airport.

The small airport in Prineville, about ten miles northeast of the Redmond field, had often been mistaken by *real* pilots because its runways were on the same compass points as Redmond's.

Coming in over a juniper-spotted butte, I began the usual procedure to set the plane down. But this time, when I felt the plane touch the narrow pavement, something seemed wrong, for the plane began to porpoise, its nose diving toward the ground and its main wheels repeatedly lifting up behind, increasing each time in height and intensity.

I knew I'd better give the engine more power and take off, or the next time the nose might just smash on the runway.

The plane lifted off with little effort under full throttle. Unsure about what I had done wrong, and too embarrassed to call the tower in nearby

Redmond to ask for the professionals' able advice, I decided to calm down and fly around a bit and try again.

That's when the storm came up—quickly, as they sometimes do in the afternoon in the mountains.

I saw the blackness moving like a tidal wave from the south. Rain won't hurt a plane, but the thunderhead that rolled toward me in the sky was ominous, boiling with wind and hail. I was already nervous, fearful that because I hadn't landed well in Prineville maybe I'd have trouble back in Redmond, too. I chastised myself for having broken my routine, not practicing a landing *immediately* before I played around.

"Better set it down in Redmond," I said aloud to myself. "Use the runway you took off from. It's closest." I went through all the procedures, trying not to rush them as I watched the blackness from the corner of my eye. I pulled the throttle partially back as planned, set the flaps, checked my airspeed and altitude, and began the descent, constantly praying aloud to quell my growing panic.

Over the runway, I flared the plane, feeling a slight settling sensation. It seemed normal—except the plane refused to land. It just kept floating well above the runway, as though the wind were pushing it, keeping it from touching down. I checked the airspeed and realized I hadn't slowed it down at all.

I had trouble keeping the plane centered above the pavement. It simply wouldn't land.

A sixties song about the poor man who rode the subway "forever 'neath the streets of Boston" flitted into my frazzled mind, and I wondered if I was facing a similar fate above ground.

I thought I might have damaged the plane somehow in the Prineville porpoise landing, and now something was keeping the plane from working properly. Not thinking clearly, I worried I might not have enough runway at Redmond (although ten thousand feet is adequate for jets, and the Rallye had been known to land in less than three hundred feet). I gave the engine full throttle to do a go-around so I could try the landing once again.

The storm was closer now.

Whirlwinds of dirt and dust rose up from the desert below me. My sweaty hand was slippery on the stick as I gripped and released it nervously. *Something's wrong with the plane!* I heard myself say aloud those fatal words of lost confidence: "I'm going to crash!"

The windsock swirled below me, and I felt a gust of wind vibrate against the airframe. Dust was blowing harder along the ground, rolling toward the airport. On my headphones I heard the flight service station attendant tell another plane that the wind was up to eighteen knots. It was coming at an angle that wasn't quite a crosswind, but it was enough to change the way I'd set the nose for landing.

I prayed, fearful now that I couldn't bring it down without a crash. I went through the landing sequence again, this time deciding to pull all power, thinking maybe I had too much speed. Maybe that was why the Rallye didn't seem to want to let its wheels touch the earth.

In hindsight, more power would have been a better defense against the wind. However, considering my response when I felt the safety of the ground, it was fortunate I had pulled off all power.

I lost control when the wheels finally touched the ground.

At eighty miles an hour, I felt the main wheels balloon up and the nose scrape the earth like a wheelbarrow dumping its load. The plane fell back on the two main wheels and then skidded right, toward the grassy area next to the runway.

Too fast!

In my mind, I could hear Jerry saying, *Slam the left rudder! Slam the left brake! Keep the wings level!*

Slow down! Oh, please, God, slow it down!

And then God did.

My heart slowed, too, to a normal rate.

Why I have struggled at times to believe in the existence of a supreme, all-knowing, all-loving, all-powerful God who cares for poor wretches despite their dalliances is beyond me when I consider my encounters with disasters.

The plane slowed. The Rallye veered to the right, and only my pumping the left brake kept it on the runway at all.

The storm had blown over, and clear, calm air followed behind. So it wasn't wind forcing the plane toward the grass.

In a shaky voice, I called the tower. "Five Four Bravo Foxtrot to Redmond tower. I'm at the end of runway two-eight, taxiing slowly. I have brakes out and steering difficulties. I'll be off as soon as I can. Over."

"Brakes out" was the only conclusion I could come to. The brakes are used to steer the Rallye, and their absence would account for the plane's not wanting to stay on the runway. There was no response from the tower, so I assumed no jets were preparing to land on top of me.

When I passed in front of the tower, I expected a call from a controller saying, "Five Four Bravo Foxtrot, your right wheel is missing." But the radio was silent as I limped on by.

I taxied to our parking spot, turned the plane, and placed it perfectly to tie down.

The winding-down sequence went smoothly. I pulled the throttle off, shut down the mags and engine, flipped off the remaining switches, set the brakes, and sat quietly, *so* grateful to be down and wondering if the fear of death really was a way to counter a stress-filled life.

Eventually, I rolled back the canopy, stepped out, and looked around. The wings were fine. Getting out and walking around the plane to tie the wings and tail, I checked the main gears, tires, and brakes. Everything looked normal. Even the nosewheel seemed fine as I ran my hands over it, looking for cracks or *some* indication of why the plane refused to move in a straight line down the runway. There was nothing out of the ordinary.

Until I stood up, facing the propeller.

Like innocently opening a closet door only to have a dead body fall out, I saw it then and gasped, tears burning behind my eyes.

On either side of the plane's nose, the propeller stretched out, then ended in a curl like the finest, crispiest, most unwelcome potato chip ever manufactured. On even closer inspection, I could see that the shaft that held the nosewheel had been damaged too. It formed a perfect S (and should have been a straight line).

Beyond the plane, I saw Jerry pull the car into the airport parking lot. I dragged myself across the tarmac, crying. He seemed unable to grasp the enormity of what I'd done. He kept saying, "What can be so bad? You're here, walking around. I can see the plane is parked over there, so what's the problem?"

Between my tears and pointing, the words made little sense until I led him to the front of the plane with his arm wrapped comfortingly about my shoulders as we walked. Once there, the tattletale propeller above the arthritic nosewheel said it all.

I tried to explain what had happened.

"You probably did the damage when the plane ballooned forward onto its nose when you landed just now," Jerry guessed, squatting down to check the damaged shaft. "It's okay," he kept saying, his arms around me then, holding me to him. "It's okay. You're not hurt. We can check the engine. The propeller can be fixed. That's why we have insurance."

But it was all so embarrassing! I swore I'd never tell a soul; but Jerry reminded me that there were businesses devoted entirely to repairing propellers and planes, so other pilots must have had accidents, too. "And besides," he added. "Now you've had your accident. Every pilot is entitled to one. Yours is over."

That left only his.

Both the propeller and the nosewheel were replaced much faster than my confidence or willingness to pilot again. Even flying as a passenger with Jerry after that was fearful for me, especially on the approach to landings.

Each time we landed I prayed shamelessly, "Please, God, please help us down safely." I tensed my foot on an imaginary brake and braced my left arm on the canopy, preparing for a crash. Jerry said the prayers unnerved him, but I told him to ignore me and just get the plane down while I shook.

I wondered how seriously God would take a prayer repeated so desperately every time I flew.

In August we flew the Rallye over the Rocky Mountains and the flat plains of Montana and the Dakotas to Minnesota for my brother Craig Rutschow's wedding, and then on to Ohio and Indiana to visit friends. We thought that forced exposure to my fear of flying would eventually make piloting a desire. But it didn't.

I hated it that something I'd begun to enjoy now meant nothing but fear.

We made several flights over our land, too, with Hansel's sleeping body curled against the blue vinyl seat in the back. I wished for his lack of anxiety, and I knew that unless I conquered my fear of flying, the plane's role as a part of *my* escape from future remoteness would be limited and would push the ranch further and further away from reality.

At least for me.

6

Retreat and Advance

A WALK BESIDE THE PACIFIC was just what the doctor ordered.

I found myself awake at 5:00 a.m., despite having stayed up late, laughing and giggling like a schoolgirl, with two friends and six other women I'd just met. We were sharing a motel suite (with only one bathroom) at Seaside, Oregon, attending the 1982 Northwest Evangelical Women's Retreat.

A retreat is meant to set people apart for a time, give them room to consider, think, make changes, and grow. Children call them "summer camps"; corporations call them "conferences" or "workshops"; and hunters and fishermen call them "weekends."

My dad, a lover of words, says retreats are misnamed. He calls them "advances."

I hadn't been sure I wanted to make the six-hour drive from Bend to the northern coast for a weekend "advance" with five hundred other people I didn't know. Strangers brought out the shyness in me, and if it hadn't been for my new friend Carol's encouragement and my colleague Jeannie's willingness to drive, I wouldn't have gone.

It was a quiet May dawn.

I moved silently, dressing quickly in the darkness, closing the motel door without a squeak. Misty salt air filled my lungs. Overhead, seagulls dipped their wings, screeching like greaseless brakes, heading toward the ocean and then turning inland in a never-ending swirl above the weather-worn cottages lining the streets to the beach.

In the distance a ship punctured the horizon. Closer in, figures walked slowly in the gentle dawn breeze. One or two jogged, their footprints erased by the incoming tide.

I walked beside huge logs, tossed like pick-up-sticks along the shore by high tide. Little birds with quick steps rushed toward the waves, then scurried back. Broken shells glittered against the beige cloth of sand.

Like someone floating with ears just below the water line, I let the roar of the ocean drown out all sound except the squawking of the gulls. I inhaled the salty dawn.

I was alone.

That morning I felt compelled to wake, to walk. It was as if my feet awoke with independent plans. Once there, beside the ocean, I felt a little frightened. The others didn't know I'd gone. I thought of the violence in the world. People get kidnapped on the beach. A sneaker wave could take me out, and no one would ever know what had happened to me. I decided such thoughts would only divert me from my retreat. I found a spot and settled behind a nubby driftwood log. The waves served as white noise as they beat against the shore; they filled my world with cleansing peace.

What should we do, God? I asked. Jerry had said good-bye to me for the weekend with a quick comment that maybe I'd come back with some great idea for what we ought to do about our lives. I stopped my packing in midair. "It *is* settled, though," I said. "We *aren't* going to the land."

With little enthusiasm, he nodded his agreement, propped himself up against the bed's headboard, and sighed. "Guess that's what makes the most sense when you put all the pieces in place." John the cat jumped onto the waterbed, his seventeen pounds setting Jerry and luggage on a seafaring roll. Jerry pulled the cat to him, absently petting John's long gray hair.

The cat had reminded me of an evening a few months earlier when, for a moment, I'd felt, again, that we *could* go. I'd been asking myself *What on earth would I do if we went to the land?* when John jumped on the couch. Just then, a word slipped into my mind.

Words do routinely run through my head—words and phrases that become the first sentence of a report or a comment jotted on a birthday card. That night in February, a single word stood alone, distinctive and unique. I felt that its occurrence was divine. The word was *write,* and the thought made me restless.

As a child I'd enjoyed writing "wretched little poems," as I called them, along with plays and short stories. My teachers had encouraged me. I'd once dreamed of writing a novel, believing that everyone had at least one good book tucked between his or her courage and time.

At work I wrote daily of professional things: letters to legislators, reports, memos, and plans—nothing particularly creative. But that night, the word *write* suggested something to pursue "once we moved to the land"—if we ever did.

Like a kitten's breath, the thought warmed.

Not a week later I'd come home testy from a trying day at the clinic to discover clothes still in the dryer, the living room cluttered, and no dinner plans made. Jerry had said he'd take care of those things when I'd left in the morning. Coming home to this disappointment, I'd lost my temper.

Yanking clothes from the dryer, I shouted at him as he stood in the doorway. "If you worked for me and weren't any more reliable than this, I'd fire you!"

"Well, I *don't* work for you," he spit back. "Besides, I did some other stuff. And I'm hurting."

"Great excuse," I cut him off, then turned to twist the knife. "If it'd had to do with hunting or fishing, you'd have done it!"

I slammed wrinkled clothes into the basket, feeling judgmental and self-righteous. A smart man, Jerry turned away, walked to the kitchen, and began fixing dinner.

Later, after a silent meal, I apologized. But I added, "I just don't see how we can even consider going to the land with all the work there'd be. You'd have to do it; I couldn't. At least not much. And when you'd hurt and it wouldn't get done, then I'd be angry and frustrated, and we'd be stuck there, alone, far from everything. It just isn't realistic."

He sighed, nodding his head in agreement, and we sat in silence.

"We still need to sell this place, though," he added later in the evening. "Then we'll figure out what to do from there."

The house would eventually sell, though it had been on the market for almost a year with only a few people even stopping to look. We knew we wanted a change, something different. I was tired and willing to move—just not to that isolated land at the end of the reptile road.

We'd parted for the retreat weekend with one thing for sure between us: living on the land was no longer realistic.

We'd said good-bye to the dream. We'd keep the land, play on it, and sell it someday. Nothing else made any sense.

Being there on the beach made little sense either. I pulled my jacket up around my neck. The air was cool. No confirming answer came. I headed back to the motel and to the rush and chaos of nine women using one shower and then making it to breakfast by 8:00 a.m.

The keynote speaker that morning spoke of trust, of learning to rely on something larger than ourselves. Her scriptural references were of Moses leading others to the Promised Land despite his feelings of inadequacy, despite all the odds against him, despite what others might think.

In the afternoon the wife of a missionary told of her reluctance to go with her husband to Africa, even when he had been so delighted, so sure of their calling. On their first trip to Africa, she hated the desolate, barren place. "Finally," she told us, "I prayed that 'his' land would somehow become 'my' promised land. I didn't think anything less than God Himself could make that change happen." She spoke of how frightened she'd been, of how difficult it was to trust in something unseen.

They were leaving again for Africa at the end of the week. She said she was genuinely delighted.

Brainwashing, the skeptic in me thought.

While everyone else went for a pre-supper shopping spree, I stayed in the room and read. There are hundreds of references to land on in Scripture, and the odds were good that just a casual opening of the Bible would bring me close to more than one. And of course, it did.

I slept little that night, taking another early morning walk along the beach the next day. I hoped that the solitude beside the ocean might somehow bring relief to our troubled future. I didn't want to hear the still, small voice within me beating on the rhythm of the waves a phrase as crazy as *Just go to the land.*

Had Columbus heard such a phrase inside his head? I wondered. *Were the Pilgrims and patriots driven by tyrants—and endless words inside themselves? Did the pioneers who crossed the continent find it difficult to explain to others why they were leaving solid homes and family and moving on to unknown places? Could they find the words to make their dreams sound purposeful and real? Or was it like a melody, hard to describe without having experienced the rhythm and beat?*

There is no way we can make it, I thought, listing the obstacles: *Jerry's back. The way we argue over little things when we have to work together. I'd be so isolated. What would happen to us? What would people think? We might kill each other and be dead for weeks before anyone even knew we'd been there.*

But I kept coming up against that phrase about the land and the word *write;* despite the difficulties I knew we would encounter every step of the way, I wanted to be obedient to God's will. The poet Rainer Maria Rilke once wrote that when we're born, God calls us by name, then sends us out into the universe. We remember little of this except God's voice beside us as we walk, saying this: *You, sent out beyond your recall, / Go, to the limits of your longing. / Embody me.* Was going to this land being sent out beyond recall? Was writing the longing of my heart? Would believing it was so help me be the eyes and hands of God? My face turned warm at such an arrogant thought.

"Would you think us crazy if I quit my job and we moved to the piece of property on the John Day River we bought a few years ago and lived there full time?" I asked my friend Carol later. We were sitting on the sofa bed we'd shared the night before in the motel. I watched her face closely for any signs of diplomacy, of covering up true feelings just to protect me.

I hadn't known her all that long, but she was family, married to Jerry's cousin Jack, a lanky man who as a boy had been like a brother to Jerry. Jerry had told me stories of their escapades as kids, hunting and fishing near the base of Mount Bachelor near Bend before it became a skiing and vacation mecca.

I'd met Carol at Kevin's funeral and remembered her comforting smile and gentle voice as she and her youngest daughter had left our home that day. Our acquaintance had expanded to friendship early in 1979, when Jerry needed surgery to fuse two of the vertebrae in his neck. The surgery took place in Eugene, where Jack and Carol lived. I'd been uncomfortable sharing space with two people I barely knew, but being with them soon became as comfortable as wearing an old sweater.

A permanent friendship blossomed that week, a friendship that would see us through danger and enormous pain as Jack and Carol became entangled in our dream.

I trusted Carol for her honesty and watched as she formed an answer to my question. Her beginning-to-gray hair made a halo of soft curls around her face, while warm blue eyes looked out at me from behind her bifocals. She leaned back against the pillows and closed her eyes. "Is it what you think God wants you to do?" she asked.

There are those who would think such a question borders on the bizarre or religious fanaticism, that only weak, unthinking, escaping people who hate to face the future use such terms to describe their major life decisions. I myself had often thought that decisions made on faith alone were absurd.

Now the absurd was happening to me.

"It makes no sense to me, but yes," I sighed.

Carol reached a hand to mine. "If it's what your heart tells you, you have to do it."

She said it so matter-of-factly that I knew she must have listened to that still, small voice herself.

"But what if we fail? Fall flat on our faces? Can't even survive? What will you think of us?"

"What's to think?" she asked as calmly as if someone had asked her opinion about serving whole-wheat or white bread. "If it's truly what God wants you to do, then God will provide the means to make it happen—maybe not the way you want or imagined it, but you'll never be deserted."

"Would you visit us there? I mean, we'd be so far away."

"Of course we'd come." She laughed. "Jack would love it. All that wide open space, the deer, the river. You couldn't keep us away!"

As I allowed the picture to form again in my mind, I saw the river and the rimrocks, heard the chukars and geese. I could feel the excitement, the assurance that it could truly happen!

I loved Carol for not asking lots of detailed questions about what we'd do or how we'd do it, how we'd manage with Jerry's injured back, or how we'd ever build a house in such a remote location. She had asked only the basic question. Everything else was superfluous to a believing, trusting, faithful soul.

The trip home with Jeannie added to my growing enthusiasm. We had worked together for a little over a year; she had been my administrative assistant. I appreciated her detailed, sequential thinking, her kind and caring heart.

She was delighted that I now seemed so sure of what we needed to do. But being practical, too, she alerted me to the highs and lows of such decisions. "There'll be some rough times," she assured me, her hand steady on the steering wheel as we eased our way through the Portland traffic on our way back to Bend. "But if you're sure, then it will happen."

Years later, recalling that trip back, Jeannie told me she really wanted to tell me we were crazy. "I could just see Jerry's back brace and you with your fake nails out there in the sagebrush. But the Lord put a check on my spirit, and I couldn't say anything discouraging. Now, looking around at all that has happened, I can see why."

A million unresolved details awaited us: selling the house, building on the land, making a living from such a remote site, managing Jerry's health needs, finding friends in an old, established community, and getting my pilot's license. We also had to say good-bye and explain to people what we were about to do and why, if we could.

We had to let go of what people thought.

"Are you nuts?" Jerry wondered aloud, surprised, when I arrived home with the dream, and now the determination, at last. "What happened?" he laughed.

The details of the weekend; the conspiracy of scriptures; the phrases and the feelings; the still, small voice; the fears; and the reassurances were all shared with him. His smile grew broader as I spoke.

He'd never given up the dream despite his declarations of surrender.

That night, as we lay curled like nested spoons in our bed, John asleep at our feet, Jerry spoke quietly into my ear. "It's just so great that you want to go now too," he whispered. "I wanted to go badly enough for both of us."

"If I went just to please you," I said, "then when things got bad, I'd blame you. I never want to be angry because you *took* me there. I needed it to be my choice. Now I believe we're going because, for whatever reason, we're supposed to.

"Maybe you don't need assurance like I do," I continued, turning to see his face in the moonlight. "You're always in control, always making everything work by yourself. I'm not that strong. Until this weekend, I just didn't see how going to the land could work. I still don't," I added, pulling the covers up over his shoulder, resting my head on his chest, "but now I'm trusting that we're not in it alone."

His hand gently swept my cheek in the darkness as we lay there, retreating into the sleep of dreamers who know they are advancing to a different kind of day.

By the next morning my enthusiasm wavered slightly. "Let's write our own ad to sell the house," I said. The real-estate contract had run out. And just to be sure I understood this longing to go beyond our recall, I told a skeptical Jerry, "I'll ask God to send us a cash buyer. If we get that, I'll know for sure we'll never be deserted on the land."

The first people who responded to the ad said they weren't sure why they'd come by. They lived out of state, couldn't retire for two years anyway, but they'd liked the sound of what I'd written, about a house that was a "plant palace," custom built, with vast windows and mountain views.

After they left, Jerry said, "They're going to make a cash offer." Two weeks later, they did, in a phone call. Even more amazing, they asked if we could remain in our house for another two years, so that they'd know the house was in good hands until they could retire.

Ephesians 3:20 reads, "Now to him who is able to do immeasurably more than all we ask or imagine, according to his power that is at work within us."

More than all we could ask or imagine. I was just beginning to understand how limitless God is.

7

Of Friends and Fire

As we became more confident about sharing our dream, we brought friends to the land. Their presence set a precedent: friends would almost always be there as we made discoveries about Starvation Point and about ourselves.

We floated down ten miles of the John Day River with a friend (and former boss) and his wife, Loring and Jeannette Cannon, and took their raft out on the gravel beach at the island end of the land. We spent the next morning getting the truck unstuck from the deep, soft sand of the flat.

In between efforts to push the truck, Jeannette inquired, "Where will you put all the people?" Her question gave me chills. Jerry and I had not shared with anyone our vision of the people who might come to the land.

After halting explanations, Jeannette sighed, relieved. "Well, good," she said. "I feel better knowing you feel this adventure is something God wants you to do."

I felt better knowing we could share the spiritual side of the land with others without everyone thinking we were crazy.

Another weekend, when we brought Sandy Maynard down, we explored the possibility of fixing up Con's cabin to live in while we built a permanent home. Sandy was a colleague and friend. Like Jerry, she had visionary qualities and could anticipate potential problems down the road.

We sat cozily in the front of the pickup one February day, her friend David on the passenger side, with Sandy and me sandwiched in the middle while Jerry drove.

Unhindered by clouds, the sun burned hot against the velvet hills, casting gothic shadows in the ravines.

When we arrived at the top of the roller-coaster hill, we stopped at my request. We could see that winter snows had washed out the steep incline even more than before. The ruts were huge—two feet deep in places. They ran like gaping wounds over the first ridge and then dropped out of sight down the steep incline to the flat stopping place at the bottom. Jerry would have to straddle them, maybe driving up on the bank into the sagebrush in places.

I took a deep breath. Then, as though preparing for an airplane landing, I braced my right arm on the ceiling of the truck cab and planted my right foot on the center hump, as if to brake. Jerry, David, and Sandy seemed unconcerned.

Jerry put the automatic transmission in low gear, and we started slowly down the hill, each of us leaning forward, peering over the truck hood. I gritted my teeth and stiffened my legs.

I hated this part.

Suddenly, for no reason, Jerry stepped on the gas, and we shot down the incline like a rabbit discovering a hungry coyote on his tail. The truck bounced and bucked, twisted and careened off the sides of the ruts at full speed.

"Slow down!" I screamed, furious with him for doing this just to prove to me that we could make that roller-coaster hill at seventy miles per hour.

"I'm trying!" he shouted back.

We plunged forward, the four of us unevenly hitting the top of the cab with our heads, then plopping onto the seat like pistons in an engine. *If we survive this,* I thought to myself, *I will walk ever after down this section of road.*

At the bottom, the truck coasted to a stop, still upright. Jerry had turned off the engine.

I surveyed the survivors.

David's glasses were askew on his face. With one arm he gripped the door in a death lock; with the other arm he held the window behind Sandy's head, like the backside of a breast stroke. He was uncharacteristically silent.

"That was interesting," Sandy noted calmly, though her eyes were the size of charcoal briquettes.

As I turned to see how Jerry survived, he said flatly, through clenched teeth, "Jane…take…your…foot…off…the…accelerator." The words were spoken with great control. I just looked at him, wonderingly.

"Your foot," he said, pointing. "Look!"

My eyes followed his finger to the dastardly appendage jammed against the gas pedal. It was my foot. While my right shoe had so carefully "braked" on the engine hump, my left foot had slipped unnoticed onto the accelerator, where I had pushed to brace myself and instead almost sent us into orbit.

I looked sheepishly at him. How like me to shout "Slow down" while I was the one speeding us up. He patted my knee, forgiving. "We would have made it just fine without your bracing for an accident."

In silence we drove the short distance up the padlock turn, through the gate to the lower bench, toward the cabin.

Peace and quiet welcomed us. A red-tailed hawk circled above, whistling his high-pitched soothing call.

Regaining our land legs, we walked slowly around Con's cabin, considering its potential. Jerry cautioned us about rattlesnakes as we explored.

"It would probably be easier to tear it down and start over," he noted from the loft where he'd climbed, using the sagebrush ladder attached to the wall.

It was like a cell inside, a good place to get cabin fever from being holed up for months in bad weather. I wondered if we could even get our stuffed couch and love seat in it, along with a table and some chairs, my books, Jerry's guns, and the dogs. "Would there even be room for a bed?" I asked Jerry skeptically.

"There's an old bedspring up here," he called down. Looking up through the holes in the loft boards, we could see him stooping under the low roof while walking gingerly around the bed. Blue sky showed above him in ragged patches.

I remembered stories of homesteaders with families of twelve living in even smaller cabins—and still inviting weary travelers to join them for the night.

Off to the side, an old chair with no seat lay on its side. (Later we would learn that the chair was Con's outdoor bathroom. He'd sit, watch the view, listen to the meadowlarks, and do his business.

When the "toilet" needed emptying, Con simply moved the chair to another scenic spot. The EPA would probably not have approved.

Climbing down from the loft, Jerry stepped outside and announced in his "I've decided" voice, "We should be able to build the hangar and house on the bench, even though it's less than a quarter-mile to the river." Our land fell within the Federal Scenic Waterways Act, which allows agricultural buildings such as barns and shops within a quarter-mile of the river, but not domestic buildings. Rules governed rotating crops, metal roofs (that might restrict fire damage), and building back from the river. But since the cabin existed when the law passed in '74, Jerry thought he could design a home on the site where the cabin had been.

The sun beat down on our faces, making us wish we'd brought sunscreen or hats.

"We're going to plant grapes on the benches," Jerry explained to Sandy. "And maybe watermelons in the sandier soil on the flat as a cash crop until the grapes mature. Then we'll clear the flat for alfalfa."

Sandy had been thoughtful. Now she spoke. "I'd consider taking some first-aid classes," she offered. "CPR, response to snake bite, that sort of thing. You could be quite a distance from any medical care. Maybe some veterinary information, too."

I had thought about Hansel and Ricky loving it here, and about cats chasing field mice in the barn. But of course we'd be unable to rush them to a vet in fifteen minutes as we had.

We returned to the truck and made a run up the roller-coaster grade. But without *my* help, Jerry failed to step on the gas sufficiently the first time, so we spun rocks out in a spray behind us, and we halted halfway up.

"You'll need a four-wheel-drive, too," Sandy pragmatically noted as Jerry backed down over the deep ruts.

This time Jerry backed halfway up the padlock turn, then slammed on the gas. We roared down the road and up the roller coaster, our bodies jostling in the cab like the pebbles in the truck bed.

"Maybe we should have taken the chair and the ladder as souvenirs," I said, wishing later that we had.

The next time we drove down, we shot surveyor grades with Jerry's transit, selecting the solar site for the house. We also brought a sluice box, gold pans, and the Pedersons, who thought we might strike it rich beside the river with the fine black sand that promised flecks of gold. But the real reason we came that weekend almost a year later was to survey the damage Marion Boynton's Christmas card had described.

I should have written you sooner, she wrote. *We did everything we could to save the cabin, but it was just so dry. Lightning downriver started the fire, and the winds wouldn't let it die. It burned several thousand acres. The men were out for days at a time fighting it. It's so hard in those deep ravines. I'm so sorry. I know you liked the cabin, too.*

We wondered what the land would look like now, without the cabin, the sagebrush, or the bunch grass sprouting up like stiff bouquets held tightly by a child's hand.

At the gate on Memorial Day 1983, we could see the effects of the fire from the autumn before. The fence that marched up the steep hill and swung down to the river, opening only for the gate, still stood. But some of the cedar posts were charred; others, having fed the hungry flames, were completely gone. Still, the fence held taut and tight, evidence that the corner posts had been set deep and strong those years ago and still held the five strands of barbed wire tightly.

The sagebrush on the flat stood untouched, but on either side of the road along the bench stood skeletons of black sagebrush remains. The gnarled, knotty stems still stood six feet tall, but their naked branches gave no shade. The dark stems stood out, etched against the new green growth of native bunch grass, as though someone had carefully cut them and placed them there.

"It's already recovering," Jerry said. We stopped the truck and took in the fresh smell of damp spring earth, admiring the softness of the green. Above us a jet hemmed its way across the sky like a needle followed by a streak of white thread.

We felt ourselves mending too, being restored and refreshed. Despite the blackened sagebrush staring at us, the decision to come here never seemed more right.

Jerry and I walked hand in hand, letting the dogs run up and over the hills, beneath the leafless sage. We rested amid a few tiny, fragrant yellow flowers that still sported bell-like blooms, although most must have sparkled earlier in the spring. Small purple flowers like phlox sprang up in clumps. Delicate spears of camass bobbed their heads in the faint breeze. Wild asters seemed to grow out of rocks. The river ran like a blue thread beyond the flowers.

I remember being surprised that so much life could come back in just one season.

Across the river we could see a tractor, toy-size in the distance. Someone moved brush, clearing the ground on a flat. Thin wisps of smoke grew out of piles of branches and grass.

Close to the base of the steep hill on the other side stood several tall cottonwood trees hiding an old house.

"We'll be clearing land like that before long," Jerry said wistfully.

I looked more longingly at the trees and the shade they'd offer. We'd discovered only two scrubby hackberry trees on our land, growing at the base of the bench, far from where the house would go.

Jerry was first to notice the black smoke and flames across the river. "He's got a real fire going over there now," he said, an edge to his voice. Steve Pederson looked in that direction. "But it's so damp, I can't believe it'll burn much."

But as we watched, the wind picked up and we could see the red fingers of flames reaching higher and then moving ominously across the neighbor's field, toward the trees.

And the homesite.

"Is someone living there?" I wondered aloud. Jerry shook his head, but we were all standing now, watching, when we saw the fire explode beneath the trees, sending sparks and flames a hundred feet into the sky.

"It's got the house," Jerry said, knowing there was nothing we could do, even if we could have crossed the river.

My heart pounded as I watched the rancher edge his Caterpillar tractor up the side of the steep hill, well in front of the flames that moved rapidly after him seeking more food, having quickly digested the dry old house.

"He's trying to get a firebreak," Steve translated for us, "to cut it off, if it gets that far."

Which it did—and then beyond, rolling close to the ground like a burning tumbleweed in the wind. Once it jumped the firebreak, the tractor stopped, its owner resigned, we guessed, to fate.

"Shouldn't we go out and call the fire department?" I asked, only vaguely wondering how far a phone might be.

Jerry shook his head. "By the time fire engines got there, it'd be burned out, hopefully at the road farther upriver."

We watched for some time as the low flames and smoke moved across the ridge, into the ravines and out again, leaving rocks exposed like pimples as it burned out of sight.

I thought of Nero watching Rome burn, and I wondered if he'd thought someone else had called the fire department. Faint smoke drifted back for hours, wrapping our evening meal and campfire in caution.

"We'll have to have a green fire ring around the house," Jerry said. "It may be the only thing that saves us from a range fire."

Sleep came uneasily that night as I thought of protections I had always taken for granted.

In the morning we walked out toward the river. Deer—and Elsie's cows—had made tunnels through the sagebrush, which had otherwise grown unbothered for the past fifteen years. We followed one to the river, Ricky and Hansel nudging closely at our heels.

The scorched remains of the hillside across the river stopped us. The fire had burned out eventually; the Caterpillar tractor's tracks reminded us of how quickly fortunes could change in this country.

The fires reminded me that we would be at the mercy of the elements here. No matter how hard we worked or studied or planned, lightning, water, wind, and sun could change it all, taking away the efforts of hard labor in a matter of minutes.

Much of our life here would be beyond our control.

It was not a comforting thought.

Jerry and Steve worked the sluice box without success, pouring pebbles and water through the long trough set in a ripple in the river. Judy and I gathered only sunburn, sore backs, and an appreciation for the long-ago miners. Squatting over our old gold pans, swirling sand and pebbles in the tepid water, we soon grew tired, stiff, and discouraged about the prospects of prospecting.

"It's going to be a mess to clear that flat," Jerry said later at the tent while drinking cold lemonade from the cooler. "And we won't have a gold mine to pay for it." He smiled.

Judy and I sat in the tent's shade, our legs stretched out on lawn chairs, Hansel's dark head competing with my book for space in my lap. His eyes begged for another walk, and his nose whistled his impatience.

Absently, I scratched his ears. "Someday," I told him, "when the house sells and we build and move here, we'll walk out there every morning. I promise."

He seemed content, his stubby tail wagging his whole body, his head burrowing deeper into my lap. His eyes closed. I imagined he dreamed of romps in the fine black sand, while I wondered about outwitting the elements to successfully homestead on Starvation Point.

8

Gatherings, Endings, and New Beginnings

IT STOOD LIKE A SLEEPING DINOSAUR stuck between the Spotted Mule Western Wear Store and the Bend Laundromat. I'd passed it fifty times without noticing its For Sale sign.

The uses of a 450-B John Deere tractor with a backhoe, bucket, and teeth escaped me. But Jerry said we needed it, and in his world of machines and construction, I had to trust him.

I'd been reading *Freedom of Simplicity,* thinking that our move to someplace rural and remote would bring something rustic and uncomplicated into our lives. The tractor—we called it Deere John—startled me into realizing we'd be *adding* to our possessions rather than discarding.

I wondered what the pioneers considered essential as they packed and planned. From their diaries, I knew the women harbored heirlooms in the cluttered Conestogas but often left the weighty things behind.

Men took their horses for transportation and as tools to clear the ground. They brought knives and axes and ropes that later made buckets or bedsteads. They took their weapons more for food than fight.

Unlike the pioneers, we would not be traveling far in miles; but in the change of trappings, we were moving almost to another planet.

"Do we really need something so big?" I wondered aloud as we walked around the machine in a billow of diesel and exhaust fumes from the traffic swirling around us. Jerry patted the machine frame like a contented husband.

Males bond quickly to machines. While I certainly felt no attachment to Deere John in 1983, Jerry had already taken his vows.

It was the length of two cars parallel parked. Shaped like paper clips, the wide tracks on either side of the yellow tractor rose thigh high. Levers and pedals operated black hydraulic hoses that hung like long, fat sausages extending from a block behind the driver's seat. The hoses disappeared inside a long metal section that angled out, tonglike, and ended in a bucket with teeth like a spaghetti grabber.

"That's the backhoe," Jerry noted. A larger bucket sat beside it, unattached.

In front, the engine was housed under sturdy yellow metal like that of a farm tractor. The John Deere tractors I'd grown up with in Wisconsin were smaller and green, making gentle noises as they pulled around manure spreaders and wagons.

"Look at that bucket," Jerry said, pointing enthusiastically at what I thought of as a scoop. He shook his head in wonder, thoroughly delighted with Mr. Deere's versatility.

"But what will we use it for?" I asked.

Jerry thought I was joking. "We'll load the dump truck with it," he said.

"Dump truck?"

"Right. We'll have to clear ground for the building sites, first the hangar and shop, then the house. There'll be a fair amount of work clearing the sagebrush off the bottom and then moving some of the dirt back that was pushed against the bench during the '64 flood. We'll need it for the water, for digging the ditches for the power lines. It can clear the benches, move rocks…" His voice trailed off as my eyes glazed over.

"Dump truck?" I said again. "What dump truck?"

"I saw an ad for one in the classified section."

The white-and-blue dump truck turned out to be rather cute. Within minutes, it was ours.

We bought it from a couple who had cleared their own ground and now had no use for the 1973 truck. "That's what we'll do, too," Jerry assured me, discounting his pack-rat tendencies. "We'll sell it as soon as we're through with it." Right.

Oddly enough, the dump truck's owners also had photographic equipment for sale: cameras, darkroom developers, and trays. Jerry's knowledge of such equipment surprised me. "I was in the naval photographic school for three years," he reminded me. "If you're really thinking about writing, the cameras could come in handy for illustrating articles. And you need a computer." The latter suggestion didn't sound negotiable.

So the dark-room equipment came home with us too. And the computer was not far behind.

Then we gathered animals, deciding to keep one of Hansel's daughters who sported brown-and-white ticking. Surrounding her stubby tail was a solid liver patch resembling a shovel, which she turned toward anyone calling her name, wagging her whole behind, begging to be scratched.

The temperamental opposite of hyper Hansel, she loved to snuggle, a habit she refused to give up even when she eventually weighed fifty pounds, her warped self-image leaving her believing she was poodle-size and so could climb and squat on any open lap. She loved food and gained weight easily. She also liked to lie around in front of wood stoves, sprawled on her back legs open to the warmth.

Her love of unsupervised butter earned her the nickname of Mrs. Butterworth-less.

I had wanted to call her Gretel because it fit so well with Hansel. But Jerry was adamantly opposed. "I won't be out in the field hunting birds with my friends and have to call 'Here, Hansel! Here, Gretel!' It'd be just too much," he said with a scowl.

"No need to bring attention to the stepmother image, either," I decided, selecting Josie as our new addition's name.

Imagining we'd take field-dressed game from the deep ravines of the ranch, we also added four mules for hunting. Henry, known affectionately as Fat Albert, came first, a pony mule who loved kids but easily dumped grown men he didn't like. He also thumped the water trough whenever it was low, reminding us to "fill 'er up." Miss Em came next, a sturdy black mule who faithfully carried her load; then came Cissy, the strong-willed one, and Blue, gentle Blue, who trotted to us whenever we entered the field, lowering her head for a scratch. Blue was the first to follow Hansel and me on our morning walks.

Jerry focused next on gathering the oak lumber we wanted for floors, cabinets, and trim for the windows and walls. My parents (though skeptical of our endeavor) scouted out mills in Minnesota and Wisconsin for us, looking for red oak.

Several vague, foreign-sounding, long-distance phone conversations about the oak passed between Jerry and my dad. I wanted to understand the decisions we were making that were taking us closer to the land, but I was limited by experience and personal energy. Thus I got an early taste of the total trust I'd eventually have in Jerry's knowledge and skill.

I was already giving hours of my life to the foreign language of the air, having recommitted myself to take flying lessons again until I'd conquered my fears and had my license.

Or destroyed the plane, whichever came first.

So while Jerry gathered oak from Minnesota and my parents delivered it across country, still with the rough bark lining the edges of splintery slabs, I flew.

After Jerry and I stacked the oak for drying in the barn, then transported it to a local mill to have it planed and cut into the hardwood-floor lengths and stairsteps, I flew.

While Jerry worked on plans, studied contour maps, outlined the airstrip at the base of the bench, and designed the hangar and the house so they'd collect the sun, I flew.

A cobbler by trade, Clint, my new instructor, looked every bit the part. A leather apron covered his broad chest as he pounded on boots and shoes, little glasses perched on his nose. Short and almost round, he had hundreds of hours of flight instruction, and his was the name we'd heard most often when we'd sought an instructor who was patient, kind, and had nerves of steel.

Soft-spoken and talkative, Clint loved teaching as much as flying, and I think he enjoyed the challenge of teaching me to land instead of hyperventilate.

He seemed to know I needed time to reassure myself that I could fly and would once again find joy in piercing skies above the desert or squeaking tires on concrete strips.

He timed each step in my mastery of the Rallye so I would win in the battle with myself.

At home I'd imagine myself piloting the plane, taking off and landing, and when my hands began to sweat and my breathing changed, I'd think of birds singing, of water rushing over river rocks, of deer gingerly stepping around the sage. And then I'd imagine flying once again until I could be there in the plane, alone, and not be frightened.

Eventually, I did fly alone again, and then for hours more with Clint, landing in crosswinds, on short strips near the mountains, or at precision points he chose at Roberts Field. We flew at night, collecting memories of sparkling towns scattered along the black desert, like a mirror reflecting the stars glittering overhead. We flew maneuvers and practiced stalls and turns that left my stomach searching for Mom's old coffee can.

The Rallye became a trustworthy machine to me, the way Deere John became a faithful friend to Jerry. I flew until the Rallye seemed predictable and friendly, and both Clint and I thought I was ready for the official FAA flight-check ride, which I passed.

At the local college, I enrolled in a writer's class taught by Bob Welch, who worked for the local newspaper. When he read aloud my first assignments, my palms sweated nearly as much as when I encountered a difficult landing. "These are good," he told me as I picked up my papers. "I think you could sell some of this." Like Clint, my writing instructor helped me overcome the battle of inadequacy. Maybe I could go to the land. And write.

Then, finally, in the classified ads (where else!) we located an oak piano and moved it into my vision of the living room in our not-yet-built home. I could see it filling empty hours without television as I plunked away, trying to regain the skills I had when I'd last played as a child. The imagined notes brought back childhood dreams of playing as smoothly as my grandma did, or my aunt Gert, who taught my weekly lessons.

Finally, by Christmas, Jerry finished drawing the plans that would be our home. We purchased work boots from Clint, along with extra pairs of jeans and shirts. The piano stood refinished in the living room; the photographic equipment filled boxes in the hall. The dogs were ready, the mules fat and sassy. The computer sat atop an oak desk Jerry had built for me, and I'd sold my first short article to a regional magazine. Deere John sat idly waiting beside the dump truck, ready.

Journal Entry, December 17, 1983

The snow lightly dusts itself off onto the junipers. Our driveway looks a perfect ribbon of white as it winds its way past the split-rail fence and out to Connarn Road. It's our last Christmas, if all goes as planned, looking at this view.

Four mules graze on snow-covered fields. The dogs are penned (unless Hansel figures out *this* gate latch, too) because of the staff party later this evening. Again, a last one. After the first of the year, Jerry will begin building our home, and by fall, we'll move in.

Food to overflowing spreads across Grandma's harvest table. I've made things without flour or gluten that I can eat, relieved to find out why I was always ill. People will arrive soon, good people, ones I've worked with now for ten years. I will miss them in the time ahead.

Many changes. Back from the army, Matt has brought his new girlfriend, Melissa, for a visit. A petite blond with a goal to work in special education, she seems good for Matt, though we worry. He was discharged for failing to complete an alcohol-and-drug treatment program.

Still, gone is the vague, foggy feeling that surrounded me whenever I thought about going to the river. I haven't placed the burden of responsibility for our happiness with the move on Jerry. I know that this move, with its sacrifice and disruption, is my decision, too. Maybe I'm trusting Jerry more, and growing in faith that we will not be forsaken there, having chosen to "go to the land and write."

By late January 1984, we were faced with one more new beginning, after Jerry spent a day at the state Capitol and learned the horrible news that we would not be allowed to build a home on Con's old site. "The agency says since no one lived in that house when it burned, we can't replace it. We can build agricultural buildings that close to the river, but not a home. The guy said it was his job to keep the land the way it was in 1974 when the law passed. 'The law allows us to hassle you every step of the way, and that's what we intend to do,'" Jerry quoted him.

"We can only build beyond the quarter mile, and there's no level place to do that. The ridges are too steep."

He sank into the recliner, dropped his head in his hands so I saw only thick white hair threaded through his fingers.

"What'll we do?" I said, alarmed. "We've already sold the house, bought all that stuff. I've given notice at work."

"I'm not sure," Jerry sighed. "Let's drive up tomorrow and see if there's any other place to build, maybe talk with some planning people."

We drove silently toward Sherman County. In the mood we were in, the sky seemed to be a weary shade of blue. Dirty, crusted snow lined the barren black roads, matching our dispositions. In Moro we met and talked with locals about the permit process and our problem. "Just build it," one said. "They'll never bother you way down there."

But the thought of living illegally washed out our pleasure. If we were *supposed* to be there on that property, it didn't seem that we should have to cheat to do it.

We wound our way down to the river, forced to change our vision or cheat.

Geese lifted up from the water. We heard them first, then watched them circling ever higher. Con's site was just too close; the benches, too, sat within the quarter mile. Within the *legal* limit rose steep hills and rimrocks. We both spoke silent prayers but saw nothing there in answer. Since we had already driven so far, we continued our trip back to Wasco, then on down the Columbia gorge to the town of The Dalles. Fifty-two miles from Starvation Point, The Dalles would be our main shopping area once we moved. *If* we moved.

We ate lunch, and Jerry called to arrange for the Rallye's next annual checkup with an airplane mechanic. He pulled out the aerial map of the property to share with Ned and Judy Pointer, the mechanic and his wife; Jerry spread it across the hood of the Datsun. "This is the river and the land," he said sadly, "but we may not be able to build there." He ran his stubby fingers across the map. His hand moved up along the road toward the gate, then stopped abruptly.

He picked up the map, held it closer.

"This ravine," he said, tapping the map with his finger as he set it back on the car hood. "Wonder why I never noticed it."

His fingers pointed at a steep ravine cut between two rock ledges that promised to be a quarter mile from the river, and maybe, with effort, made level enough to house a home.

Briskly, we drove back to the river, our spirits lifted, the sky much bluer now. With tape measure in hand, we walked the ravine. We'd exercise our calf muscles traveling to a house built here; constructing it would be tricky. We stood in the shadow of the ridge, realizing the house could not count on sun for heating. No hangar could be attached this far from the landing strip.

But the site *was* beyond the quarter mile, and legal.

While Jerry marked the distance on the map, checking and rechecking with his transit, I caught the view. We'd be higher up here, farther from the river, but we could see the entire canyon. On either side would be outcroppings of lava rock, old and nubby, with scattered growth of bunch grass spearing out from the shallow soil.

Behind us, straight up the ravine, ran the reptile road as it began its descent through the canyon. Toward the river, we'd gaze across to a wall of exposed rock set stiffly in the hillside that stretched up almost a thousand feet.

In just two years we'd spend months looking at that view, unable to do more than lie there, staring, letting our bodies heal as we recovered. But that was in the future, in a time we could not see. On that day in January, the view was new and welcome, an answer to our prayers.

A breeze rustled the low grasses surrounding my feet. Maybe it'd be cooler here in the summer, catching a flutter of wind. Jerry smiled and signaled me to come back to the car. He'd have to redesign the house for this new site and construct a separate barn and hangar, probably where Con's cabin once stood. We'd never get a new loan and permits for the house by the time we needed to move from the Bend home, never mind construct a house to move into. Interim arrangements would have to gel.

The building would be arduous, but all the pieces could fall into place. We'd gathered what we needed for our dream; we wouldn't need to cheat. Now wide awake in this adventure, we were finally ready to move on.

Part II

ARRIVING ON
STARVATION POINT

Even old rats, when given new challenges,
grow new brain cells.

—JANE'S RAT WISDOM

The homestead under construction. Notice the hangar/barn in the background.

9

Take Nothing for Granted

THOUGH WE DIDN'T MEAN TO, we made several false assumptions that came from comfortable living and having a menu of choices and gifts. For example, we thought Jerry's building experience and proper planning would keep our distresses under control. We didn't anticipate the power of the elements, the wind and the rain, and we underestimated the value of the things we took for granted.

On the land we would learn that the rules were different. Elements could not be controlled, no matter how much we planned, and priorities shifted rather quickly.

Dennis Gant and his yellow lab, Kipper, spent the night in their van, though it's questionable how much sleep they managed with the wind howling around their ears like Niagara Falls tumbling over the edge.

Jerry, Hansel, and I slept in the eight-foot camper we'd moved to the land and set on two wooden sawhorses. The windows rattled in the gusts, and the vents clanked against the roof.

Jerry spent weekdays in the camper, opening cans, cooking on the small stove, and using camper water sparingly for drinking and washing.

In March, he and Dennis had brought the camper, Deere John, and the dump truck to the land. They had used the tractor to pull the dump truck and Jerry's Chevy out of the mud-bogged road as it wound through the wheat fields on top.

I wasn't delighted to learn that the road was impassable along the flat. I had thought only the section as steep as a cow's face that dropped into the canyon would be treacherous, and then for only a few days a year. But I'd made the trip safely the night before, taking a needed break from the packing and the hassles of leaving and grieving work.

Dennis and Jerry spent the week working on the foundation for the hangar, barn, and shop, the first building to go up. Tomorrow the cement trucks would lumber down the hill and deposit the concrete for the floor.

Jerry slept contentedly despite the wind. Hansel rested curled up on the floor, a privileged visitor, since Ricky and Josie stayed home. I slept little, sure the wind was not just noise, but push and shove.

The little camper rocked on its fragile base as the gusts hit, blowing swirling sand against the metal sides like pelting raindrops. Just before daylight, someone seemed to pull the wind's plug, and it suddenly stopped.

Dawn cracked open like a ripe watermelon: rosy, crisp, and aromatic. I stuck my head out of the camper door to inhale the morning. Hansel peeked around my legs to check the river view. Meadowlarks warbled their song that friends from Wyoming translated as "Laramie is a pretty little town." The eastern sun warmed my face as it rose above the river.

"Coffee's on," Jerry called out the window to Dennis. We watched Dennis's lanky, Levi-clad legs stretch out the end of his van, pausing. Kipper barked his impatience, needing help to move his arthritic old bones out into the dust.

A California transplant, Dennis had been a craftsman working as a carpet layer until his knees gave out and he began applying his skills to home building. He'd stayed with a neighbor in Bend for a number of years, and we'd become acquainted with his gentle voice, his easy smile, his inquisitive, detailed style.

As he had built his own home, there were phone calls to Jerry about ways to manage problems in structure and design. His learning curve was high, and Jerry liked being around him. He'd stopped by one evening, wondering if we'd need some help building on the land—an answer to another prayer.

In his early thirties, Dennis approached life as an opportunity to learn something new, and then he remembered and applied the lessons. He'd agreed to help with the shop and barn and, we hoped, with the house later on in the year when it was finally designed and the permits acquired. And his bride, Sherrie, would have a chance to decide whether she wanted some months of remote living with strangers.

Dennis unwrapped his slender six-foot frame from the van and tenderly helped Kipper out. He checked the dog's water and food supply before his sandy hair and brown eyes appeared in the doorway of our camper. He stepped over Hansel, folding his body, cowboy boots, and knees under the small kitchen table.

"This is the day," he said, his good looks smiling in anticipation, his hands wrapping around the steaming coffee cup Jerry handed him.

"I hope," Jerry said, concern sounding in his voice as he set a stack of pancakes in front of Dennis and checked his watch.

We'd chosen one of the wettest springs on record to begin building on Starvation Point. In April 1984, that rain was manna to the winter wheat, but it left the reptile road soft and murky. Traveling on it was a treacherous adventure, like driving on intestines.

The last few days had dawned without rain. The wind howling at night dried out the road some, leaving water puddling in the dust. But Jerry, to feel secure about the safety of the big trucks on so soft a surface, had convinced the cement contractor to drive down the day before.

When they arrived, the trucks would back up against the wooden forms that created the outline of the building. They'd dump their mixture of gravel, sand, and cement onto the leveled sand and then drive off, all in less than an hour.

We waited now for the arrival of the trucks and of a cement worker from The Dalles, who would help us finish out the heavy, wet mixture, creating, leveling, and smoothing the floor that would support the airplane, Jerry's shop equipment, and, eventually, farm machinery. In the back would be a small room we'd fill with darkroom equipment one day. For now, though, we planned to secure all our worldly goods there, stacked to the ceiling while we built the house.

On the bank above the foundation, I took a picture, imagining I'd photograph the events of the day. Hansel whistled and whined for the walk I'd promised as soon as the foundation was poured. He sat at attention beside me, leaned his head into my knee, then stood up and wandered off, sniffing birds beneath the sagebrush.

We waited for the big trucks.

Finally, we heard a pickup—not a cement truck—and then saw it pull onto the bench next to the construction form. Two men stepped out, facing Con's old homesite. They looked around, and I motioned them to join us at the camper, but they signaled back that we should come up to them.

Reading the sign on the side of the pickup, Jerry said, "It's the contractor, but not the one who came down yesterday."

We followed Jerry rapidly up the short, steep hill.

"Ain't gonna do it," the contractor said to Jerry as he approached. He scowled, and I pictured him with a cigar in his mouth, chewing in irritation. "That road's a mess. My trucks'll sink outta sight! Can't believe he said we'd do it!" He disliked the decision of his partner, the one who'd ordered out the two trucks now sitting at the top of the winding grade.

One had started down, and at a hairpin turn (where the old car body lay on its side to keep the corner from sinking during the rains) the truck had sunk in close to the edge. The driver had barely backed out and wanted no part of coming back down.

Jerry protested, and there was a brief discussion and then silence. Finally, the cement contractor said, "That thing work?" He pointed to our cute dump truck. Jerry nodded. "Well, drive 'er up there and we'll pour the cement in. You can bring down a few yards at a time. Won't be so heavy on the road. Stuff's hot, so let's get going." He headed up the hill.

"I'd tell him to take it back!" Dennis said as we walked back to the camper, aware of the work ahead. But it was Saturday, and Jerry seemed to know they'd have no place else to put "hot" cement, a mixture getting ready to set up as hard concrete. It looked as though we'd have trouble getting anyone to come down any other day anyway, so we needed to take what advantage we could.

The ascent and descent of cement in the dump truck began.

It is a little over a mile from the barn to the top, where the twisting, winding road begins to sink down into the canyon.

At the top sat the two cement trucks, their center sections whirling like a child's top, twirling the gravel, sand, and cement. Through a funnel contraption, they filled the truck's dump box less than half-full, and Jerry began the slow drive down, across the fake cattle guard, around the bends, inching down the roller-coaster driveway and up the other side, through the gate, back to the foundation.

The first load went fairly well, though Jerry had to back over some of the forms he'd so carefully laid as a foundation, the lumber splintering with the weight of dump truck and concrete. The dump bed raised up slowly, Jerry pulled a lever behind the cab, and stuff as gray as dental silver, with the consistency of pancake dough, poured out.

While Jerry left for the next load, Dennis and I and the cement worker, who had just arrived, began spreading the sludge with shovels, collecting small chunks on our boots and pants. When sufficiently spread out, we leveled it off with a long board—a screed—held at each end and scraped across the top of the concrete, like a baker creating a level cup of flour with a knife.

Panting, we'd just finished when Jerry arrived with the second load.

This was going to be a long, photo-free day.

At the sixth or seventh cargo of cement, Dennis noted that the concrete was getting thicker, harder to work and screed. The cement worker brought out a gasoline-operated gizmo that looked like a large metal hoop skirt. He skated it across the top of the goop, and it shook the concrete, moving and smoothing the pebbles into deeper pools of silver.

"How many more loads"? I asked as Jerry reported that the first truck was empty. Jerry counted his up-and-down trips, scanned over how much we'd filled up, and looked puzzled.

"The cement's not filling as much of the space as it should." He stopped to measure and turned with a horrified look on his face.

"The floor's going to be three and a half inches thicker than I set it for!" he said, alarmed. He measured an untouched side again and paled. "I measured it just last night, and it was fine." He ran his hands through his hair, upset, before concluding, "The wind must have blown away two inches of sand! I just can't believe it!"

I could. I'd heard it pitting the side of the camper all night.

They had to explain to me what this meant: There wouldn't be enough cement to cover the foundation, and the floor would be thicker than it needed to be and more expensive to finish.

Quick alterations were devised. The shop, darkroom, and back of the barn would get cement while it lasted; the front half would go without until some later date, maybe when the house foundation was poured—if it could be.

My shoulders began to ache around eleven. The pulling and pushing strained every muscle I had. Dennis and the cement man worked steadily, pacing themselves, moving the thick silver mud under skies now as gray as the concrete.

Hansel checked in with me, whining at times, but wisely staying out of the wet smudge.

Around noon, Jerry said they'd run out of water in the second cement truck, having dumped 250 gallons each during the morning, trying to keep the cement from thickening up in the trucks. They needed more water.

I looked at him, wondering where he thought we'd get any with no electricity and no well or spring yet tapped.

He handed me two five-gallon plastic containers and sent me to the river.

In the high water, the river overflowed its banks and then receded, leaving behind a slow finger of flow that couldn't get back into the river. It worked its way around the bottom of the bench, not far from our campsite, where it would eventually sink in or evaporate.

Hidden by sagebrush, it was deep enough to sink a five-gallon can into on its side. I held the jug down with my foot, pulled it out of the muck full, and laid the second one in. Then, with a can in each hand, I carried the eighty pounds of water up the steep hill to the waiting dump truck.

Jerry drove the ten gallons up the hill and dumped the water into the cement truck on top, hoping to keep the stuff fluid while they poured another batch of concrete into our cute little truck.

Fatigue showed on Jerry's face.

I knew the rough ride up and down the hill would be killing his back. He said nothing, just kept going, knowing that to stop would literally mark our failure in concrete.

At each trip down the hill, I refilled the water cans, admiring the pioneer women who must have done this kind of hard work daily; I decided such activities would cause—or make one wish for—an early death.

Jerry drove back up the ravine, chewing on a sandwich; the three of us stopped just long enough to eat a late lunch.

The cement worker, a man in his late forties, slipped open his shirt to dry off the sweat. Sitting across from me on the bumper of his truck, he leaned over to pick up a container of water.

That's when I saw it.

A long scar ran the length of his chest, from the top of his sternum, out of sight near his belly. It was pink and raw as fresh shrimp.

"What on earth did you do to yourself?" I asked, impolitely pointing.

He looked down at his body. "Open-heart surgery," he answered, taking a bite of his sandwich.

"How long ago?" It looked so fresh.

"Been out about six weeks," he said.

There were lines on his face I hadn't noticed before, and sweat beaded across his furrowed brow.

He'll die here! I thought. But I said, "Does your doctor know you're out here, doing this?"

He nodded, brushing a crumb from his sliced chest. "If he wants to get paid, he has to let me work. No insurance. Wife and kids to support."

Risking his life for "no insurance." Was it really worth that, forcing himself to work less than two months after his lifesaving surgery? For him it was, I guessed. At least, here he was. Without the luxury of sick leave or benefactor to pay off his debt, his choices were few.

As a contractor, Jerry kept disability insurance, and I'd always had health coverage provided by my employers—dental, vision, sick leave, the works. I knew what it cost to provide it for my own staff in 1984, budgeting 33 percent of a salary for benefits, which most employees never considered as gains.

Until that moment, I hadn't considered what a loss it would be—no health insurance or sick leave—and I wondered if I'd push myself as hard as he was if I had to, returning to work so quickly after death brushed by my side.

We'd face that same decision not two years later; but on the day we poured the concrete, it was just a wondering thought for me—but not for the hardworking man resting from the work.

We returned to our task as Jerry brought another load back and handed me the water cans. The water weighed more each time, and so did the truck. Each trip meant more hardened concrete stuck to the sides of the dump box. The stuff that did come out looked chunkier, no longer partially fluid. Our arms ached trying to maneuver it, level it.

At six o'clock, the empty concrete trucks headed back, the floor looked as level as it would get, and the heart-surgery worker drove home, still alive.

Globs of immovable concrete, like volcanic rocks, clung to the sides of the truck's dump box. We tried a shovel and pickax, but concrete, like the concept, gets its name from its immovability, its hard rigidity. I understood why.

It would take Dennis pounding Deere John's bucket against the hardened sludge in the morning, over and over like a powerful pick, to remove the rigid rocks and return the dump truck to its normal state. Like an attractive, smart model, it had proven itself not only cute, but capable in its first call to arms.

At dusk we surveyed the less-than-smooth floor, and Jerry and Dennis outlined how much work we'd have to do on that mile of road if we were ever to get concrete trucks to come down to pour the foundation for the house.

Then, as a period to our sentence of hard labor, Hansel made a quick dash onto the floor, leaving one or two footprints we were too tired to smooth out. He was lucky we had river water to clean his paws with.

That night my arms shook with fatigue. I needed help just getting undressed; I was unable to lift my arms without Jerry's aid.

"Will everything take twice as long, be twice as hard to do here?" I asked as Jerry pulled my sweatshirt off over my head. I'd thought building the barn would be the least of our worries.

"Can't get much worse than this," Jerry said, trying to reassure me.

Little did we know.

10

Summer Mist

SHERRIE AND I GATHERED goose guano scattered across the gravel bars that sliced the summer river like ancient Indian spears. We stuffed the pale, hard little sausages in our oversize T-shirts. In tennis shoes and shorts, we sloshed through the shallow river sections back to the trailers, broke up the natural fertilizer, and mixed the droppings with the volcanic dirt.

Then we planted the garden.

It was August 14, 1984.

Our two trailers had taken over the spindly ailanthus grove at the Boyntons' river place. Dennis and Sherrie had rented out their Bend home, and we'd worked out an hourly wage we thought we could afford to pay Dennis as our jack-of-all-trades. He worked partly for the experience of homesteading.

Sherrie, his wife, turned out to be a fringe benefit we couldn't have done without.

In August, Jerry towed the fifth-wheel trailer we'd borrowed from my parents. Dennis and Sherrie followed with their seventeen-foot rig. The dogs, cats, and I brought up the rear in my parents' van, traveling down the gravel that turned to dirt, winding down the rocky, rutted sections to where Bart had first exposed us to the river. We'd have water and power at the Boyntons' river place. So Jerry decided pioneering would be more comfortable there.

Black smoke filled the sky in the distance as we drove, evidence of range fires in the east. I spoke encouragingly to the cats in their travel pillowcases and the dogs in their plastic kennels. But I was saying prayers for safety for us all.

We weren't sure if the trailers could make it around the sharp bends or scrape past the rock outcroppings that reached like grabbing fingers out into the narrow road. Barely registering any movement on the speedometers, we crept carefully down the steep grade, pulling up like a load of Gypsies before Bob's gate next to the river, surveying our home for the next two months.

Here Jerry and I lived with a river view, miles from locals, but close neighbors to Sherrie and Dennis, sharing the basics of water and work. The Boyntons lived on top and kept the river place to graze their cattle. They let us settle there temporarily while we made our own land more livable.

In the beginning, time drifted by like a mist around the four of us. We woke with the first blush of sun against the basalt cliffs, ate, worked until we tired, and then slipped into bed and snapped the lights out before the bugs that smelled of eucalyptus swarmed like dark confetti around the lamps.

We listened to the geese that summered on the river. Coyote howls at night echoed in the rimrocks like a hundred voices.

I stopped wearing my watch.

Our environment was cozily arranged. Power that ran Bob's irrigation pumps made our lights glow and the refrigerator-freezer and washing machine hum. The latter two sat in Bob's machinery shed, next to an old rowboat inhabited by a smelly pack rat, which Hansel barked at frequently until Jerry's .38 Special gave us back some peace and quiet.

Water came to us from the old homestead well.

Sherrie and I looked after the home front, planted the garden, washed clothes every day, hung them on a line stretched between our trailer and the shed, cooked, and looked after the men. We drove ten miles three times a week to pick up the mail when it was delivered, and made gofer runs into Wasco, Moro, or The Dalles.

Jerry parked the Rallye under the protection of the century-old walnut tree, where it sat secure even against the night winds. He used the plane to fly out for parts for Deere John or the truck, sometimes spending the night, then gently buzzing our site so we'd have time to move Bob's cows through the gate to another lush green pasture before he landed, stopping quickly just short of the fence.

Once we both flew out, the engine racing to gain full speed through the thick grass. We had to be off by the walnut tree or we'd never clear the fence. As we approached the tree, I held my breath and closed my eyes. The tires sailed just a whisper above the barbed wire. Jerry grinned at me as we climbed, so sure was he of his plane.

That summer marked the first time in my adult life I could remember not "working" or being in school. I read and wrote thank-you notes to colleagues and friends for the good-bye gifts they'd given us, gifts like a computer modem and two King Crimson maple trees we'd plant on our homestead.

I wrote letters, a necessity with the nearest phone at least ten miles up the grade, and rested.

It's been said that two years are needed to adjust once a family moves to a new community. I wondered if the effects were cumulative, since we'd be moving four times in all.

Everything had taken longer than planned.

Electricity—which we learned would cost us $7,200 to connect— couldn't arrive from across the river until we'd dug the trenches for the lines; but building a place to store our things in became a higher priority.

Beginning in April, Jerry lived weekdays at Starvation Point, while he and Dennis worked without electricity to frame the hangar and shop, using my dad's noisy generator to run the air compressor, power tools, and equipment. Then we moved from Bend to my parents' home on my sister's ranch near the town of Sisters, while they traveled back East. From there we moved to the trailers on Boyntons' river place, then to Starvation Point.

The road hadn't been worked on.

The house plans weren't complete either. Jerry had learned of an experimental program to test energy-efficient homes, and if he designed the house to fit the ravine *and* to qualify for the program, we'd be reimbursed for some of our costs. Computers built into the house would test how much electricity we used and how effective the new building procedures might be. We'd save money on electric heating, which we'd decided on, since we were so far from a wood supply.

Jerry's brother, Ellis, helped build one week but swore our dream site was "the jumping off place for the end of the world." With no water for washing, and the dust and wind overpowering, Ellis had said, "Jerry's crazy for moving there. And Jane's crazier for agreeing to go with him."

Jerry and I convinced ourselves that sacrifices preceded bliss.

The men worked long, grubby hours, and by the end of April their efforts materialized into the hangar, shop, and barn, a combined building with overhangs on either end for parking machinery, boats, and whatever. They built a small, enclosed darkroom into the back.

We made more than twenty trips from Bend that summer, stacking essentials under tarps in the sagebrush or under the shop overhangs.

On one trip, driving a load along the reptile road following a rain, I watched Jerry straddle the two-foot-deep cuts in the dirt, and I began my usual hyperventilating. Jerry stopped the truck, put his arm around me, and let me cry. Then he said the words I'll always remember, the words of choice: "We don't have to come here. We can go anywhere. Sell this place. It doesn't matter. I just want you to be happy."

I knew he meant it. He'd actually spent an afternoon with my manicurist, Wanda, learning how to form my fake, silicone nails, a sign of his tender caring, his wanting me to be happy out in the boonies.

"No," I'd said, sighing deeply. "I know it's where we're supposed to be. I have to find some way to live with the road."

We'd finally loaded all our household goods into two gooseneck horse trailers. The scent of hay, dried manure, and our own sweat clung to the boxes.

With careful arranging, all the household things we thought we wouldn't need for a year were now stacked to the ceiling in the darkroom of the hangar.

It was startling to discover that we had so many possessions—yet planned to survive nicely with most of them jammed into a small, basically inaccessible room.

After leaving Bend, we'd lived on my sister's ranch in my parents' A-frame home for three months, a half-hour drive from my job. I had time with my sister Judy Hurtley; our mules were feeding off the Hurtley fields; the dogs slept in the house. Surrounded by my parents' things, I had a sense of closeness to them, even though they were traveling for the summer.

And now, at last, we were at the river.

The slower pace without the outside pressures made it easier to give myself to Jerry, to cook for him, read to him, rub his sore back.

In the little trailer, we slept like spoons in one of two single beds separated by a small nightstand.

Initially, Hansel and Josie sprawled *between* our beds while Ricky stretched his longhaired body in the narrow opening of the galley kitchen. Harvey and Puffin, the cats Dave and Sharon Larson had given us, draped themselves wherever they wanted. But in no time, the cats slept outside because the dogs had taken over.

I'd awaken in my twin bed in the night unable to move, feeling the hot breath of bearded beings against my face. The aroma of Hartz Flea & Tick collars on either side of my pillow informed me that neither beard belonged to Jerry.

We'd tried tying the dogs at night, but they barked constantly at the coyotes, and Hansel had chewed the side mirror of the Datsun as a sign of his irritation. Letting them loose inside the trailer until we fashioned some kind of kennel seemed the solution.

That's when they took over my bed, and Jerry invited me to share his.

Ever after, until we moved into the finished home, Hansel and Josie slept at eye level with us, on their own twin bed, while Jerry and I cozily coordinated our turns on the other twin, an arrangement we found quite pleasant when the thermometer dropped below zero.

The trailer was cramped with essentials: a couch, a drop-leaf table that couldn't open because the desk, computer, and printer took up most of the room, and a card table for eating. Jerry usually ate his meals sitting on the couch. I sat on the desk chair that swiveled between the desk and table.

A television sat precariously on a counter; the VCR barely fit on a shelf beneath it. We made do without a microwave oven in the narrow kitchen. Our trailer had a little gas stove and miniature oven and a good-sized refrigerator. A stainless-steel sink separated a short stretch of white counter space.

Small wood-paneled closets framed the top and sides of the trailer, giving us a fair amount of storage—considering we were moving from almost twenty-eight hundred square feet of space into less than three hundred.

We had air conditioning (if we endured the noise), and both electric and propane heat were available for later.

But the saving grace of the trailer was the bathroom in the back. It had a closet, a sink, a full-size tub, a shower, and a toilet that worked just like Con's chair, emptying into a large hole in the ground. We quickly forgot to look much in the little mirror above the sink; we were always startled by the dust and dirt that thickened our hair and covered our faces that summer.

With only a five-gallon hot-water heater, however, the tub offered only the illusion of long, luxurious baths in the wilderness. Still, it beat the solar-heated bath we prepared in an old porcelain tub buried beneath Bob's trees. Sherrie and I filled it with well water, and by the time it was warm enough to dip into, Bob's cows had discovered it, consuming all but the bubble-bath bottle.

The Gants' trailer was smaller than ours, but it housed a double bed over a table seating four. It had a larger stove, a smaller living room, and a larger-capacity hot-water heater. Eventually, we planned meals together, deciding which oven or refrigerator could manage which menu.

When Jerry and I wanted long, hot showers, we visited the Gants.

When they wanted to watch a video, they visited us.

During the long summer days, Jerry and Dennis reworked the rocky road that wound down the canyon to our future home, moving gravel and water to stabilize the powdery holes. The work was tedious and dirty, with the temperature hitting nearly one hundred degrees daily.

With Deere John, they loaded the dump truck with rocks and dropped them along sections of road most likely to be slick in the wet season. Then they crushed the rock with Deere John's tracks, driving rock shards into the dirt. When the rock still sat on top of the road, they borrowed a six-hundred-gallon plastic tank from the Wasco fertilizer company, placed it on the back of our pickup, and filled it with water from Bob's well. Through holes drilled along plastic pipe, they released water onto the road as they drove, wetting the rock and sand into a natural cement.

The gravel didn't reduce the steep grades or the roller-coaster driveway; but we hoped it would decrease the depth of the ruts washed into the steep sections during the rains.

Higher up on the grade, the men cut the corners of the reptile road wider so the concrete trucks would be willing to drive down to pour the house foundation.

With the road passable, Deere John went into action again, scraping entangled sagebrush and digging trenches across the flat, preparing for the power yet to cross the river.

Sherrie and I could help little with this kind of work, so we took long, early morning walks, talking and exercising the dogs.

The basalt rocks stretched high into cloudless skies, heating the canyon like an old stone oven by midmorning. Next to Bob's dirt road, thin bunch grass covered soil spread partway up the rocks, a perfect habitat for chukars and deer.

One day I found myself climbing the steep rocks above the road, hand over hand, carefully picking my way across a shale slide, with Sherrie giving me worried directions from below. I thought of snakes as I reached for each handhold above my head, sweat dripping into my eyes, the sun burning my bare shoulders. I also thought of dying when my footholds slid out from under me, and I hung momentarily in space.

"To your right!" Sherrie yelled from below until my foot found a toe-hold in the rocks. I rested, thinking after all this effort to get to the river, it would be ironic to die on the rocky cliff, all for Josie, whose curiosity had outdone her courage.

She'd climbed the tall, red-rock cliffs on an easier grade, coming in from above. Then she'd dropped down onto a ledge 150 feet above us and stood there barking, ready to jump over. I'd sent Hansel up above her, and he barked and whistled at her, trying to convince her to climb up, away from us, but she refused.

So there I was, inching my way across the cliff until I was above her, call-ing her up. Then I was sweating my way back down with her, marveling at the things I found that I could do here on Starvation Point.

Jerry left the .38 Special with us to defend ourselves against snakes and other predators. I used it once, after the dogs came home with porcupine quills stuck to their noses. They developed a special bark for porcupines after that. Once Sherrie and I both heard it and went charging from the trailers. The dogs had cornered one beneath a sagebrush, frantically barking, mov-ing in and out against it, getting closer and closer to the dangerous quills.

I forgot that the first two rounds in the revolver were shot shells for snakes, and when I pulled the trigger, the animal fell back with a sickening, high-pitched squeal but didn't die. I shot again, at closer range, still forget-ting the spattering shots, dogs yipping in my ear, the pink underside of the porcupine bleeding, my heart pounding. But it didn't die.

The third round was a soft-pointed bullet, shot at close range. The poor animal finally stopped squealing.

I felt sick.

The single slug would have done it quickly, without pain, if I hadn't for-gotten to roll the chamber.

Sherrie and I buried the porcupine, knowing that even dead, the animal could hinder curious calves and deer that would starve to death with a mouth or nose full of quills.

We watched for rattlers and feisty badgers that populated the river-banks. The rattlers kept us constantly staring at our feet when we walked; the badgers—never known to back down—made us grab dogs and beat hasty retreats if we saw their backs of rolling fat guarding their holes.

We basked in the silence.

I liked Sherrie, not just because she loved the dogs and cats, but for her quick thinking, common sense, hard work, and energy. She was Matt's age. But she only vaguely remembered him, because she had dropped out of high school in her junior year to work full time and had later finished her GED. I took it as a compliment when later I was mistaken for her mother by the locals.

She had an artist's eye, reflected both in the photographs she shot and in her use of color and craft in decorating their small trailer. She remembered things. She asked questions. We shared the frustration of being married to older men who thought "experience" should bear more weight than "feeling" in decisions of opinion.

Jerry called Sherrie a "long, tall drink of water." Her slender model's body looked as at home in jeans and cowboy boots as it did in a slinky dress. She was a natural beauty despite her self-criticism that ranged from "bad teeth" to "pooches on my thighs."

Ah, to have such pooches.

Other people could have been intrusive, but we found our family extended easily by the Gants. In the late summer evenings, the four of us, surrounded by bouncing dogs and curious cats, carried our Ivory soap to the warm river, scrubbed away the dust of day, threw Frisbees in the water, and floated on our backs, toes pointed toward the rose-tinted sky.

Later we played games of trivia, scooped hoarded gluten-free ice cream (brought 160 miles from rare trips to Bend) from the shed freezer, and came to know the Gants as good friends.

The garden gave up its peas and lettuce.

In a world of want, we had everything we needed.

11

Power and Running Water

SHERRIE AND I WANTED to be closer to the action. We wanted to help harness the spring, work on the house foundation, be part of the pioneering. The arrival of power made that move possible.

On power day, the Columbia Basin Power Company sent trucks on either side of the river to set the poles. On our side, the truck steered slowly across the flat, following the long trench Dennis had dug with the backhoe.

On both sides, men in hard hats and leather utility belts spent the hot, dusty day digging the holes and then sinking the forty-foot poles into the ground. Strong guy wires braced the poles, holding them to stand against gusting winds, snow, and ice storms.

The second day, electricity actually arrived across the water, thanks to primitive tools: our fishing boat, rope, and cable. Three heavy wires stretched across the John Day River. They were raised, one wire at a time, by a man in the power bucket perched precariously above the water.

The men ate their lunch, dropped a fishing line into the water, and delighted themselves with the first steelhead catch of the season. The scent of blooming yellow rabbit brush blended with the late summer heat.

They spent a third day setting transformers in the dust, to take electricity to a pump house being built at the base of Con's hill. Someday we'd also have water where now the refrigerator-freezer, washer, and dryer waited in the sagebrush. Power would also feed the shop and barn, and eventually move on up the trenches to the house on top of the steep hill.

The linemen draped the rolls of wire into the deep trenches between the river and the barn, encountering only two rattlesnakes basking in the cool of the trenches.

By day's end, we turned on a switch in the shop, and the wonderful words *Let there be light* took on a totally new meaning! The simplest thing, flipping a switch, seemed so miraculous, given the work and the wait.

On a sunny late-September day, we left the shade and security of Bob's place and moved the trailer again, creeping along the river road. Dennis and Sherrie had taken their trailer out to travel during deer season for a few weeks with family and friends.

We were alone with our land.

The pickup pulled the trailer steadily through the neighbor's field to avoid half of the roller-coaster grade. In certain seasons such avoidance was possible. But halfway up the other side, near the padlock turn and within a few feet of the fence and our new land, the wheels spun in our newly laid gravel and rock. Then we stalled; our pickup was unable to pull the heavy trailer any farther up the steep hill.

I could just see the trailer slipping back, dropping over the side, plunging our worldly goods into the river. My daymares could be quite vivid.

Deere John rescued us, as it would so many times, when Jerry hooked on a chain and used the tractor to pull our home the rest of the way up the hill.

We lived in the trailer at the house site for a few days, getting used to the view. We hoped to finish laying water pipes in the same trench as the electrical wire before taking the trailer down the steep hill to a green area at the base of the bench.

For power that next week or so, we ran the gasoline generator, turning on the noisy machine for an hour in the morning and evening, giving us energy to run the small water pump in the trailer and charge up the battery for lights. We became more cautious with water, too, now that Bob's well was so far away. We filled five-gallon cans when we went into town, dumping the fresh water into the trailer tank for drinking and cooking.

Moving the trailer from the house site down the hill toward the shop took the better part of a day. Jerry was concerned about being able to hold the trailer on the steep section without a four-wheel drive, so Deere John was commissioned once again. Jerry drove the tractor to the tongue end of the trailer, picked it up with the bucket, and wrapped a chain around both. Then he informed me that I'd be instructing him as he backed the trailer down the almost vertical sections of road, past the shop to the pump house. "Since I can't see where I am, you'll have to signal me which way to turn."

I paled. Every woman in the world knows why.

My mind was wild with possibilities. *What if the chain breaks? What if the trailer goes off over the edge? What if the tractor can't hold the trailer on the steep slope? What if I signal wrong?*

Standing off to the side, I nervously instructed Jerry as the trailer jerked and twisted against the bucket, sliding, inching its way down the hill. When it started to tip or was thrown off by a boulder or got too close to the deep ruts, I signaled, and he managed to pull it back onto the road. I sighed in relief at the bottom.

"Look good?" Jerry yelled from the tractor.

"Looks fine," I yelled back, waving my hand in agreement.

"Put blocks by the wheels," he yelled. We began leveling our home with jacks and blocks of wood.

Finally, the jacks were set firm in the ground. Jerry disconnected the tongue from the bucket and backed Deere John out.

"What will keep the trailer from tipping off the jacks in the wind or something?" I asked Jerry.

"You worry too much," he answered irritably.

There wasn't any wind. But the trailer was moving.

"It's going!" I shouted to Jerry as he stepped out from under the tongue just in time to watch the trailer tip forward, tongue and nose crashing into a cloud of dirt, bending the tongue under while sending the bathroom end of the trailer—and all its contents—popping up toward the sky.

I'm sure my heart stopped.

Why do the terrible things I imagine keep happening?

When the dust settled, it took Jerry only seconds to figure out what had caused the calamity. "You put the blocks and rocks *behind* the tires, instead of in front," he said disgustedly.

He sighed, started up the tractor, and we started all over again. *I really don't belong here,* I thought as we worked.

My heart beat more slowly, steadily, palms no longer wet with sweat, as I fixed our first dinner in the minimally damaged trailer. There was so much to learn. I was so easily frightened by the machines and distance and weather and elements.

What have we done? I wondered, knowing this was only the beginning.

Water issues came next. The spring had been located. I'd been sitting in the shade of a sage bush that autumn day, reading, completing morning devotions that I noted kept me calmer as I faced each new day. Nearby, Jerry and Deere John cleared sagebrush.

A strange buzzing interrupted my reading periodically. I couldn't localize the sound, though, so I ignored it. (Later the sound materialized again as a three-foot-long, emerald-green rattlesnake as thick as Jerry's arm appeared. Jerry buried the head, and Sherrie and I planned to skin it for a hatband, until we realized it would have intestines and things, so we changed our minds.)

I sat oblivious to the snake as Jerry uncovered a dark murky pool of water in a hole about fifteen feet below the surface. Peering over the side, I caught my reflection in the black sludge. Sagebrush roots and a dead gopher floated in the water. Dirt and pebbles dribbled from the loose sides into the hole. I stepped back. "That was Con's reservoir?" I asked. Jerry nodded.

"But it doesn't seem like much water," I said.

"He probably didn't use much," Jerry said. Then more to himself he added, "I wonder how much water is really there."

"Don't you know?" I asked, the creep of alarm moving up my neck. This would be our *total* water supply for washing and drinking and cleaning. Had we really made this major move without the assurance of accessible drinking water?

"We'll just have to see," Jerry answered, running his hands through his hair. He gathered his optimism and described how we'd place a wide piece of plastic tubing into the hole, slide a submersible pump down the center, and pump out water until it ran clear. I couldn't imagine how it would work. "We should have it contained by the time Dennis and Sherrie get back from deer hunting," he said confidently. "Have a little faith."

I peered apprehensively again over the edge.

It was also deer season on our ranch, and water and power took a sideline to the sport. Jerry filled his tag opening morning, assuring us of meat for the winter. We dressed out the animal and hung it from the rafters in the hangar. Then Jerry cut the meat off the bone while I put it in freezer packages. The wrapped venison sat stacked in the freezer, which stood in the middle of the sagebrush. We cleaned up the camper, aware once again of the water shortage, then returned to the task of burying water lines from the incomplete pump house to the dirty black hole Jerry insisted on describing as our water supply.

During Dennis and Sherrie's absence those weeks, we tried several methods to harness the spring. First, we pushed the dead gopher aside and lowered a submersible pump into the hole. The pump tapped the hole dry within a few minutes.

This was not good.

"Not enough water stored there," Jerry said, and he set about digging the hole deeper with the backhoe. But the work also made the hole wider, and now the pit I peered into was ample enough to bury the Datsun.

Next, we drilled holes in a loop of six-inch plastic pipe and dropped it into the hole. Jerry was sure sufficient water would be stored in the loop to provide our needs for washing and cleaning and drinking, so he dumped gravel back into the hole around the pipe. He set the pump into the pipe and, with power from the pump house, switched it on.

It sucked out all the water in seconds and pulled sand as fine as mustard seeds into the pump. Jerry spent two hours fixing it.

Then this ingenious man created a flapper valve to slosh the water into the loop, hoping to swirl the sand around in the water, diluting it, until eventually the water came up free, without sand.

The shaft simply filled with mud.

We then bought a sandpoint—a copper-screened, pointed, narrow steel pipe—recommended by the old-timers we discussed our water problem with. We pounded it through the plastic pipe, down into the water standing in the hole. In shallow water tables, sandpoint wells were well known. Jerry's eighty-eight-year-old father had stood on his own garage roof years ago, pounded a sandpoint into the ground with a hammer, and received gushing fresh water for his reward.

But our sandpoint hit rock and bent.

"I didn't think steel would bend like that," Jerry complained as he yanked the long pipe out of the ground with Deere John and a chain. "We must have hit bedrock."

Jerry next began the process of digging out the hole once again, and this time the work seemed dangerous. The worked dirt and sand failed to pack as it had before, and the sides around the water hole caved in.

Over and over again. Meanwhile, the laundry piled up.

In honor of old Con, I should have washed as he did: by hand, sloshing shirts in tubs of steaming John Day water, laying them gently across breast-high sagebrush to deodorize and dry, while meadowlarks flew by to sweetly serenade me.

I vowed to find some other way to honor my predecessor's spirit. As a result, washing clothes became a pioneering experience confounded by Jerry's creativity. His first suggestion was to fill two five-gallon water cans with river water and pour them into the electric washing machine sitting outside, beside the pump house. "Ten gallons to wash and ten to rinse ought to do it," he said confidently.

It didn't.

While we used barely four gallons weekly for drinking (courtesy of the faucet at the Wasco Chevron station) and heated three to four gallons daily for cleaning and dishwashing (courtesy of the river), it took fifteen gallons to wash a load of clothes and another fifteen to rinse.

After wrestling with the river to fill the first five-gallon can—similar to the day we poured the shop foundation—I knew I'd never make it.

I also knew why pioneer women died young.

With seven loads of wash looming before me like Mount Hood, I suggested hopefully: "Why don't I drive to a Laundromat in The Dalles?"

Jerry was insulted. "There has to be an easier way than driving fifty miles," he concluded.

A way was found.

We hauled the gas generator to the river, along with heavy red-and-black licorice-looking wire, lengths of plastic pipe, and the submersible pump. The pump sucked river water into the six-hundred-gallon chemical company tank. We turned it off at the three-hundred-gallon mark, pulled everything out of the river, loaded it onto our aging pickup, and bumped along the road to the trailer. We would have brought more water, but the tank sat on a lame trailer that complained least at three hundred gallons.

We stopped the truck halfway up the hill, just past the washing machine that sat amid sagebrush, next to the refrigerator-freezer.

Lengths of plastic pipe were then connected between the water tank and the open washing machine. (Fortunately, we had a top loader. Our labor-saving technique is not recommended for front loaders.) I held the pipe and braced my feet, Jerry pulled a lever, and water gushed through the gaping hole, saturating our clothes in the machine.

Water has such power as it pushes through those pipes! It took all my strength to keep the pipe over the machine. I worried that the brakes on the truck might not hold, or that the tank would tip, but then, Jerry said I worried too much.

When agitation began (the machine's, not mine), I yelled, my creative husband stopped the flowing water, and we rested until the rinse was ready, watching until the biodegradable soapy water poured out onto the ground.

Then we began again.

The meadowlarks surely thought we were missing more than running water.

Once while filling the machine, the trailer did tip, toppling over the washing machine and the refrigerator-freezer. The freezer door flew open and out coughed ice cream and venison, which mingled with the clothes floating down the stream created by the spilled water. The appliances lay in the dirt like wounded mummies, all bandaged in white.

Amazingly, while the washing machine looked slightly like a parallelogram after that, it did run quieter than it had before we made our eventful move to pioneering. And though the refrigerator had a gash down its left side, its wound would be hidden between cabinets when the house was finally finished. The front and center still glowed clean and white.

So did our clothes, much to my surprise, though with every washing, one piece of clothing would come out with strips of fine black dust tucked within its folds.

After Sherrie and Dennis returned, we began taking bets on which item of clothing would catch the river dirt (it was usually Jerry's back brace) and have to be beaten again in the machine. Still, I never thought that river water would conquer as well as it did the alkaline dust and powdery dirt that, like us, were permanent residents of the river ranch.

But after laundry day each week, I knew I'd be pleased when the wait for water was over, when electricity and the washing machine were safely mated inside the house, and when *running water* referred to something more efficient than our racing around with pumps and pipes on the days we attacked the laundry.

12

Thanksgiving Day Blessing

EXCEPT FOR MEALS AND DAILY WALKS with the dogs, there were few routines besides work. Time no longer draped around us like a mist. Instead, it became a driving torrent without relief. We began a dozen essential projects, which made life a muddle of middles.

Though harnessing the spring was important, we set it aside for the house foundation, which we needed before the fall rains ruined the newly built road and kept the concrete trucks out again.

Jerry and Deere John began cutting, carving, and scraping the earth from the side of the ravine, creating the designs he had drawn on paper, pawing and spreading the dirt like a giant dog uncovering a buried treasure.

From my perch partway up the rocks, I watched them, man and machine, noting the fall colors of sage and bunch grasses, watching the John Day rise from rains a few days earlier upriver, counting the increased flights of Canada geese heading south beneath wispy horsetail clouds. Winter whispered in their wings.

Together, Jerry and I set a double row of wooden forms like the Great Wall of China, encircling the perimeter of the dirt, creating an outline of where the house's corners would be, where the porches would jut out, where the hot tub would sink into the bathroom.

Then we began the process of shooting grades to Jerry's perfectionistic liking and positioning twists of steel to strengthen places where a boulder protruded into the foundation or the grade changed.

Jerry assured me that a good foundation—as in a relationship—is critical for long-term survival.

When Dennis and Sherrie returned, we drove ten miles up the reptile road to a neighbor's barn for the closest phone to order cement. Jerry chose a different company this time. Two trucks were scheduled to arrive on October 26.

Memories of the shop foundation fiasco swirled vividly in my mind, and I slept fitfully that night in our twin bed, waking with prayers on my lips.

In midafternoon, under a drizzle-threatening sky, Jerry and Dennis drove to the top of the hill to meet the first truck, which was driven by a thin, wiry man dressed in work jeans and jacket. He followed them cautiously down the reworked grade. But when he saw the roller-coaster driveway, he balked.

A discussion ensued.

Plan B went into effect.

The truck would turn off and follow the bottom of the bench through a neighbor's field, coming back out at the base of the roller-coaster grade.

"You oughta warn people about that driveway," the thin man snarled, stepping from his truck when it finally stopped below the house. "My partner's not going to like it." His eyes turned upward toward a truck winding down the road above us.

"Go up and warn him about the grade," Jerry said to me.

I spun the red Datsun's wheels, racing to meet the second truck, muttering about what to say and that I'd been directed to say it. "They want me to warn you about the hill," I said nervously to the second driver, a bigger man with a barrel chest.

"What hill?" he said as he followed me to the top of the grade and looked down.

"That ain't no hill," he said, his eyes sparkling. "I'm an old elk hunter—seen lots worse than that!"

Agile for his size, he hopped back into the cab. I drove aside to let him inch his loaded truck down the gravel-covered hill, and watched him wind up the padlock turn and through the gate toward the house, with no help from Deere John.

Elk Hunter stopped, stepped out of his truck, and walked quickly up the hill to the foundation maze. Apparently, Thin Man had attempted to back his truck up to the side of the forms, but the hill was too steep and his wheels had spun.

He was eying the cute dump truck.

Not again! I thought.

Elk Hunter listened to the conversation, surveyed the possibilities around him, and like a man used to making things happen, announced, "We'll use your tractor over there to pull the trucks backward up the hill and hold 'em there while we unload." He pointed to Deere John, and Dennis moved quickly to hook the chain to Thin Man's truck.

Within minutes the truck was beside one set of forms. A long funnel dropped from the rolling container on the back of the truck holding the swirling cement. Elk Hunter yelled, and the sludgy silver stuff that we'd build our home and future on poured into the forms.

With shovels, Jerry and Dennis and Elk Hunter pushed the mixture as far along the forms as they could, especially filling the corners, until the cement filled the China Wall.

Thin Man left immediately and silently, but Elk Hunter backed up so his truck could be pulled backward up the hill. Sherrie and I were drafted with additional shovels to push and pull the sludge. Sweat beaded quickly on our brows despite the cooling dusk. The second truck's concrete finished filling the foundation and poured the form shaping the hot tub and the pads that would support the two porch edges. And still there was concrete remaining for a pad beneath the sagebrush: Hansel, Josie, and Ricky's kennel.

As Elk Hunter left, Sherrie and I began finishing the edges of the kennel pad with trowels, feeling pretty proud of our skills, while the dogs sniffed around, inspecting the portion of their new quarters without leaving their footprints.

Dennis and Jerry pushed the edge of daylight leveling the concrete. Then they set steel bolts that pointed toward the darkening sky to anchor the foundation to the wooden plates. The bolts would secure the eventually finished walls against fierce winds.

When a tired but happy crew finally wound its way down the path to the trailers, the first stars lit the way. Raindrops patted gently on the metal trailer roof as we slipped between the cool sheets, relieved that this concrete phase was over.

But a hundred other projects waited for us in the morning.

"We need a separate pasture for the mules," Jerry announced. "You'll have to build a fence across the bottom of that side hill to meet up with that old cedar fence that goes up the ravine."

Fence-building is a primitive task. Like an embarrassed native displaying Stone Age tools for pictures in *National Geographic,* I found only archaic methods worked.

I'd built a fence in Bend, once, over flat ground. When finished, it had been a task with satisfaction attached, like admiring perfect rows of canned peaches on the pantry shelf.

But there was no easy way to haul wire and seven-foot metal posts up a rocky slope whose shallow soil held together sparse bunch grass and sage. Straining, I could carry five posts up the slope at one time, leaving black-and-blue tattoos where they bounced against the tops of my thighs.

The fence-post driver, that steel tube with narrow handles sticking from its side that I pounded on each post, felt as if it weighed as much as Henry, the smallest mule.

A straight and perfect line along a side hill is a challenge. If I avoided rocks, it took eight driver jolts to get the post into the ground. I quickly lost my goal of setting them exactly seven paces apart. Often where the post was supposed to stand, the tip of a huge rock buried deep beneath the surface poked its nose above the soil.

It took two days to sink eighty-five seven-foot metal posts into the rocky soil halfway up the side hill.

That part finished, I clipped two red insulators, like red bugs, to each green post. Finally, I rolled half a mile of heavy wire beside the posts, wound the wire through the insulators, plugged in the electricity, and checked for grounding to ensure the electric fence would work.

As I walked the old fence line, my appreciation for the first fence builder grew. Where did he gather so many wooden posts in a land barren of trees? How had he carried them up this hill—or did he roll them down? How long had it taken him to attach four rows of barbed wire around this forty-acre site?

I admired his crudely built rock cribs that still kept the fence's corners tight, and I admired the way a wire clutched a huge rock to keep a post erect where the shallow soil refused support.

An old whiskey bottle was buried beside one post. Perhaps this primitive task is easier to handle if one's numb.

As I climbed along the old fence, I fixed an occasional loose staple that dropped its wire too low to be of use. And I smiled while untangling a perfect X formed by wires strung between two posts, knowing that a fleeting deer had snapped the wires together as its hooves cleared the fence.

At the top of the hill, I rested and looked down the barbed-wire fence toward the river, a breathtaking view. The old fence, with its wood and wire, looked much better than my metal fence; it was straighter and more natural. It would last longer, too. But a bond had grown between me and the sturdy soul who'd formed that finer fence. I understood his labor, his commitment to give quality to what might seem a lowly job, his wish to leave a lasting, useful gift to those who followed. More, that artisan had stepped from the past to teach me how to read the landscape, to behold the details that gave it depth.

Jerry ordered roof trusses for early December, putting the pressure on finishing the walls. So much needed doing before winter! In between house framing, the septic tank waited for burial and hookup to the house as soon as we could harness the spring. We needed to winterize the trailers so we wouldn't use up all our money paying for electric heat or have frozen water pipes—if we ever had running water.

We hoped to clear ground for the airstrip so the plane could be close by and safe in its hangar, instead of being twenty-five miles away, tied down outside at Wasco's little airport.

A large D8 Caterpillar and its operator had been hired to create twin dikes at the end of the property to protect the field from the high water we expected next spring. The operator worked diligently, hoping to complete the job before becoming bogged down in wet mud.

The pump house wasn't finished; the washer and refrigerator-freezer still sat out in the middle of sagebrush.

We continued to transport all but our drinking water from the river, boiling it for washing dishes and ourselves, running it cold over dirty clothes, stepping over one bucket in the kitchen and another in the bathroom to operate the toilet.

Dropping our faces into the sink, we took turns pouring boiled river water over our heads, rinsing the dirt from our hair. Showers were a past luxury.

We raced the winter season.

The river could well freeze over. None of us relished the idea of chopping holes in the ice or running out of drinking water while being stranded by snowed-in roads.

Clearly, we needed water and more hands.

Russell Hiatt joined us the day the water tank toppled onto the washer and refrigerator-freezer. He brought us his considerable experience as a builder, rancher, photographer, rural survivor, and (thank you, Lord!) well driller.

With Jerry's height and build, and close to his age, Russell fit the picture of a construction worker: lean torso, crinkle-wrinkles around his hazel eyes, thinning dark hair, powerful arms and legs, and wide, hammer-managing hands.

Like Jerry and Dennis, Russell was a jack-of-all-trades who made his living mostly erecting steel buildings and remodeling homes. In the spring, Russell guided "dudes," as he called them, down the wild Owyhee River in eastern Oregon, maneuvering the angry spring rapids, serving as transporter, camp maker, snake chaser, nursemaid, and cook to people craving the taste of wilderness for a week.

He smoked a pack of cigarettes a day, though never once inside our trailer. He preferred his tea in a fragile porcelain cup and saucer, slept fewer than five hours a night, took no breaks during the day, and was every inch a hyperactive workaholic who drove five hours home to Cove to be with his family every other weekend.

Russell helped frame our home, living in the little camper until Christmas, taking his meals with us, returning to help Sheetrock the inside walls the following February.

He also found himself helping with the water supply, when his introduction to homesteading included meat and ice cream floating across the flat with our clothes.

"Trouble with the laundry?" he asked in a clipped, scratchy voice, a master of understatement.

In late November, Russell, Dennis, Jerry, Sherrie, and I surveyed the water hole, which by then was large enough to encompass Deere John, both trailers, and the house. We described the litany of events already attempted in harnessing the spring.

Russell said we were lucky the sandpoint hadn't worked, since he'd known of springs simply following an underground hole through bedrock out into an abyss.

"I think we've got to find a way to keep pumping the water out so you can dig the area deeper and actually get the gravel and mud out. Then we'll put something in there for a reservoir of sorts," he said.

After a discussion of possible methods, Jerry drove seventy miles to rent a mud pump. On a crisp fall morning, the men set it into the wet cavity, turned it on, and Dennis began the precarious process of reaching into the gaping hole with the backhoe to pull out the wet gravel and mud around it.

Neither Sherrie nor I could watch for long—and not just because there was laundry to do. The tractor sat so close to the soft, wet, sagging edge of the hole that each of us harbored visions of the huge machine sinking, toppling tractor, Dennis, and curious dogs into the hole.

The sides continued to cave in, but fortunately Deere John didn't. The mud pump, however, sucked a rock past the screen, sending a high-pitched squeal blasting above the noisy clanking of the backhoe.

What's wrong now? Sherrie and I wondered while Jerry and Russell pulled up the pump.

"Never seen anything like it," Russell noted. "There's no way a rock that size could get through the screen."

He was thoughtful as they cleaned out the pump and somehow managed to put it back together, dropping it back into the hole. We watched as the pump once again sucked the muddy liquid up seventeen feet from the water to the surface and forced it out through a fist-size hose, which created muddy streams along the flat that rivaled our laundry drainage.

With the hole sucked dry, we could see three veins of water as thick as a boa constrictor pouring into the cavity. One flowed down from the house ravine, the others from either side. None came from the direction of the river, confirming that the water was spring fed and not overrun from the river. "The water moves in veins of sand," Russell told us, pointing. "The more you pump the water, the more the veins will flush themselves of sand and eventually bring just water."

I still found it hard to believe we would eventually have drinkable liquid from the gopher grave.

Sherrie and I checked progress periodically and once noticed that the water had suddenly stopped flowing out of the pump. We peered over the edge, then waved our hands to signal that something was wrong.

Once again, the men scratched their heads as Russell donned hip waders and dropped down a ladder into the hole. "The suction-line screen is gone," he called up, his voice echoing from the deep hole. Prickles ran up my neck as he told Jerry, "It shouldn't be this hard. Somebody down here doesn't want you to have water."

"It's futile to try to find that screen in the mud and the sludge," Dennis said. "It could be in that pile over there." Our eyes moved in unison to the mountain of sloppy black clay he'd been making for days.

They debated what to do next: take the pump back, rent a larger one, try something else. Finally, Russell, the optimist, suggested they try to find the screen, even though it seemed like looking for the proverbial needle in the haystack.

As he and Jerry lowered themselves into the hole, now filling thigh-high with dark water, a verse of Scripture came to mind. First John 4:4 would drift into my thoughts often in the days ahead: *He who is in you is greater than he who is in the world.*

We could only hope.

Stepping gingerly, sifting, reaching, and pawing, using only their wide hands to feel, since they couldn't see in the murky water and mud, they sorted, until miraculously, Russell pulled the little gem of wire mesh, the length of a ruler and just as thin, from beneath the sludge, with a grin wider than the hole we'd dug for water.

There was cheering in Mudville that night after Russell and Jerry put the pump back into commission.

After several days of digging, the hole was deep enough, and we began pumping the water into a fifty-gallon drum so we would know when it was finally clear of sand and mud, and could estimate how much water would be available to us each day.

We pumped seventeen gallons of water a minute, a more-than-ample supply, even for a family of four.

As we dumped the drum of water onto the dusty flat, the sun flashed against the barrel's bottom, where pinprick flecks of real gold rested. "Seventeen feet down," Jerry laughed. "That's how deep we needed our sluice box to be when the Pedersons were here last year!"

It was as close to the gold rush as we'd come.

Still, the spring wasn't harnessed.

Within the week, Jerry and I drove to Bend, bringing back from a junkyard a steel cone that resembled the first Gemini space capsule. It had once been the top of a sawmill's sawdust burner. While Russell and Jerry hammered on the house, Dennis burned rows of holes into the steel with the welder to allow water to pour into the cone without caving the sides in. When it was finished, they gently lowered the cone into the hole, using Deere John as a crane.

The sides held.

On a day when Dennis and Sherrie were gone, Russell, Jerry, and I picked up smooth river rocks from the flat, abandoned there during the flood of '64. We washed them, then plopped them gently into the water hole, making a floor for the cone. Clear water rippled over the rocks.

Next we lowered to the cone's top a two-foot-wide metal culvert, wide enough to hold one of us should we have to crawl down into the reservoir someday. It also would allow us to drop a bucket into the hole to lift water out by hand if we had to.

One end of the culvert rose like a short smokestack above what eventually would be the alfalfa field.

Finally, we sank the submersible pump into the culvert, attached wire from the pump to the pump house, and then attached the water pipes in the trench that ran from the pump house to an opening in the culvert to meet the cool spring water.

Russell laid a sheet of plastic around the outside of the cone and the culvert to prevent ground water from contaminating our fresh spring supply. Then, with Deere John, we began filling the mountain of dirt back around our reservoir.

With great anticipation, Jerry turned the switch at the pump house, and we held our breath on that day before Thanksgiving until crystal clear, fresh spring water poured into our lives.

The next morning, as I showered in the trailer for the first time in months, I knew the luxury that liquid really is—the refreshing water pouring over my hair, slipping down my shoulders, pooling in suds at my feet.

This land was carving us, it seemed, molding us, changing our characters, making us see differently and do more than we'd ever have imagined we could.

Or dreamed we would need to.

We would never take water for granted again on our homestead. I would never turn a shower on—anywhere—without a moment of wonder. And no other Thanksgiving on Starvation Point would ever be as special as that first one, which blessed us at last with life-giving water.

13

Only Remotely Isolated

THE COMPANY WE KEPT surprised us. We hadn't expected many visitors to travel to our isolated spot. The visits introduced us to the tenor of our neighbors, their character and kindnesses, telling us that even while living so remotely we were still connected to the larger world.

Nell drove down the first time just to say hi. After that, this widowed kindergarten teacher with her straight shoulders and short, curly hair brought her friends and neighbors down the reptile road to note the progress of the house building, check out the condition of the river, and share the usually warmer temperatures of the canyon.

Nell had seen the activity as we were building in the spring and, once we had moved, knew the traffic had increased on the road running through her family's wheat land on top.

She wasn't shy about wondering why we were settling in such a remote spot, but she seemed satisfied when we explained that homesteading was something "we felt we had to do."

As building progressed, we gave tours of the house, touting the experimental techniques designed into the structure. Eventually, Nell could take guests by herself around to the computerized gauges, pointing out the slick vapor barrier, the walls built with two-by-six lumber and extra insulation, and the triple-pane windows.

She never stayed long, always coming with a specific purpose—often inviting us to dinner. Then she said good-bye, driving up the dusty road out of sight, headed to some other worthy project.

Nell lived in Moro, twenty-five miles away, but her family farmed much of the wheat land we drove through before starting down the canyon. That first fall, her family constructed a large shop near the power-line graveyard and later moved a small trailer to the site for use during harvest. For two weeks each year, they were our closest neighbors.

Bruce, Nell's son, usually arrived at their shop by midmorning, where he'd work on equipment. Then, weather permitting, he'd disk or seed or spray the several hundred acres of land the family farmed each year.

Tall, with thinning blond hair and a wispy red beard, Bruce was in his late twenties, married, with a tow-headed infant named Zachary. Bruce usually wore bib overalls, reminding me of a grown-up Dennis the Menace.

More laid-back than his mother, Bruce preceded his visits by a roaring ride down the grade on his all-terrain vehicle, the whining machine stopping abruptly in the dust beside the house.

His visits seasoned our lives and nourished us. We enjoyed his comfortable discussions about the house construction, his peppery comments about the community, his explanations of who in the county was related to whom, and his spicy descriptions of childhood adventures, including the spine-tingling tale of his two rattlesnake bites while walking through wheat fields as a child of five.

We all peered curiously as he pulled up his pant leg so we could gaze at the scars on his calf. We decided he must have been a relaxed child to have survived the double dose of venom.

That fall Bruce showed Jerry how to start the old International tractor he kept at his shop through the winter. "The road gets pretty bad," he warned us. "You may need to use the tractor to pull yourselves out."

It was Bruce who had driven us to the phone nearest Starvation Point, in David and Millie Moore's barn. "They won't mind if you use it," he said, grinning, "as long as you don't make long-distance calls."

The Moores didn't mind, and would have told us so themselves if we'd been home the first time *they* drove down the grade to visit us. We'd actually met them several years earlier, just after we'd bought the land, on a tour of vineyards in the Columbia River region. Assigned to a carpool with them, we had talked most of the day about wheat, grapes, and the pesticides that helped the former and harmed the latter.

Attractive, slender, with salt-and-pepper hair, Millie drove their Cadillac around that day while stocky, chatty David leaned his arm over the backseat, talking. He had quickly figured out what land we'd bought, realizing we would actually be neighbors to their property, even though they lived on the other side of Moro.

In later years, as we got to know them and we had our own phone, they would sometimes call to find out if the bird's-beaks, those first purple blooms of spring, had begun their show, or if the geese were gathering on the gravel bars.

"Need anything?" David would ask when he called. Then he and Millie brought milk or ice from town and joined us on the deck for an afternoon of waiting on homemade ice cream.

The first time we used their barn, set in the midst of an endless wheat field, we noticed dozens of phone numbers scratched into the wood by previous phone users. Over the years, water and mud had washed into the Moores' doorless shop during the spring runoff and raised the dirt floor so that the once waist-high benches were now at knee level. The phone on the post sat slightly above belly-button height. And buried beneath boxes of parts and oil filters lay the curly edged phone book.

In the corner, empty boxes and cans reached toward the ceiling in a triangular pile that Hansel barked at when he wasn't guarding the door. I imagined it housed a fat pack rat or a rabbit. The barn phone was seven miles closer than any other one we'd known about, making the calls for inspections and supplies and parts less burdensome after Bruce led us to the barn.

Marion Boynton insisted we also use their phone, a few miles farther down the road, when I once described an interview from the barn phone on a cold windy day. "The guy asked if he could call me back," I said, "because some New Yorker was trying to reach him." I'd told the president of a company who had agreed to speak with me, "I'd really like to finish this interview. It took me an hour to get here in a four-wheel-drive vehicle, traveling through mud and snow; I'm standing here in a barn straddling water and ice, and the wind is whipping around me because there are no doors. I'm freezing my fingers, so I can hardly write, and my ears are cold."

There was a long pause.

"You *are* out in the boonies, aren't you?" he said, then added cheerfully, "I'll have the guy from New York call back."

He'd been fun to interview after that, and the story had sold; but the memory of the cold phone remained.

"Just come to the house whenever you need to," Marion encouraged, showing me where she kept the key. She prepared tea for me when she knew ahead of time I'd be there.

Bob and Marion, the original owners of our land, set the standard for the kindnesses we'd come to know. From the beginning, this retired, wheat-ranching couple kept us in their prayers and reached a hand to us before we even asked. Early on, when Dennis and Jerry were working on the shop and I was still living in Bend, I'd called Marion, picturing her small frame running in from the garden to answer the phone. "I haven't heard from Jerry," I said. "Have you seen him?"

Marion hated the road and had a dozen other things to do, but she knew I would not be reassured until someone had seen Jerry and knew he was alive. "Do you want me to drive down there and check?" she asked without hesitation. And then she did it, seeming to understand my daymares without question.

Bob, tall and weathered in his western wear, was also quick to give his time, tools, and memories of how he'd farmed our land those years before the flood.

A year later the Boyntons would be our local mainstay, spending hours at our home when devastating injuries incapacitated us. But the first year we lived at Starvation Point, I spent several nights at their home, too, waiting for daylight and a frozen road to travel on rather than risking the slick, sloppy grade in the dark.

The condition of the road also introduced us to the Coelsches and Spencers of the 97 Ranch. They stepped off their horses to visit us while at the river gathering up their cattle one day. They farmed wheat land above us, too, and we shared a property line with them, down through a steep ravine behind the shop. It wasn't fenced, because neither of us wanted to tackle the task on such a rugged ridge.

We'd seen these two couples—a brother and sister and their spouses—on horseback on the hills, their cowboy hats bobbing as they moved cattle gingerly down the steep slopes in early summer, herding the cows to greener ground. Eventually, we worked out a shared arrangement where our mules ran in their field and their cows meandered onto our land for water we provided them from our spring.

But the 97 Ranch also had access to a shortcut to the gravel portion of the road. With permission, we could leave the dirt road, drive behind Bruce's shop, and pass through a padlocked gate. Then, paralleling an old road cut deeply with washed ruts, we drove through tall sagebrush that swiped against the side-view mirrors and doors, bumping over rocks, eventually dropping off a bank, avoiding a ditch, and reaching—amazingly—gravel.

Once on the gravel, the road ran through the old Drinkard place, up through another locked gate, and out to Baseline Road, only five miles from pavement.

Some years later, when the satellite dish arrived on a little cart behind a small foreign car, the driver fouled up his directions, found the gravel road to the Drinkard place, drove through surprisingly unlocked gates, and miraculously managed the drop-off, ruts, and rocks, in awe that anyone would call the obstacle course a driveway. "You did say the road was pretty bad," he answered sheepishly when we questioned why he kept coming.

Fortunately, he was able to repair the breaks and bends in the satellite system that resulted from his detour.

During the winter we frequently called the Coelsches and Spencers to seek permission to take that shortcut to the gravel. While it *was* treacherous, it allowed us—using tire chains—to avoid almost two miles of slippery intestine sometimes mistaken for a road. It made our trips for mail a fine adventure three times a week as well.

Edna, with a deep chuckle and always-cheerful words, was Moro's local postmistress. This slender brunette wore braces on her teeth, readying herself for a fun retirement just a few years away. She knew everyone in town and acted as the local information center. If anyone wanted to know who was building on Starvation Point, Edna could tell them.

That fall, when Ricky, our English setter, decided to go hunting on his own, wearing a collar tag bearing only our Bend address, we feared he was lost forever. But a note in the mail from Edna brought him back. "Your dog's at the Simantels'," she wrote, attaching the phone number.

Ricky had traveled six miles downriver to the ranch where the Oregon Trail crossed the John Day River. The Simantels had cut the burs from his coat, doctored his cut and swollen pads, and said he'd been ready to hunt for them the next day.

Ricky's loyalty was to hunting, not to the hunter.

By car, picking Ricky up was a fifty-mile round trip we made more than once, until finally, some years later, Edna couldn't find Ricky for us. He disappeared on a hunting trip of his own and never came home.

Edna told the DeMosses about us, too.

Soon after, we received a note in the mail with a stamped, self-addressed envelope from Curly and Vada. *We heard about you down there on the river and understand you take kindly to visitors. We'd like to meet you if that's all right. Just use the self-addressed envelope to let us know a good time.*

Edna and her husband, Andy, joined them on their trip out, a visit that brought encouragement, warm hugs, and kindness from people who behaved with everyone, I think, as though they'd known them all their lives.

The DeMosses were of an old family in Sherman County. Retired wheat ranchers, they gardened and traveled and formed the basis for a good portion of Moro's social life, even when they drove their motor home to Arizona for the winter.

For us, their visits were always punctuated with the oohs and aahs noting our progress. It was comforting to know *they* didn't think we were crazy in the least.

Another letter introduced us to Patty Burnet and the Barnstormers, a local theater group. "Wanted to welcome you to Sherman County and tell you we're always looking for people interested in a little theater."

We received encouragement, too, from our neighbors on the other side of the river, the Mikkalos, who waded across the water one warm day when the river was low and Jerry and I had driven Deere John to the water rather than fight the tangled sagebrush.

Neil stretched his hand out to Jerry, introducing himself and his petite wife, Jullie. "We've been watching your work over there," he said, pointing to the shop. "The building going up. Is it a house?"

"Not yet," Jerry had told him. "The house will be up on the hill, back in the ravine."

They'd been delighted to meet us, said they'd thought about building down on the river themselves, but the road on their side was also quite treacherous, and Jullie would begin driving to The Dalles to work as a nurse three days a week when her maternity leave was over. She didn't want to drive on a risky road.

Someday their newborn baby, Paige, would go to school, too, and doing so from the river would be burdensome. They'd built a log home instead, high above us on the other side, out of sight. We learned that the power line that marched precariously down the hill to the river came from their ranch before it reached us.

Jerry and Neil discussed our hope to clear the flat and plant alfalfa, which was what Neil would do on his side in the spring. The Mikkalos farmed the wheat fields on the ridge across the river and ran cattle, too. While the men explored irrigation options, Jullie and I talked of our lives. She hoped to quit working and stay home permanently; I said aloud that I hoped to write.

With the Mikkalos, a kind, Christian couple in their late twenties, we reminisced about the day of their fire, when we'd felt so helpless watching Neil struggle with the flames. "We wish we could have helped," we offered, but the Mikkalos understood.

Then these new people made offers to help us in our lives. We never dreamed their hands and prayers would one day be so needed and appreciated so dearly.

But we didn't meet for years the people who best epitomized the character of our newfound community, though their kindness touched us that first fall.

Sherrie had decided to drive back to Bend alone one weekend to see her family. It was December. A skiff of snow had fallen. We watched her leave and waited until we saw the truck wind up around the last twist above the house. Sure of her safety, we returned to our work.

On Sunday the weather turned foul. It snowed, and the wind blew bitterly, as though chipped off an iceberg. We worried, almost hoping Sherrie had decided to stay another day.

But by dusk she arrived safely with her story to tell.

Halfway between Grass Valley and Moro, a truck had passed her, kicking a rock into the radiator and draining it. She'd pulled aside, gotten out, and begun walking, her jacket collar pulled up over her thick brown hair, her shoulders hunched against the wind. "I didn't know where I was walking to," she told us. "I couldn't call you, and I only know Bob and Marion, but didn't know their last name."

A car carrying a middle-aged couple passed, then turned around and came back. When they asked how they might help, Sherrie told them of her dilemma.

Then they began the remarkable saga.

First, they drove her to their home in Moro, where they exchanged vehicles. Then they drove their pickup back for Sherrie's truck and towed it to their home in Moro. In their garage, the nimble-fingered man finished draining the radiator, welded the hole shut, refilled the reservoir with water and antifreeze, and after devoting their entire Sunday to a total stranger, sent Sherrie on her way.

"Can I pay you or something?" Sherrie had asked. "Is there any way I can thank you?"

They'd shaken their heads no.

"Just pass it on," the woman said at last. "That's how we get by out here. We just pass it on."

Sherrie replaced the antifreeze a few days later, leaving it at their house; but she never got their names.

Marion told us later that it was the Moreaus who lived in the big yellow house in Moro.

When we first considered moving to Starvation Point, the thought of living so remotely was intriguing; yet the isolation frightened me as well. How could we have known there would be so many people like the Boyntons, Nell and Bruce, and others like the Moores and the Moreaus, all willing to set aside distance and time to touch us with their kindness, and teach us, with those rare gifts, the difference between being isolated and remote?

14

News and Entertainment

WHILE WE WERE NOT ISOLATED, we did concern ourselves about becoming insulated, an island unto ourselves.

Survival: seeking water, clearing ground, washing clothes, and providing for shelter consumed our time. With ease, we could forget about the hostages taken in the Middle East, ignore the nation's growing budget deficit, discount Oregon's slow recovery from recession, ignore the perils of an East Indian mystic's commune attempt to influence county elections seventy miles upriver.

Water rights, land use, government, and rules were not something far removed from us, though we lived physically far removed from them. We needed to know about costs and markets: the price of steel would affect the cost of farm equipment; people's interest in cholesterol could affect the price of beef. Events would have an impact on us even if we didn't know about them, and it seemed better that we shouldn't be surprised. Besides, to be people of faith offering salt and light, one must choose to be in the world.

For the first few months, we continued our subscription to the *Bulletin,* the daily newspaper covering the Bend area and some regional and limited national news. We considered subscribing to the *Oregonian,* Oregon's premier paper, upping its 99 percent coverage in literate Sherman County; but our day started at 6:00 a.m. and continued at a fast pace until we fell into bed around 7:00 p.m., leaving little time for perusing the paper.

A subscription to the weekly *Sherman County Journal,* written, printed, and distributed in Moro, seemed to match our pace, especially since some surprisingly similar stories were often reprinted from week to week, allowing those of us who missed them once to discover them later.

When we shopped in town, we treated ourselves to the *Chronicle* or the *Reminder,* published daily in The Dalles, and once in a while, we splurged on the Sunday *Oregonian,* a fat bundle that left us longing for a landfill closer than thirty miles away or a recycling center nearer than fifty.

Visitors soon discovered that an ideal gift for us consisted of any newspaper less than a week old, which they took with them when they left.

Any paper we might have subscribed to would have arrived several days late, since we drove the seven miles to the mailbox infrequently, and storing paper for recycling proved tedious. Burning old papers could take hours of watching, which we didn't have.

Still, we missed knowing about what was happening in the world and having pictures to put with names and places. The radio in the trailer picked up distant stations in a crackling fog. Our best news came from the car radio on our twice-monthly trips to The Dalles for supplies.

My parents drove down one weekend in the fall and spent the night sleeping in their van. The next morning, as they worked with us, Dad killed the fat green rattlesnake that had serenaded me by the spring. The next evening they lavished us in luxury by parking their van beside the barn so we could hear the debate between vice-presidential candidates Geraldine Ferraro and George H. W. Bush. It was a historic event.

Dad ran the engine off and on to keep the heater blasting warm air while Jerry and I huddled in the backseat, listening to Bush's barbs and Ferraro's fervor, creating our own pictures of the reporters and candidates in our minds.

We'd tried to listen to one of the presidential candidates' debates earlier that fall. I'd actually found a station on the trailer radio and had listened to the preshow discussion while I boiled a pot of water for tea. I sent Hansel and Josie to their "room," to lie quietly on their bed.

This is living! I'd thought, sinking into the couch, feet propped on my desk chair, hands wrapped around a hot cup, the fragrance of my pepper-mint tea filling the air.

But just as the show began and Mondale and Reagan were introduced, Hansel turned over on his bed, misjudged his distance to the edge, and flopped off, his seventy pounds landing with a thud on the floor between the beds. He picked himself up, shook his wiry brown body and floppy ears, and then, with great dignity, stepped back onto the bed, turned around three times, and plopped down as though nothing had happened.

While his fall had apparently done *him* no harm, it had knocked Mon-dale and Reagan off the air. Far in the distance the candidates' voices cut in and out. I turned the knobs, thumped the radio, and jumped up and down, thinking if Hansel's jolt could vibrate a wire loose, maybe I could jar it back.

The only thing I jarred loose was Sherrie, who heard the commotion and walked over to investigate. Jerry arrived too, fiddled around with the radio, took the speaker box off the wall, checked some wires, but couldn't fix it. Mondale and Reagan were gone. Even rushing out to the car was futile. That radio couldn't pick up any station covering the debate. I came back inside, chilled and frustrated.

Jerry tried to comfort me, telling me he knew who'd win, no matter how well both men might do; but I was surprised at my disappointment. I didn't want to become a close-minded recluse, unable to carry on conversations about what was happening in the world whenever we ventured out of our canyon. "We could get rid of the dog," Jerry suggested with a smile.

After Hansel interfered with our radio reception, Jerry and I compro-mised, subscribing to a monthly newsmagazine that we read together, huddled in bed, after a long day of work. We would read as we listened to the wind howl outside the trailer and be comforted by the snores wafting across to us from Hansel and Josie as they rested on their blue-covered mat-tress. Month-old news gave it all perspective.

Keeping up with the news became a whole new kind of entertainment, along with some other activities we discovered that first fall.

Russell brought along his slides of trips down the Owyhee, and the Gants brought out their photo albums. We crowded into our trailer, stepping over dogs and people's legs, to sit and look and listen, renewing the ancient art of conversation. But when we dusted off the VCR and joined the video generation, news and entertainment made the most interesting rural mix.

At first, we picked up movies at the region's only video store, in Wasco, twenty-two miles away. The young couple who operated the store catered to rural folks by letting us keep movies from Monday until Thursday. But we still missed television—news, specials, an occasional *Hill Street Blues,* sporting events. I even missed commercials.

In the remote reaches of Sherman County, though, only an expensive satellite dish would bring TV. And our budget just didn't allow it. So like every rural survivor, we turned to our families for help.

Mom volunteered first. We delivered several blank videocassette tapes to her when she offered to "borrow your sister's recorder, copy things from TV, and mail them."

"Just record movies, Mom," I said, trying to keep it simple at first.

The first tape arrived a few weeks later with *The Adventures of Marco Polo Part I* written on the side. "Could be a problem," Jerry noted, "if she doesn't record parts two and three."

On the big night of our first television in months, we finished the dishes early, then Sherrie and I made up a giant batch of popcorn while Dennis lifted Kipper into our trailer. We sent Ricky to the bathroom (so "the boys" wouldn't fight), and sent the drahthaars to their "room." Jerry lay on our bed, and Dennis, Sherrie, and I squeezed onto the couch, our feet draped over Kipper's sleeping back.

We innocently pushed the tape into the recorder, popped the corn into our mouths, turned on our set, and began relishing television.

We watched young Marco waiting for his father; we watched young Marco meeting his father; and finally, we watched him racing to the ship when he learned his father was leaving town. Just as young Marco pleads breathlessly, "You're taking me with you, aren't you?" the entire ship was hit with a snowstorm of static fuzz. The tape had run out!

"Mom," I said gently when I called her from Moore's barn the next day. "You can set the speed to record up to six hours on one tape. And, by the way, did Marco go with his dad?"

"How should I know?" she said. "I never watch TV."

We tried another approach. "Just tape something from public television," I suggested. "But try to record *all* of it."

The next tape had *all* of a month-old news hour.

At last! We could see what Geraldine Ferraro looked like!

It also had the National Drum and Bugle Corps Competition, which we watched desperately one rainy Sunday afternoon. "Why are we looking at this?" Jerry asked. "We don't even like drums and bugles." Before I could answer, the same snowstorm that wiped out Marco's ship hit the marching field—just before they announced the winner.

We knew there was no use asking Mom who won.

My sister took pity on us next. "The boys watch a lot of TV," she said, "usually the whole program."

A few weeks later, she sent three full tapes. We should have been suspicious about the notes attached, however: *Movie about famous woman, I think, Last half of Kirk Douglas movie from other tape, and ????*

But we were pioneers and used to taking chances.

"Let's watch the famous woman movie," Jerry suggested.

According to the title, it was *The Patricia Neal Story.* The list of stars rolled up the screen, followed by a slender woman in a forties bathing suit pulling herself from a Hollywood pool.

Suddenly, more credits whizzed by. It seemed strange.

It got stranger as we realized *this* movie was about a woman writer who couldn't get a job with a chauvinist editor, so she dresses up like a man. "Well, at least it's at the beginning," Jerry commented wryly.

And it *was* rather interesting, especially when she/he was supposed to go out of town with the boss. But we'll never know what happened, because we were abruptly returned to *The Patricia Neal Story*. Patricia had already had a stroke and a baby, and they kept referring to things that had happened while we were away watching a writer in drag. The star was shown in London, receiving innovative treatment for her stroke, when miraculously, Marlin Perkins from *Wild Kingdom* appeared on screen.

"What's Marlin Perkins doing in London?" I asked.

"What do transplanting ostrich eggs have to do with stroke treatment?" my husband responded.

Before either of us could decide, *The Rockford Files* rerun came on. "Maybe Rockford will solve this mystery," Jerry laughed.

That movie also began at the beginning—and ended with Patricia Neal giving her closing speech. "Well, at least we saw the end," Jerry said.

An arcing microwave oven was beginning to look good in comparison.

Eventually, we found solutions. We encouraged my sister's taping as comic relief—and then for real television we tracked down detail-oriented people who liked to finish things.

Ken Tedder sent us television news and features with the footage marked where programs started *and* finished, and only the commercials were missing. Blair taped *Mystery* and *Masterpiece Theatre* and anything else we circled in the public television magazine we mailed to her. Another friend in Madras recorded *Hill Street Blues* and sports events.

So on New Year's Day that first year, we didn't watch the Rose Bowl— we cheered the *entire* Fiesta Bowl from the week before. And really, we didn't notice the difference, because no one had told us who had won.

Best of all, we rediscovered books, including the Bible, which we began reading chapter by chapter that first fall. Even now, years later, I often read aloud to Jerry from a wide variety of books. We stay up late, reading, unveiling mysteries, well into the night.

And we count ourselves privileged that the "news and entertainment center" we love best still consists of a friend, a light, a book, and a bed.

15

Weather and the Road

"IT'S RAINING," I WHISPERED to Jerry, waking him in the night with an anxious elbow to his back. He groaned, more from the disturbance than my information.

Like me, he could hear the hard rain pelting the metal trailer roof, could feel the tension in my whisper. But he just said, "There's nothing we can do about it," and pulled closer toward the little window next to the bed, tugging the covers onto his shoulders and off mine.

I snuggled around him but wasn't comforted enough to sleep.

As a child, I had believed that if I imagined all the awfuls and terribles that might happen in my world, and considered how to manage them, then maybe they couldn't happen.

Unfortunately, I always overestimated my control and underestimated my imagination, leaving real life capable of many more awfuls and terribles than anything I could dream up.

On the homestead, the weather and the road were two terribles that challenged both my imagination and control.

Tomorrow the truss truck was due, traveling north from Bend, bringing the triangular, steeplelike wooden structures, built so long that they rested partly on a truck bed and partly on a small trailer pulled behind.

A huge crane sat on the truck, and with it, the driver would lift the trusses from the trailer and set them on the second-story walls of the house as gently as a child builds a tower from twigs.

But first the driver had to get here, sliding along the dirt road, crossing the cattle guards, rattling down the steep ravine above the house, rounding the switchbacks, and struggling up and down the roller-coaster grade. He had to do this without losing his trailer or a truss.

I was imagining the worst and hoping it wouldn't happen.

By some quirk, we had chosen the wettest fall on record to build. While most people think of Oregon as wet and rainy, the largest part of the state's land mass isn't. Historically, only eight to ten inches of rainfall watered Sherman County each year. In November, an inch and a half was normal.

The November we homesteaded, more than three inches of rain fell. It poured on the wooden floor decking, covering the insulation, seeping between the boards, and soaking the fiberglass. It ran down the road from the house to the trailers, turning the powdery dust first into slick slime, then into gooey black mud, tarry stuff that stuck to our boots, giving us inches of extra height and slowing our steps to resemble those of Frankenstein's monster. Pioneer women must have pulled their skirts up high to keep the gooey mud from clinging to their hemlines, I decided.

The rain drenched the dogs, who panted in steamy repose in the galley kitchen or slumbered on their bed surrounded by beads of caked mud.

It soaked the men, who were working feverishly to erect the side walls of the second floor before the trusses arrived.

As things turned out, the trusses wouldn't appear before either snow or cold weather, as we had hoped. The week after we harnessed the spring (and I could discard the bucket of water kept in the kitchen for boiling and cleaning), we'd encountered both, with an inch of snow and minus-zero weather.

We'd spent *that* day running my blow dryer under the trailer, pointing it at the pipes that were frozen solid. By late afternoon the end of the dryer had melted, but it still blew out heat. Finally, for supper that night, we had water again, though I needed a new blow dryer.

Not two days after it warmed up to the teens, it snowed—big, leafy-looking flakes that fell in the silent night, freezing and covering the tracks we'd left in the gooey mud.

Sherrie and I were sent for supplies when the next morning broke clear but bone-aching cold. Only an inch or so of snow had fallen in the canyon, but it was enough to cover all but the black lava rocks poking their noses out of their sidehill beds.

We were up early for the trip, leaving before 8:00 a.m. in Dennis and Sherrie's pickup.

Underneath the snow, the frozen road provided good traction. "We don't need to use four-wheel drive," Sherrie said confidently as we made it easily up the roller-coaster grade.

We rattled across the fake cattle guard, twisted up the hill, and crossed the second, then third cattle guard to the flatter section of wheat fields before we stopped. We took pictures of the road, sparkling crystal white in the morning sun, with one set of deer tracks down the middle, so fresh we could see the tiny clumps of snow her hooves had left on the edges of her prints.

It was so pristine, we hated to mar it with our tire tracks, but we needed to head on. We passed Bruce's barn, wound our way under the power lines, and chatted, relieved that only an inch or two of snow had fallen. *If this is the road in winter, it isn't bad,* I thought, forgetting to think of the worst in order to prevent it.

As we passed the last long curve, almost two miles from the barn and only a mile from the gravel road, the snow suddenly got deeper. Sherrie gave the truck more power. Snow sprayed ominously up on either side of us. The truck engine ground down as Sherrie tried desperately to throw it into four-wheel drive, and then we plunged headfirst into a snowdrift as solid as a mud wall.

We looked at each other cautiously, neither wanting to believe that we were stuck. Sherrie spun the wheels a few times; we rocked our bodies trying to urge the vehicle onward.

"I'll get out and push," I said, stepping out and dropping through a crusty pack of white up to my knees.

The road had gone from supporting two inches of snow to two feet of it.

I stomped around to the front to push, breaking the drifts with my shins; I stomped around the back to push. No luck either place.

Sherrie got out, and we looked underneath, gasping as we viewed the snow packed solid against the bottom of the truck. Stomping the snow down in front of the wheels did nothing but raise a sweat beneath our coats. Bouncing on the back bumper while Sherrie tried to step on the gas just burned up fuel. We had no kitty litter or any other abrasive item to put beneath the wheels for traction.

We weighed our resources and options. Jerry and Dennis wouldn't be expecting us home until sometime late that evening, so we couldn't count on their rescue. We could walk to the nearest phone, about three miles away, but we had no guarantee Bob Boynton, our closest savior, would be home.

We were on our own.

"Do we have chains?" I asked.

No.

"We don't have a shovel, either," Sherrie said, mumbling under her breath. "And I left my gloves home and my warm boots, too."

"Maybe Bruce has some tools back at the shop," I suggested. Sherrie checked on Kipper lying inside the shell on the truck bed. Then we set off, she walking in her high-heel leather boots, her mittenless hands swinging in the cold, and me with warm boots but only thin kid gloves to cover my aching fingers. Puffs of air like cartoon conversations hung outside our mouths as we huffed along. Our boots crunched against the snow. The bright sun flashed from the white world to our faces, making our eyes ache.

Distances are deceiving in the West. After walking toward the shop for what seemed like hours, we still hadn't reached it, and I understood how the pioneer women could write in their journals that they'd seen the mountains and kept thinking they'd reach them the next day, not in the two weeks it really took them.

Bruce left no tools outside his locked shop. I chastised myself that I hadn't listened to much of what he'd explained to Jerry about the International tractor and how to start it. Sherrie and I looked around the machine, expecting some miracle, I think, some recognition of how it might work without a key, but had no luck.

Sherrie's feet hurt and were icy cold by the time we made it back to our stuck truck. We'd taken extra water for Kipper, and we drank some of it now, concerned about dehydration.

"What do we have in this truck, anyway?" I asked as Sherrie turned the engine on to warm us up.

"We have a camera, Kipper's rug, his plastic water bucket (a child's sand-and-water version), and Dennis's carpenter's level," Sherrie said, looking into the bed of the truck.

She saw me eying the long steel rod that told carpenters if their work was in balance.

"Dennis'll kill us if we hurt his level," she cautioned.

I didn't think we had a choice.

"So, how about if we put the rug down and I lie on my back on it under the truck?" I offered. "I've got gloves, so I'll pound with the level, break away some of the snow under the truck."

"I'll use Kipper's water bucket to scrape the loose snow and dump it away from the tires," Sherrie offered.

We took no pictures as we set about our tasks.

A cold, unmelting sun arched lazily across the sky while we worked, pounding and scraping, pounding and scraping. Sherrie's knuckles burned with the cold; my kid gloves developed a hole in the palm where a blister grew from thrusting the heavy steel level into the snow over and over.

Neither of us panicked. I might have, alone; but sharing disaster made it bearable. And working through the crisis, I formed a bond with this woman I'd come to like and respect.

Every now and then we stopped. Sherrie stepped into the truck, I bounced on the bumper, and we tried to rock the truck away from the clinging snow, usually without success.

But by midday we had won.

Such cheering! I waved from behind the truck, leaning against the cold, wet level as Sherrie twisted and turned off down the road, Kipper's old bones bouncing about in the back. Sherrie drove the truck onto the stubble field, where the snow was just inches deep, and stopped.

On safe ground, we danced around in the snow like worshipers at a Bacchus feast, delighted with our accomplishment, having conquered the elements.

It was a moment of joy neither of us would ever forget.

Safe, we took pictures of the snow depth and the treacherous road, smiling at our former peril.

The wind must have drifted snow over the road, we decided later, after we'd driven to The Dalles for our errands and back.

"Good thing to know," Jerry said, "that that section drifts shut. Best to drive in the stubble, I guess. Next time, make sure you've got chains and a shovel," he added. We both vowed never to leave home in the winter without shovels, chains, sleeping bags, warm clothes, food, and water.

"Sorry about your gloves," he finished.

At least they protected my manicure.

Since we were standing in front of him and unharmed, Dennis found the status of his level to be of more interest than our adventures or my gloves. "Did you ruin it?" he asked, turning it over gently in his hands.

Sherrie was indignant that he showed so little concern for our welfare, especially once he knew the level had survived. But Dennis simply demonstrated a clearly western trait: he had absolute confidence that we women could take care of ourselves, so he focused on the problem at hand.

Now, listening to the rain pinging harder on the roof, waiting for the truss truck, I tried to feel confident, remembering how we'd outwitted the weather that day.

The warmer temperature had relieved the road of its burden of snow, leaving slush and water behind. Now it rained, pouring on the truss truck on its way to the Point.

The men continued work on the house during the morning, readying themselves, until close to noon, when Randy, a Nordic-like, wild-eyed blond, arrived driving the truss truck. Mud sheathed the truck's tires, and globs of the black, wet sludge freckled the side of the trailer, blemishes that refused to be washed off by the incessant rain.

A wheel was missing from the small trailer he pulled.

Stepping shakily down from the truck, he said, "That road's terrible!" Then he described in detail the slipping and sliding he'd endured, the tight squeeze of the long truck around the sharp corners, the wheel that broke off at the ravine above the old abandoned car.

"I just want to get these set and get outta here," he urged, "so I can get back to pavement before dark."

The men worked quickly despite the rain, pulling the truss truck backward with Deere John to reach the tall walls and walking carefully across the rafters covered with the wet vapor barrier, which now were as slick as ice.

Russell and Jerry had set lots of trusses, but these were steep and deep to compensate for the angle of the roof and the extra insulation required in the experimental house. Their hammers hit the nails true, ringing out across the ravines.

By four o'clock the trusses were set enough to allow Randy to leave.

"We'll follow you out," Jerry said, "in case you have trouble."

Randy nodded and swallowed as Jerry gave one last piece of advice: "Keep your speed up—especially after that last curve, just as you reach the top. It angles badly, and in this mud, if you slow down, you'll slide."

We followed Randy, watching the truck and trailer hinge around the switchbacks, speed up the steep grade, and bounce over the tops of boulders jutting out in the road.

My heart moved into my throat. I imagined the worst, remembering when Sherrie once drove off the road while watching deer in the distance. Two wheels had dropped over the side as the truck balanced precariously, teetering. In a cold sweat, Sherrie gingerly removed herself and Kipper and shakily walked a long distance to Dennis and Deere John for the truck rescue.

I said my prayers for Randy and his truck, when, at the section in question, he slowed.

Perhaps he began to lose traction in the mud, maybe because the thought of keeping up his speed in the slimy muck was so frightening that he couldn't imagine that quicker would be better. Or maybe the muck was simply too thick for the truck to go any faster. Whatever the reason, Randy began to slide.

We could see it from behind, the smaller trailer with only three wheels slipping toward the edge of the road and the drop-off beyond, followed by the truck and trailer.

Please, God, don't let him go over.

I saw Jerry's jaw tighten as he mumbled encouragement, "Gun it, Randy, gun it!"

But Randy didn't. The big truck and its trailers continued to slide closer and closer to the edge that topped a ravine several hundred feet deep.

Then, by the grace of God, the truck stopped.

Randy eased out of the cab, even more wild-eyed than before, but talking with Jerry and Russell about what to do next. Meanwhile, Dennis calmly drove his vehicle back down the grade and began driving Deere John up the road. Sherrie got her camera out to capture the sight.

I sat in the truck, frightened by an event so close to my imagination, wondering if I were truly meant for pioneering, for living where all the work and worry could not control the world.

Eventually, Deere John arrived to save the day—again—pulling Randy from his rut straight onto the road, setting him back on his course toward pavement and Bend. Other drivers who delivered lumber and supplies later that year on summer days, when the road ran hard and dry, said they couldn't believe the road could be as bad as Randy said it was.

But any of us who drove the grade in winter knew Randy had no need to use his imagination to embellish the truth. And I knew that my imagination was too small to control the elements on Starvation Point. That didn't keep me from trying.

16

Pit Bull Protection

EVERYONE SAID IT WAS the wettest, coldest winter in memory. Each December-morning sky resembled the bottom of a goose: gray, mottled, and heavy. We awkwardly wrapped Christmas presents purchased at our new fashion center—the Sherman Co-op Farm Store—listening quietly to the rain.

We studied the river as it inched its way up the dirt banks, wondering if it would reach the dikes in the spring, when the snow melted in the high country, or if we'd discover how secure the dikes were before Christmas.

The dikes were critical to our homestead. Without them, the river could pour across the flat each spring, carving a channel that would eventually make the flat an island. The John Day, the second largest drainage system in the country without a dam on it, was a land-hungry river. One dike reached across the upper end of the property, stretching out toward the river to a massive dump of dirt and sagebrush. A second dike pushed up out of the gravel and dirt of the flat about three hundred feet behind but parallel to the first. Both were wide enough to drive on, though so rocky no one would want to. Their height made a great walking trail for Hansel and me, affording us a fine view of the river and the flat.

Jerry had engineered the dikes based on the water lines and erosion scars left on the flat over the years. The first dike would hold back high water as it rushed around the bend during the spring thaw in the mountains. The second dike would prevent the high water eddying around the land clump from spreading across the flat.

With the water at normal levels, the dikes appeared abandoned, left in the midst of a sagebrush flat. With the river in flood stage, we hoped the dikes would be closely attached to—though not overwhelmed by—the muddy water.

"At least that's one thing we finished without a hassle," Jerry noted, remembering that the D8 Cat had completed the tasks without getting stuck in the mud.

Of course, he spoke too soon.

It was Bob Boynton who told us.

A state official had driven with Bob, following a complaint that Bob had done work within the quarter-mile limit without a permit.

"When we came around the bend above your house," Bob related, "the state guy came unglued! 'They can't build there!' he said. I told him that you'd used our phone sometimes to call for inspections, so I knew you were legal. He said you couldn't be, and then he saw the dikes, and I thought he'd have a heart attack. Sorry," he finished lamely, adjusting his Stetson, hating to be the bearer of bad tidings.

Even though we knew that we were legal, Bob's news was a chunk of coal in our unhung Christmas stocking.

The letters arrived two weeks before the holiday, embossed with official Oregon State seals. I'd sent dozens of "official" letters to people as a public administrator. But I'd never realized until we got one of our own just how helpless missives from the government can make the recipients feel—especially when they arrive on a Friday, leaving a whole weekend to stew about them. This one said:

This is to inform you that the Division of State Lands...requires a
permit prior to the removal, filling, or alteration of fifty cubic yards
or more of material within the banks of all natural waterways of the

State. We ask that you call or write and tell us what you know about this matter.

The second letter was more ominous:

The Division of State Lands has informed us that your development within the John Day Scenic Waterway may be in violation of the Scenic Waterway Act. Please file the [required] notification with this office before you continue with your project.

In other words, cease and desist.

My palms grew wet as I read the signatures of the state officials. My old fears were renewed. Jerry was just angry.

"We've got permits!" he thundered. "We haven't done anything within the riverway!" He stomped around, causing the dogs to scurry for cover on their beds. Eventually, he announced we would just ignore the letters.

But I knew that government could seem like a pit bull terrier, attacking in the dark, biting and holding on, thinking it was protecting, just doing its job, then being unable to release its death grip, even when it finally recognized its master.

The master usually had to find a way to help the pit bull loosen its gripping jaws.

So I wrote back long letters quoting the statutes and administrative rules as we understood them, especially informing the officials that we'd done "nothing within the waterway or to its banks." Then we waited—and worried. I would rather have fought rattlesnakes than those administrative rules.

A response arrived with a copy of an attorney general's ruling and a request that we meet to discuss our "alteration of the riverbank."

We assured them of our desire to meet but disclaimed, in writing, any work *within* the riverbank.

It wasn't to be resolved before Christmas.

Dennis and Sherrie had driven the only four-wheel-drive vehicle on the ranch when they left for holiday visits with family and friends. Russell had put chains on his small car for the run up the grade and home to Cove for Christmas. We planned to spend Christmas day with Jerry's parents, who lived three hours away. We hoped to see Matt and his girlfriend, Melissa, as well.

Jerry's parents worried about us, although I wrote weekly to assure them of our progress. They were anxious for us to get a phone. His mother and dad were small and round and loving, resembling the couple atop a wedding cake who had sampled some of the frosting below.

Christmas was especially important to Jerry's mom, a Christian evangelist, and we looked forward to sharing it with her. The holiday also occurred as we began craving a meal served on a real table surrounded by family, shoes not covered with mud, the promise of a shower not rushed by the shortage of hot water, and a mailbox without threatening letters.

Christmas Eve oozed into Christmas morning, dark and gloomy; the sky blended with the dense fog rising above the river. In the mist, we loaded the dogs into portable kennels in the back of the pickup, stacked the presents behind the seat, and headed out to Christmas.

I came to terms with the road that day.

Every time I had experienced danger on the road, I had marked the spot in my mind, sure that once we passed *that* section, we'd be safe. First there was the roller-coaster grade, then the edge Sherrie had almost gone over, then the spot where Randy had lost a wheel, and where the cement trucks had turned back. Then came Randy's rut, where the truss truck almost slid off the road, followed by the hyperventilating spot near Bruce's barn; I'd hold my breath from there until we passed through the Coelsches' gate, slid through the sagebrush, and dropped over the steep bank onto gravel.

By the time that first Christmas morning rolled around, every inch of the road was a terror.

The slush was deep, the mud slick, and the grade awash with melting snow. The truck slipped and spun its wheels; mud and slush splashed against the windshield, blinding us as the wipers groaned.

I jammed my arm against the cab roof, right foot forward, bracing myself. We had to slow to make the sharp turn that led to the ravine above the house, and though Jerry gunned the engine, the truck simply couldn't get enough traction in the slimy sludge. Mud flew, dogs bounced, the truck slid sideways, and I screamed as Jerry managed to stop us just inches from the edge of the nine-hundred-foot ravine above the house.

"Get out and push," he directed.

I stepped gingerly around the truck, with only a foot width between it and instant catastrophe over the side. I pushed, but I couldn't keep my footing in the slime. The truck simply slid the other way, spattering me with globs and slush, but gaining no forward ground.

I assumed we'd turn back and spend Christmas in the trailer. But Jerry said, "We'll have to make a run for it."

"A run for it?" I asked weakly.

"I'll back down around the bend and pick up enough speed to pull up this last grade," he said. Then he added confidently, "Come on, get in."

I couldn't move. I simply stood there, mud caking my jeans and jacket, terror tightening my face.

"You go," I croaked. "I'll walk the rest of the way up and meet you at the top."

As Jerry inched his way back down the hill and around the bend out of sight, I climbed the bank above the road. From that height, I could see the challenge of the muddy reptile road.

Standing there in the drizzle, scared and waiting, I wondered why I wasn't with my husband in the truck. How could I be so disloyal? Did I think I was needed to dial 911 should he go over the side? Did I so mistrust his judgment? Would he be there if he thought it wasn't safe? I should have been with him, I decided. If my best friend went over the side, I wouldn't want to carry on without him.

The engine roared, the nose of the truck shot out from around the switchback, and Jerry and the dogs sped by below me, slush and mud flying every which way, wet clumps flung against the dog kennel like snowballs against a picket fence.

The truck twisted in the roadway, but with the added speed, Jerry straightened it and kept moving forward until the truck disappeared safely up the grade and around the ridge.

I exhaled great gasps of air.

"Come on!" Jerry yelled, appearing at the top of the ridge, swinging his arm in an arc. I slid off the bank and took off running, my feet struggling to stay upright in the muddy tracks his tires had left, breathlessly praying *Thank you* with each step I took.

After the initial adventure, our Christmas holiday was a pleasant event. It also was a time of reconciling myself with the road. It had become a symbol of my life, always something I had to worry about, fearing the worst, lying awake in the rain, planning and preparing, but still unable to control. From that first Christmas Day onward, I accepted the fact that to stay on Starvation Point and achieve our dream, I had to see the road for what it was, just a path to someplace else, just a byway with good strips and bad strips and unexpected rest stops. I had to trust that our being on it had some meaning, that we'd be protected and directed until we reached our final destination.

The return of Russell and the Gants, and the arrival of 1985 with its flurry of activity, kept our minds from the road or the dikes. Then, for each of us, homesteading moved into a kind of routine.

Jerry fixed pancakes for Russell and himself each morning. Dennis joined them for coffee and tea, the three deciding on the day's work and then heading to the house as dawn washed over the rimrocks.

If we could help, Sherrie and I were assigned tasks, such as staining the siding sage green, turning ourselves into Jolly Green Giants in the process. Later we walked up the steep path to the house, followed by sniffing and meandering dogs. If our skills were not needed there, we'd bake cookies, fix lunch and dinner, or I'd write, with Hansel curled under the desk beneath my feet.

If we made supply trips to town, they began early, before the sun thawed the road by noon. Once, Jerry and I arrived home, arms loaded with groceries, only to discover the dogs had locked us out of the trailer.

"We've got to get that kennel fixed," Jerry mumbled. The trio barked at me as I tried to enter the trailer through the air vent on top. They cheered me on, but my bottom was too big to slip through. A window left ajar and a sliced screen finally permitted entry to a chorus of loud, yapping dogs who were never left alone in the trailer again.

Jerry and I still straddled dogs sleeping in the galley kitchen while we cooked, and we had to wipe their paws off each time they came in or out, which occurred often, since only one animal was permitted out at a time. If we forgot, all three of them explored on their own, keeping us awake nights waiting for the scratch on the trailer door announcing their return.

Several times daily the litany sounded: "Ricky, in." "Hansel, out." "Josie, stay!" "Harvey, no!" "Puffin, down!"

Sherrie thought we could put the rhythm to music.

The rhythm of our routines continued too. Then a day was marked on the calendar. Jerry and the state officials had worked out February 20—the day I turned thirty-nine—as "dike day."

"Another rut," I said.

"Have a little faith," my husband urged.

While we waited, Dennis and Russell—neither liking the height—

inched their way across the plywood on scaffolding to cover the trusses; they carried hammers and shingles while hanging precariously from their perches like the geese nesting in the high rocks across the river. Then the men finished roughing in the electrical wiring and plumbing, and we, wearing surgical masks to protect our lungs from the fiberglass filaments, shoved insulation between the wooden studs.

Because he hovered at our heels, Hansel wore a mask as well, tolerating our snickers at the nurse's mask that made him look like *M*A*S*H*'s* "Hot Lips" Hoolihan with floppy ears.

While we worked on the second floor, the dogs watched from below. Ricky, Kipper, and Josie snoozed in the occasional sun streaking in through the high windows while Hansel whined and whistled through his nose at the bottom of the ladder, begging to be carried up to where the action was.

The first day he appeared behind us on the second floor, we each accused the other of bringing him up. Eventually, Russell was the one who had to carry the squirming, uncooperative dog *back down* the ladder.

But the next day I watched as Hansel painstakingly stepped up the ladder rungs, whining and whistling nervously as he climbed, then jumping onto the second floor and barking proudly with his self-taught success. He even learned to walk down.

While we waited for the official's visit, we wrapped the inside of the house with a required vapor barrier; the white plastic bulged against the thick insulation, the two held together by black stringy glue. When we finished, the wind whistled in toward the walls, and the plastic huffed inward, but the barrier held, keeping the drafts on the outside decks.

Sheetrock arrived next, on a truck wearing clanking chains on all four of its dual tires. Dennis met the truck at 7:00 a.m. near the mailbox and led it the seven miles down the snowy grade.

Our arms ached as we hurried to unload the heavy chalky boards so the truck could get back out to the gravel before the road thawed.

My sister and parents delivered the mules the next week. The animals, though contained by my primitive fence, ran happily up and down the hillside.

But the unresolved dike debate wore on us like a bur beneath Blue's saddle. We only briefly thought about what we'd do if the state insisted we stop building or tear down the dikes. We couldn't afford to do either, nor could we afford to pursue a lengthy legal battle.

February arrived like a long-awaited rainbow: beautiful, with promises of good things to come. But the river ran muddy and full, inching its way up the side of the first dike. The road on top through the wheat fields reportedly resembled a rushing river, too.

I could just see the official getting stuck in mud.

On the appointed day in February, we waited anxiously until four o'clock before Jerry drove up to the top, looking for an official stuck at Randy's rut or near Bruce's barn. But the road ran empty through the fields.

He continued out to the mailbox, where another embossed letter explained why we had waited in vain: "I regret that I will not be able to meet with you on February 20, 1985 at 1:00 p.m. However, I would like to re-schedule my visit with you for March 7, 1985."

Another two weeks to wait and worry. Oh, how we longed for a phone.

Then we decided it was just as well the official had changed the date. At least by March, the road should be more stable.

The men finished hanging Sheetrock and began pounding hemlock on the walls. Sherrie and I selected wallpaper. Jerry and I made the molding that would trim the windows and frame the doors and floors.

They were dreary, time-consuming jobs that didn't keep my mind from the dangers of the dikes.

March came in quietly, like the tiny yellow flowers and wild phlox that magically appeared one morning along the steep banks. "Yellow bells will be out next," Marion predicted. Sure enough, their fragrant tiny blooms soon dotted the ground beneath the sage. The sun burned warm against our faces. The river receded away from the dikes, back into its normal channel.

The "official" arrived as scheduled.

He was younger than I imagined. His uncallused hand reached out to shake Jerry's—a desk person, sent out to visit the wilderness, a man representing one of eighteen agencies with jurisdiction over the John Day River.

He apologized for canceling the previous trip and told us as he scanned the canyon that he'd never been to this part of the scenic waterways area before.

We walked silently with him to the dikes. He looked and walked and measured with a tape, then picked up soil and rocks and rubbed them between his fingers. He crossed over to the riverbank, then came striding back slowly to where Jerry, Hansel, and I stood, checking the distances, seeing if we were really building legally.

"Are you mining the gravel along the river?" he finally asked, eying the dump truck suspiciously.

"Mining?" Jerry asked incredulously. "We're definitely not mining!"

Apparently, the state was concerned that we might be excavating the smooth river rocks left on the flat, selling them to some faraway place.

"We could barely get cement trucks to come down here, let alone load trucks to move out gravel," I told him.

"I guess there isn't much market for rocks this size, is there?" the official agreed, dropping the cantaloupe-size stone.

"We want to put the land back into production," Jerry told him, "like Neil is doing across the river." We could see our neighbor and his crew of workers with big scrapes and tractors, clearing sagebrush, leveling and preparing his piece along the river for alfalfa.

The official's eyes narrowed, his jaws set tightly in protection.

"You can't move ground without a permit."

"How can we rotate crops, then?" Jerry asked, reminding him of the law and its allowance to convert grazing to cropland. "Cows grazed here. Now we want to plant alfalfa."

"You can't change anything from the way the land looked in 1974, when the act passed," the official said. He nervously pushed his glasses up his nose.

Jerry said, "The state can't stop us from making a living on our land. Maybe we'll have to settle this in court."

I winced. We were in no financial position to do that.

The official rocked uneasily from foot to foot but assured us we wouldn't have to go *that* far and promised a written response within a week.

It was several weeks, actually, before we heard. But once we opened the letter, we did not complain about the wait, for the officials had come to the interpretation we had believed in all along: we had built legally and had done nothing in the river or to its banks. We'd left no silt or sand to strangle the fish, done nothing to injure the birds or wildlife habitat.

"Since you have done no work within the riverbanks," the letter read, "it has been determined that we have no jurisdiction in this matter."

The pit bull had loosened its grip.

17

Murphy's Law

MURPHY—AS IN MURPHY'S LAW—must have been a homesteader, for in March, everything went wrong.

Strong winds shook the trailer daily, rattling windows and anything not tied down, including a two-hundred-pound septic tank waiting to be installed, which disappeared one night. We found it halfway to the river in the morning. It took Deere John and Dennis all morning to bring the runaway back to the house and stake it to the ground.

Dad brought his Case tractor to the ranch to disk sagebrush into the ground, and while it had worked perfectly the day before, it wouldn't on our ranch.

"Is there a black hole here," we wondered, "where healthy things come to die?"

Something happened to Deere John, too, that same week, and at first we were delighted that Dad's trailer was present and large enough to haul our machine out for repairs. But halfway out the reptile road, the trailer spring broke. Still, Dad and Jerry fixed it in a matter of hours and continued easing it on into town for repairs—then ran out of gas on the way home.

Mom and I wore surgical masks again to sand boards, this time for the wainscoting and cabinets, but the sanding belts kept breaking, forcing Jerry to make five-hour round trips into Portland for the unusual replacements.

On one trip, a black mass chased Jerry's car as it left the mailbox, appearing as a black spot with pointy ears in the rearview mirror as he drove away. It was odd for a dog to be way out here, but maybe someone hiked nearby and the dog waited, Jerry thought.

But it was still there when he returned five hours later, so Jerry opened the door; the frisky black Scotty jumped in and huddled on the floor on the passenger side, only its pink tongue distinguishing it from the darkness of the car.

Jerry brought it home and handed the squiggling solid body to my parents, who'd recently lost a dog. "Oh my!" Mom said with happy surprise at such a perfect gift.

But since it was our Murphy month, she soon exclaimed "Oh my!" again, this time with some distress, as she noticed the underside of the dog. It was a squirming glob of fleas, and an oozing mass of sores, pus, and blood drained beneath the Scotty's tail. Her little eyes were dull beneath the stringy fur. She panted hard in between grateful licks of Mom's face.

Mom and Dad made several fifty-mile round trips nursing the little dog that week, scouring Wasco for flea powder and shampoo, medicine and tick collars, putting sparkle back into Sparky, as they named her. Ultimately, Sparky was something good that came from Murphy's March.

When Jerry sent Sherrie and me to Wasco to locate hay to tide the mules over, we stopped hopefully at the Farm Store. "Just let me finish up here," the clerk said, "and I'll call around for you."

What luxury to have a phone to "call around," I thought. But he didn't use a phone. He just raised his voice to the clusters of men standing about near the oil filters and tractor parts in the store. "Anyone got any hay to sell?" he yelled.

One man did, and Sherrie and I followed him out of town to an old church in a locust grove, beautifully wainscoted inside, but now used for his storage. "Where you living?" he asked. When I told him, he said, "Really?

All winter down there? Why?" With all the hassles we'd had that month, I had a hard time forming an answer.

The hassles weren't over. Next, the dump truck developed a broken axle while it carried a load of gravel needed for the septic tank leach fields we would put in later in the spring. In taking the axle out, bolts in the hub sheared, resulting in more trips to Wasco for repairs.

Then the hydraulic lines on Deere John decided to retire, and even with all new parts, Dad and Jerry needed hours to get it to work again. "I've never seen anything like it," Dad said. "The simplest things…"

Dennis worked on the tile in the double shower upstairs, the hot tub and shower on the first floor, and in the entryway. The mud refused to set up in the damp house. Dennis spent a month on what we all agreed any-where else would have taken a week.

The rain no longer threatened the inside of the house, but water had accumulated beneath the insulation in the floors, caught in the vapor bar-rier. Jerry drilled holes throughout the plywood floor in my future office, and with turkey basters, Mom and I began sucking the water out through the woodpecker-size holes.

The work was boring and our fingers cramped, until David Moore, hearing of our plight, offered us his wet/dry vacuum cleaner. We stuck the hose through the holes, sucking out more than forty gallons from that one room alone.

"Just think how long those turkey basters would have taken," Mom observed as we lugged the heavy container of water sloppily down the stairs.

The electric fence I'd built kept getting unplugged, and then the mules would disappear. That caused me to give up designer jeans as a casualty of ranching. The pockets couldn't hold the wire cutters, pliers, hammer, gloves, and fence insulators I needed to check the old fence line and my new one each time the mules got away.

I gave up fake fingernails in March. Jerry only siliconed my nails one

time, and while he'd done a marvelous job, long nails were just too imprac-
tical on the homestead, always popping off and chipping, getting lost in the
dog food.

The dogs discovered ticks by the dozens, making me wonder what the
parasites had lived on before we'd arrived. Several times a day we ran our
hands over the dogs' bodies, feeling for the telltale lumps, then pulling until
we held the greedy, bloated insects in our hands.

"The family that picks ticks together sticks together," I noted, trying to
laugh the day we took more than a hundred ticks off Ricky.

"Maybe I'll write a book about this place and call it *The Tick and I*," I
told Jerry.

"Or *Pickin' Ticks*," he said, executing the disgusting things beneath a
rock.

We checked our beds each night, performed body searches of our own,
reminding each other that our days of a hundred irritations could have been
worse.

When the parts manufacturer sent us a wrong part for Deere John—for
the second time—and I had to drive to David's barn for still another call to
a man who didn't like talking machinery with a woman, I thought for sure
God was punishing us for something we'd done wrong.

Then Dad drove over Hansel, and I was sure.

He didn't mean to, of course. We'd tied Hansel to Dad's truck for the
day, and he slept beneath it, digging a hole for himself in the cool, shaded
dirt. But Dad forgot about the dog when he started the truck and started to
drive away.

Hansel's wrenching screams brought us rushing from the trailer. He
paced back and forth, howling, whining, and limping.

Dad quickly untied him. "Poor Hunzie Bunzie," Dad said as we ran
gentle hands over the dog's body. Hansel stopped howling. He seemed okay.
"He must have been asleep in that hole he dug," Dad said, looking back at
the tracks of the truck.

A Pollyanna would say, "How fortunate! Hansel was saved by sinking in the mud."

We debated about driving Hansel to the veterinarian. Whether or not to take an animal to a veterinarian had never been an issue before we moved, but the distance and condition of the road were all considerations now. Later we learned that a vet came once a week to the courthouse in Moro and would meet ranchers there with their sick stock. It would save us fifty miles in later years.

Our consideration of whether to take him in reminded us of an earlier time, when Sherrie and I had acted as vets for the cats. Harvey, the skinny longhaired cat as gray as evening fog, had moved to the Point with us, but he disappeared within a day of our settling in.

With no luck, Sherrie and I had called and searched, walking the steep riverbanks, carefully stepping over rocks in the ravine, hoping to find Harvey and not a rattlesnake.

That night, Jerry said Harvey would probably become a coyote's lunch.

But on the second day, when Hansel barked and barked at a spot behind our trailer, refusing to leave the tall, dry cheat grass even when I pulled on him, we discovered Harvey, curled into a fluffy ball that groaned when we lifted him. A tennis-ball-size growth swelled from the side of his throat and face.

We wondered if he'd been bitten by a snake.

Harvey stayed in our trailer for the afternoon, lying on the orange carpet behind my desk. But later we heard a mournful screech. Sherrie and I rushed into the trailer in time to hear Harvey wail again. We found Harvey in the bathtub, pus and blood draining from his head onto the porcelain surface.

Oddly, he seemed better. He'd apparently scratched open his wound and now could move around more easily.

"But his eye's still swollen shut," Sherrie noticed as he lay draped over her arm outside, his long, tail hairs separating in the gentle wind.

Harvey let us pull his eyelids gently apart. Inside, we saw the cat's golden iris—plus a tiny gold fleck, out of place, to the side.

Sherrie reached in with her long fingernails and gently pulled at the tip of the fleck. It was the end of a cheat grass, twice as long as her nail. It must have entered Harvey's throat, swelled up, and come out in his eye, a strange progression. It surprised me that a little cheat grass could cause such damage.

Our remoteness didn't seem so friendly then.

"Dennis has some stuff the eye doctor gave him," Sherrie remembered. We gently squeezed Dennis's salve into Harvey's eye, and Harvey recovered without complications.

Perhaps Hansel would recover too, if we just watched. I'd nursed him through a cold during the winter, giving him half an aspirin, some children's cough syrup, and leftover chicken soup.

He seemed well enough to go for walks within a day or two of Dad's drive-over, though he was a little stiff at first. Within four days, he was running and jumping as he had before, racing ahead, hyper as always, turning to see if I followed.

We walked along the river that Murphy-March morning, then headed to the dikes and up over the steep bench that would someday nourish grapes.

I'd enjoyed the arrival of a few purple wildflowers and the fresh scent of new growth when I heard a strange gurgling behind me and turned in time to see Hansel stop. He looked strangely at me and then dropped heavily to the ground, his front paws stiff. He began to shake violently, and I gasped. *Water hemlock! He's gotten into water hemlock!* I thought. *Or maybe he's been bitten by a snake!* I looked around for the reptile, certain Hansel must be poisoned.

His body shook so violently that he was forced onto his side, his paws digging impressions in the soft earth, his eyes a road map of red streaks, the whites a bloody pink.

I stroked his head, shaking, knowing he would die.

All the disappointments of this place rushed quickly through my head:

the delays, the hard work, the dike debates, the water, the wind, and the rain. *How much more can we endure?* I wondered.

Maybe we never should have come.

"J-e-r-r-y!" I screamed at the top of my lungs, not wanting to be alone. My voice just echoed against the canyon walls.

I started to move toward the trailers on the other side of the bench, but Hansel was still in convulsions, his mouth foaming, dirt catching in his frothy whiskers. I knew he'd be dead in seconds; I didn't want to let him die alone.

He couldn't hear me or know that I was crying, just wishing now that it was over. I patted him, my hand jerking with his body.

Suddenly, the jerking stopped, and he began breathing in quick, gulping, gasping breaths as he continued lying on his side. I stepped back, afraid to be hopeful.

Then, menacingly, Hansel stopped the rapid breathing, sat halfway up, turned vacant eyes toward me, lowered his head, curled his lips back, and growled a low, foreboding, threatening warning.

He started toward me, low to the ground, black lips baring canine teeth.

This dog is going to attack! I thought. *He survived, and now he's going to kill me!*

I backed away slowly, giving him the command to "Stay!" but not really believing that he would.

He hesitated just long enough for me to put space between us. Out of his sight, I ran toward the trail, screaming for Jerry.

Jerry had to tell me to calm down so I could tell him what was wrong. "Get the gun!" I cried, a mass of jumbled feelings. "You'll have to put Hansel down! He's rabid or poisoned or something. He had convulsions and then growled and started to attack!"

Jerry looked confused, pointing behind me.

Hansel was trotting down the hill, looking confused himself, then sheepish when he saw me. Jerry spoke to him, and he nuzzled his hand like a horse. He came to me, then sat in heel position and looked up with frightened eyes as I cautiously scratched behind his ears.

Sherrie and I drove to the barn to call Hansel's former veterinarian in Bend.

"It could be a sign of internal pain," she said. "Or maybe he's hypoglycemic. Was he running hard before the seizure? Or he might have a brain tumor."

"Should I have brought him in after the truck ran over him?" I asked guiltily. She assured me that was unlikely to have caused this reaction several days later.

"Should I bring him in now?" I asked. She was 160 miles away, but I would take him to the doctor who knew him best if that was necessary.

"Not really," she said. "If he seems fine now, he probably is. If he has another seizure, you'll have to make that decision. It'll mean blood tests and x-rays to find out for sure. You may want to meet the veterinarians in Goldendale, across the Columbia. They have a good reputation and are closer. But Hansel may just have eaten a chicken bone that caused him extra pain," she finished reassuringly.

I hovered over him for months after that, expecting another Murphy, waiting for the worst. But eventually I stopped worrying each time we took a walk, announcing instead that he'd "made one more day without a seizure."

Yes, we decided, Murphy must have been a homesteader. And the spouse who helped him find the positive in every flaw he probably called Polly—short for Pollyanna. How else could they have survived?

18

Moving In

IT SLITHERED DOWN THE SANDY PATH just below the house. I'd been waiting for it to happen, to see if I'd recognize it and know what to do this time. It stopped, curled, and coiled. I stopped, stepped back, and yelled, "Rattlesnake!" It slithered under a rock next to the well-walked path. I took a deep breath.

The first snake I'd seen had been coiled in the middle of the dirt road just a month before, at the abandoned-car curve. I'd stepped out of the Datsun, tried to look for the triangular head and the blunt tail with rattling buttons Jerry warned me about. Then I began throwing rocks, stoning it to death.

But because it hadn't buzzed when it coiled, I asked Jerry to drive back with me, to make sure it was really a rattlesnake.

Jerry was furious when he saw the dead snake lying in the rocks. "That's no rattler! It's a bull snake! Bull snakes kill rattlers, so don't *ever* kill a bull snake. Don't you know what a rattler looks like?"

"Would I put myself through this if I did?" I said, feeling like a naughty child. "Why do you think I asked you to come back with me?"

He calmed down, promising to find me a picture so I could imprint "rattlesnake" on my brain. "Guess I shouldn't have cut the heads off and buried the others before you saw one," he added.

Now, but a month later, close to the house that would provide such peace and comfort to us when we moved in on Memorial Day, I recognized it all right: a rattler.

Jerry puffed up the hill behind me. "Where is it?" he said. I pointed under the large rock.

"You're going to have to start carrying the .38," he cautioned. "Better go get it."

As I looked in the trailer for the .38 Special, I imagined the line, *In the spring, she began carrying the pistol.* It would make a great opening for a historical novel—or a hysterical one. What a strange life we led.

I handed Jerry the Special and reached down to pull the rock back that harbored the snake. I jumped three feet instead when Jerry yelled, "Don't touch that rock! It'll strike!"

Instead, with his high western boot, Jerry rolled the rock with his foot and, with one shot, did in the rattler coiled in the shadow of our house.

The next week we moved in.

The cabinets weren't yet hung; the hot tub was tiled but unfilled; and we had no phone yet. But we had running water, floors, and electricity. And except for a small bull snake that dropped at my feet from the top of the storage door and slithered away to my scream, we saw no new snakes.

We have only one picture taken inside the trailer during our almost yearlong stay: moving day. Dogs are sprawled on their bed; Hansel is licking Dennis's face; Sandy is squeezed next to the door while Jerry, in bathrobe and uncombed hair, eats an early breakfast on the card table. They all look cramped and uncomfortable amid the clutter.

A friend from Bend, Sandy Maynard, drove up with one Norwegian elkhound and a mostly springer spaniel (with a bad perm), and helped move boxes from the storeroom into trucks and vans for the short drive to the house. Then she began unpacking dishes and towels we had not seen for a year.

Parke and Marilyn Miller, friends from Bend, delivered asparagus ferns and spider plants kept healthy for us at the clinic and were now ready to flow from the loft above the kitchen and from the window ledge in the stairway landing.

The washer and dryer left their abode in the pump house that day and moved up the honey-colored stairs to the hall outside our second-floor bedroom. The refrigerator slipped perfectly into its spot in the kitchen, its gaping wound covered by a cabinet and a calendar. My grandmother's maple bedroom set fit perfectly in the rose-papered guest room.

We marveled that the couches, chairs, and bedding bore no mouse or moth holes from their year's storage, especially since the mules' saddle blankets, stored in the shop next door, had been a mouse feast.

We gingerly wrapped the piano in a quilt and rolled it into the bucket of Deere John, who tenderly carried it up the hill and deposited it on the back porch, unscratched. It took little effort to roll it into its place of honor on the oak floor of the great room. I uncovered the ivory keys and softly plunked out an almost in-tune melody.

That evening our helpful friends sat outside eating supper with seven dogs sprawled around the cedar deck. Who could have guessed that piano music would someday echo off these rimrocks, floating lazily to the river beyond? What luxury! A pioneer woman's wish to bring her family heirlooms across the mountains had never made more sense.

We slept well that night in our hand-built home. In the morning the first blaze of sun cut across the rock outside the bedroom window and poured across our faces. Jerry had set the house perfectly in the ravine, and we were grateful for another silver lining. Our skill at finding silver linings increased on Starvation Point, an ability we found critical not two weeks after we'd moved in.

Dennis and Jerry worked outside on that still June day while Sherrie and I chatted in the computer room. Then we heard the strange crackling. Looking out the upstairs window toward the rimrock, we gasped.

The entire hillside outside our bedroom was ablaze!

Memories of Neil's nightmare burned fresh in my mind as we tumbled down the steps, yelling for the men, conscious that the dogs were inside, aware that the wind was suddenly blowing hard, in great gusts, swirling smoke and flames.

Dennis was a ghost in the smoke, already dragging a hose up the hillside; Jerry slammed a shovel against the flames near the driveway. Sherrie ran for the van and sped out the road, racing the fire, heading up the grade to the barn phone and the volunteer fire department, twenty-five miles away. I climbed the hill awkwardly in the wooden clogs I wore, gasping in the smoke of bunch grass and sage, smashing flames with the shovel and praying, *Please, God, make it go out!*

At the top of the rocks, we thought the fire was out as Dennis and I watched the last flame hit the rimrock ledge and die. Panting, we climbed to the top, my shoes smoking from the heat, eyes burning and watering. We looked over the edge.

We saw not an answered prayer there, but a wild, wind-whipped fire on the bench below us. My heart sank. I looked for Jerry through the smoke and fire, and Dennis and I scurried back down the ridge toward him. "Grab the tractor!" he yelled above the wind and howl of fire. "See if you can make a firebreak beyond the end of the field!" With his first words, Dennis already ran.

By the time Dennis and Deere John reached the end of the burning field, the flames were beyond it. "Maybe the road will stop it," Jerry said hopefully, "if it doesn't jump the dirt."

As we raced toward the gate, Bob appeared on the other side of the smoke, just above the roller-coaster grade. He'd met Sherrie and brought his shovel on down, scraping dirt on the edges of the flames, keeping them from moving up the hill, where we joined him, coughing and gasping through the scorched sage.

At the road, the flames, cornered like a cat, moved low, this way and that, planning a way to sneak out, then reluctantly gave in.

"What happened?" I asked hoarsely as Jerry's smudged face approached me through the smoldering grass and sage.

"Burning trash," he said wonderingly. "No wind at all! A whirlwind. Down the ravine. Picked up burning stuff. Dribbled it across the grass." His hands swung about, punctuating the scenario.

As we sighed in relief, we saw then the parade of pickups and trucks, tanks of water and hoses in their beds, inching their way down the grade behind a lone red 1940s fire truck. My eyes watered with gratitude.

They were our neighbors, and others we didn't know, answering the alarm.

"Always wondered about people who would build so far out," said one neighbor, new to us, a grin on his face as he shook Jerry's hand.

"Usually a good idea to burn your weeds," another drawled into the wind, "but most of us wait till it's a calm day."

"Gives us practice in mopping up," another added as they went about watering the edges of the fire, glad the danger was over, free to enjoy the break in their day.

We were amazed that so many shopkeepers left their stores and so many ranchers abandoned their fields to wind down the reptile road to help us, less than thirty minutes after Sherrie's call.

"Now that you've had your fire for the year, you can relax," Marion said, another Pollyanna who appreciated silver linings.

We were thankful the wind had blown *away* from the house that day, away from the shop and barn. Toward the west there would have been no roads for miles to stop the fire or keep it contained. Since the fire had burned east, our driveway and the roller-coaster grade had saved us.

That night we showered out the smoke smell, appreciating the luxury of long, hot showers, shaking in relief that the fire was out with so little damage.

I hoped that we were finally finished with disasters.

The cough and smell and taste of smoke still lingered a few days later at our scheduled open house, expanding the meaning of housewarming. We had invited every local person we could think of who had visited, sent encouraging words, or helped in a dozen different ways with the septic tank or the dikes or the road or the water supply or finding dogs or appliances. We wanted to say thank you.

Without a phone, we hadn't bothered to ask for RSVPs.

Sandy came a few days early to assist with fixing food. She helped with veterinary duties, too, when Josie scratched at the door at 3:00 a.m., her face a white halo of porcupine quills glowing in the moonlight.

It took three of us until dawn to pull all the quills out. Sandy held Josie's head, I straddled her squirming, squealing canine body wrapped in a blanket, talking softly, while Jerry cut the tips and pulled the quills from her mouth, her teeth, her tongue, her nose, her chin, and so close to her eyes. With bloody fingers, he filled a cereal bowl full with the extracted quills.

Josie wasn't the only exhausted one.

Dennis and Sherrie arrived early too after being away a few days, and they mysteriously headed down to the shop. "We have to finish our surprise," Sherrie said happily as they walked the path down the hill.

I was upstairs getting ready when Sherrie whirled into the house, slamming the front door behind her. Through the window opening from our bedroom into the living room I could see her, and I knew she was distressed. "What's wrong?" I called down to her, fearing more disasters; but she was silent as she stomped up the steps.

"He says I've ruined it!" she said, deeply upset. "We worked so hard on your housewarming present, and now I've ruined it!"

"*You* are our present," I said, putting my arms around her as she cried. "Your being here is our present. Nothing you could ever give us could mean as much as all the love and care you've put into this house. Nothing. We simply could not be living here without you."

And I meant it, even after they presented us with their poignant gift, a needlepoint piece Sherrie had stitched of a house with an apple tree, a swing, and a Scripture verse: *Except the LORD build the house, they labour in vain that build it.*

Dennis had framed it with discarded pieces of the very oak molding Jerry and I had cut from the logs, that Sherrie and I had stained, and that he and Jerry had trimmed every window and door with and outlined every wall.

Jerry hung the piece in the front hall, a rare gift from rare friends. I couldn't see a flaw, though Sherrie said it was on the back—the perfect place for a mistake soon forgotten.

More than fifty people braved the road that day, filling the house to eat and laugh and take tours, good-naturedly kidding us about the blackened field next to the house, complimenting us on the computers monitoring our electricity use.

My sister arrived with a video camera to record the occasion, including the Mikkalos' arrival by boat across the river, a decision that saved them fifty miles of travel time. "My mother-in-law wouldn't let us bring the baby," Jullie said, regaining her land legs. "She thought we were crazy to come across that river in flood stage in a rubber raft."

People spent the afternoon talking and laughing and eating on the river deck, commenting on all the changes we'd made to this desolate spot and giving us suggestions for keeping snakes from the house: "Put lime around the perimeter; they won't cross it" and "Get some guinea hens or pigs…or peacocks."

I personally liked the pig plan, since we had only two trees for a peacock or guinea to roost in.

These were good people, these neighbors and new friends whose lives had crossed ours in special ways. I liked having them here. I began to feel as though we belonged.

After the party, Dennis and Sherrie stayed on a few more days, helping hang kitchen cabinets—without doors—and installing the ceiling fan and the garbage compactor. The dogs got their housewarming, too, when we stretched chain-link fence around posts to finish their kennel.

Then Dennis and Sherrie left.

It had been a remarkable matching of personalities, our living so closely for ten months. Like family, they had shared all our joys and frustrations, understanding as no one else could the labor of our dream. Even now, years later, their spirits live in every room of our home, touching us daily as we work and remember the laughter as Sherrie and I stained the fiberglass doors over and over again, the tears after Hansel's seizure, the shared frustrations of Dennis and Jerry as they solved each structural problem, the goodness of finding people to work with while never once sharing a cross or irritated word.

We said sad good-byes. I felt a prickle of anxiety as they drove their van out the drive and I realized we were truly alone in our home. They had done so much, had been such an important part of our building, that I wondered if we could make it here without them.

"It feels strange, to finally be here by ourselves," I told Jerry as we stood on the deck looking out across the flat to the island, listening to the river gurgle.

He nodded. We stood there quietly in the late evening dusk. "I love it here," he said. Then he said aloud the little fear I also harbored in my heart: "I just hope we can survive."

Part III

SURVIVING ON STARVATION POINT

Be like the fox who makes more tracks than necessary,
some in the wrong direction.

—WENDELL BERRY,
"Manifesto: The Mad Farmer Liberation Front,"
The Country of Marriage

Jerry, Jane, and granddaughter Mariah—happy homestead times.

19

Reaching Out on Our Own

"You'd better sit down," the Public Utility Commission official said. I thought she was being overly dramatic, but I sat. "I'm about to give out the highest estimate for a residential phone-line hookup I have ever given. Are you ready?"

"Sure," I said.

We'd been told it might cost as much as four hundred dollars to bring the phone wire across the river with the power line, and that our monthly bill could be as high as a hundred dollars. But the price would be worth it, we reasoned. Survival on Starvation Point would be much easier with a phone for reaching firefighters, veterinarians, family, and friends. If I wanted to write seriously, I'd need a phone for interviews and editor contacts.

We eventually had to call the Public Utilities Commission for help.

It should have been a sign to us the previous fall, when the power line had arrived and the phone had not.

The official cleared her throat, preparing herself. "The utility wants $65,000 to install your phone," she finally blurted out.

Silence.

"Are you there?" she asked, worry in her voice.

"You're kidding, aren't you?"

"I'm really not." Her voice became professional again once she realized

I hadn't fainted. "I even spoke with the head of engineering, and he says they'll need to stand poles for fifteen miles, from where the nearest private phone line is now. There is a party line across the river, but it's full, so you can't use it. Then they have to hang the line on the poles and come across the river—at about twenty cents a foot. You can imagine how many feet are in fifteen miles."

I could imagine.

"I've asked for an engineer to come down to see if there isn't an alternative. I'm really sorry," she finished, leaving her stunned listener holding the receiver.

I thought about how I'd complained when we had waited two weeks for phone hookups in the office, never imagining that something so familiar would be beyond our financial reach. We checked into solar and mobile phones, but the canyon depth discouraged their success. The computer modem wouldn't work with a solar phone, anyway. A real phone was the only answer.

A few weeks later we were surprised at the trailer by a tanned-face man who introduced himself as Wally Hoblit, a Pacific Bell engineer.

He wore a frazzled look, not uncommon in country where cars lack air conditioning but the dust requires closed windows. The late October afternoon heat hadn't helped.

"You really want a phone down here," he'd said kindly, looking out across the river.

"Not at sixty-five thousand dollars," Jerry said.

Wally looked thoughtful. He turned to check the steep hill ending in a rock ledge behind us, then scanned the scar left on the ground by the powerline trench snaking its way over the bench and across the flat to the river.

"Why don't you consider bringing a line from the mailbox, on this side of the river? That's only seven miles or so," he said.

It was a good idea.

Wally told us the cost for the phone company to bring the poles from the mailbox might be as high as $18,000. We winced. "This is pretty far out," he noted.

Then he suggested that it would be cheaper if we dug an underground trench ourselves, through the wheat fields, down the rock-infested slopes, to the house. "The trench has to be eighteen to twenty-one inches deep. In the rocky places, you'd have to use a backhoe," he cautioned. "We'd come out and hook the splices together," he continued, wiping the sweat from his forehead. "We would get the phone working and then accept the line into our system."

It sounded simple enough.

But first we needed to get an easement from the county to dig along the reptile road. And second, we needed the weather to hold: no rain and no frozen ground.

The road was a slimy river of mud the November weekend we spoke with Lloyd Gossen, the Sherman County Road Department boss, about trenching along the road. Lloyd knew every rock and hill, every dirt and gravel road that crisscrossed the fields of his domain. He didn't mind being called at home and, understanding the time constraints, said he'd talk with the county commissioners, who would have to grant the easement, over the weekend.

Jerry got the go-ahead on Monday. "Do we need something signed?" Jerry asked, a little surprised at the speed of this governmental response.

"Nope," Lloyd said. "We know that you know what you have to do, and you've agreed to do it; so just do it."

Jerry smiled, hanging up the barn phone. "It's the way government ought to work," he said.

But it continued to rain. Hard. Good for the wheat ranchers; terrible for the road.

The D8 Cat we'd hired to dig the trench was ready, and Wally had ordered the wire. But it continued to rain, sending water gushing and gouging into the dirt road. Wally said the man delivering the wire was afraid the muddy road would hold him hostage until spring, so he had turned around and left. A week later he tried again, leaving the wire at one of the first bends. "The spools are smaller than I ordered," Wally said into my ear at the barn phone, "but I think it'll be okay."

The wire might have been okay, but the ground wasn't.

The first week in December the temperature dropped to minus-eight degrees, ending any plans for a phone line in 1984.

All winter we drove twenty miles round trip over that treacherous road to the barn phone, shouting into the receiver while Hansel barked at some unknown assailant hiding beneath a stack of empty oil-filter boxes. We kicked aside drifts of snow blown against the post that held the plain black phone. We straddled water as it rushed between our feet during the spring runoff, and we survived wind that whooshed through to freeze our knuckles when we were placed on hold during business calls. After all that sacrifice just to "reach out and touch someone," we were ready to have the phone line buried—maybe—by Easter.

March. The weather was ready; the Cat was available. But our dream of having a phone became a nightmare of frustration.

We went blithely through the scheduled mid-March phone-installation day. Jack Tedder, Jerry's cousin, and his wife, Carol, chose March for their first visit, and Jack volunteered to ride the back of the Caterpillar, watching the pulley drop the precious phone wire three feet into the ground. He exchanged spools as needed, while Jerry marked the splices and ferried the new spools to the tractor.

Carol and I packed lunches that we enjoyed in the middle of the reptile road beneath a perfect cloudless sky, using an empty spool for our table.

Most of the day was spent digging the seven-mile trench. At dusk the Cat headed down over the rocky ledge behind the house, its trench-digging stinger sinking deeply into the rocky soil, keeping it from tumbling head over heels. We all held our breaths, grateful when the operator stepped out safely at the bottom. The long scar left on the hillside resembled a giant zipper.

Carol and I happily planned for phone service within a week or so, thinking that at $85 per hour for the Cat, we'd accomplished our task rather cheaply.

Jerry threw the cold water of reality on our faces by informing us that there were several areas so rocky, they'd have to be dug with the backhoe. In other places, exposed wire would have to be reburied.

With shovels, Jerry dispatched Carol and me the next morning to close the zipper over the wire. We imagined a two-hour task.

At noon, when Jack brought us water and lunch, blisters tenderized our hands. Our legs ached from stepping on the wire inside the trench as deep as our hips and then pulling dirt over it and ourselves before stepping out and moving on down the rugged hillside.

"Just think," Carol sighed. "Some people work this hard every day for pennies."

"At least we have a nice view," Pollyanna added.

The river was a spring-blue ribbon. We watched as the Spencers and Coelsches rode their quarter horses cautiously behind cattle on the side hill. Succulent green leaves sprinkled the ground, promising the purple blossoms of bird's-beaks.

But by four o'clock the day had lost its luster.

"Better set June for your new goal," Jerry said. He and Jack were as tired as we from covering line through the wheat fields and replacing fences taken down for the big Cat.

Over the next weeks, in between putting finishing touches on the house, we drove Deere John to the sage land on top and redug sections of the phone line. In some places where even the backhoe couldn't dig, we chopped trenches around boulders with pick and mattock, sometimes clawing shards of rock out of the way with our hands, startling at chipmunks, and warily watching for snakes.

We were assigned our very own phone number, which we gave out to everyone, believing that soon, any day now, we'd be reaching out to touch them.

When Jerry decided the lines were ready, we called for a splicer, who was not happy to be exiled to the wilds of sagebrush and rattlesnake country for the three days in June it took to do the job. "This is never going to work," he snarled.

Unfortunately, he was right.

When the lines were spliced, they provided the sounds of waves hitting the shoreline over scratchy, distant voices.

The phone company refused to accept the poor quality of the line. I tried not to sound desperate when I called Wally from the barn a few days later.

"What are we going to do?" I said, swallowing back tears of frustration.

Wally's answer was the epitome of diplomacy, his phrase a gentle camouflage for hopelessness. "Common sense will prevail, Jane," he said.

Of course, I thought he meant the line could be fixed.

Of course, he meant we'd have to do it over.

Wally and the head of construction for the phone company drove out a few days later with high-tech equipment and tested the lines, which showed a tiny slice every few feet in the cable. Perhaps it had been damaged as it came off the pulley, or the yanking and pressure from the big Cat had been too much for the fine line. Or perhaps the wire was defective.

"We'll provide bigger, heavier wire and a cart to manage eight-hundred-pound spools," Wally offered, "if you want to rent a digger like the phone company uses and lay the wire by hand."

The mere thought exhausted us.

Then Ken and Nancy Tedder energized us.

They had no idea what they were getting into.

We didn't know that Jack and Carol Tedder of the first phone line would connect again through their son and daughter-in-law. We'd spent little time with the younger Tedders. In fact, for their wedding a few years earlier, we'd sent them an electric coffee grinder, not knowing that neither of them drank coffee. But it was summer, and the senior Tedders had raved about Starvation Point and had so intrigued those two thirty-something physical education teachers living on Oregon's wet southern coast that they said they'd help.

In July, after a flight in the Rallye over the mountains to Salem for a mental-health-related meeting, I flew to Eugene to pick up Ken, a man as tall and lanky as his dad. We planned to pick up Nancy later in the week. Ken and I flew over the Cascade Mountains in a clear July sky. We set the little Rallye down without incident right in the middle of the Wasco strip.

Jerry rented a trencher—a machine slightly larger than a garden tractor with a long stinger at its end covered with teeth and a chain that gouged into the earth and left a four-inch-wide, twenty-one-inch-deep trench in its wake. One had to stay with the noisy diesel or it wandered, and it dug only a few boring feet a minute. Behind it, the parched July ground often caved in, and we had to dig out the trench again before laying the cable.

The phone company delivered the eight-hundred-pound spools of wire, placing one on a small cart we pulled behind our new four-wheel-drive pickup we'd purchased the month before. Ken dug, Jerry drove the truck, and I pulled the wire off, gently laying it into the trench.

After the third day of Ken's stay, having made barely a mile of the needed seven, a bearing failed in the trencher. There were no parts available, so we returned it. Then we all flew to pick up Nancy.

Jerry located another trencher in Hood River, seventy miles away, and while he and Ken drove to get it, Nancy and I slowly became acquainted.

"This could be a hard week," I cautioned, "working with people you don't know all that well."

Lean, attractive, and private, Nancy smiled. "I've been wondering about that," she said. But the ice was broken. She talked about her work, family, and marriage. I told her about living here, leaving my job, my fears, my frustrations, and my growing faith.

What neither of us knew then was how hard labor would bond us. Much later we'd discover how tragedy bonded us, too; but by the time Ken and Jerry returned, late in the evening, with their woes to share, Nancy and I were good friends.

The trencher in Hood River had taken a while to load, they reported. And just as they were pulling out, they had noticed a loose chain that couldn't be fixed, despite all the time they spent trying. So they rushed to pick up another trencher in Goldendale, Washington, fifty miles in the other direction.

"It looks pretty old," Ken said. "I don't know if it'll hold up in these rocks."

"Maybe it means it's already successfully trenched a lot," I said, still suffering from a terminal case of Pollyannaitis.

For the next eight days in July and August, the routine was pretty much the same. We arose early, threw venison into the Crockpot, packed four lunches and lots of water and sunscreen, fed and watered the dogs in their kennel, and headed up the hill.

Ken trenched.

Nancy, Jerry, and I cleared the narrow ditch of any rocks, roots, or rodents and then laid the seven miles of wire in the trench, checking each inch for flaws. Periodically, Jerry drove Deere John's bucket back over the trench, pulling dirt over the newly laid cable.

The trencher broke down often. First the brakes, then the clutch, sometimes a tooth or two. Each time the men managed to fix it, and it rattled on, a few feet at a time.

Dust clogged our noses and throats. Sun burned the backs of our ears. Between the cattle guards, we dug with picks again, digging where no ripper tooth could go. Jerry's back ached from riding the rough tractor, and he rested often, leaning back in the truck.

When the boredom of the trencher's droning got to us—or we had to kill time during its repair—we composed limericks.

There once was a couple from Coos Bay
Who thought they'd relax at a hideaway.
But instead of relaxed
Their bodies were taxed
And they only swam once in the John Day.

On July 31, our ninth wedding anniversary, Jerry gifted me with three rattlesnake buttons taken from reptiles crawling in the trenches. "Such a romantic," I said, holding the light-as-eggshell rattles in my hand.

About two miles from the house, the trencher broke another tooth, and Jerry finally expressed his discouragement. But for the first time, I wasn't worried. Odd as it was, I knew that God would not make us survive here without the phone.

Curlews whistled and swooped toward us as we jury-rigged the machine for the fiftieth time.

Near the end of the second week, the old trencher still rattling away, Jerry and Ken dug the trench that left the road, slicing instead down the steep hill, off to the side of the zipper. One of the men balanced the trencher while the other steered.

Nancy and I were sure we'd both end the day as widows—and almost did when the trencher tipped and Jerry went tumbling down the ravine we now call Death Valley. He stood up, gave a shaky wave, and rejoined Ken, who was still clinging to the upright trencher.

Early the next morning, Nancy, Jerry, and I dragged the heavy wire up the steep hill, laid it in the trench, and then repeated what Carol and I had done for a day, covering the wire with dirt by hand. Large daisylike flowers bloomed out of the rocky, shallow-soil hillsides, their leaves rattling like reptiles in the dry summer heat. Nancy and I startled frequently and always looked before we stepped or sat.

All this so we can answer a wrong number at 3:00 a.m., I thought, watching Ken chug the trencher up the center of the driveway.

Ken and Nancy would leave the next morning, no matter how much we'd accomplished; but we agonized when, within twenty feet of the house, we ran out of cable!

Jerry snarled that Nancy and I had pulled too much up on top, and he didn't want to splice the wire because "that's where we'll have problems later, at the splices."

We compromised, with Ken digging a trench across the corner of the yard and Jerry, Nancy, and I taking turns lying on our bellies in the dirt, digging a trench by hand beneath the porch, trying to get the dogs to dig where we wanted.

"If God had wanted us to talk to people thousands of miles away," Jerry observed wryly as we finished, wiping a smudge from my face, "wouldn't He just have given us larger ears?"

By evening the younger Tedder contribution was complete. We celebrated by rubbing one another's tired feet and acknowledging the gift of our special friendship.

Jerry flew them home in the morning, knowing we had only a steep quarter-mile section to complete with the backhoe. But that short section took us another eight days, new hydraulic hoses, and many prayers to complete, as it was the rockiest and steepest portion, just above the old zipper scar. Once, faithful Deere John dropped one of its tracks into the two-foot-deep phone trench on the steep slope, and I gasped, standing below, close enough to see the whites of Jerry's eyes grow in horror in tandem to my prayer. Then, as in slow motion, the heavy machine righted itself with Jerry still safely on his seat.

Our first call—after a pleasant lineman came out to splice the lines and another worked overtime to hook up the phone in the house—went to Ken and Nancy on August 23,1985; a second went to Wally, our adopted engineer.

David Moore was one of *our* first callers a day or so later. He rang to tell us he'd discovered what Hansel barked at all those months we'd used the phone in his barn. That day he'd found and killed a four-foot rattlesnake stretched between the door and the black phone.

20

Long-Distance Blessing

As Jerry's dad would say, the August day was already "hotter than a hijacker's pistol," though the sun just peered above the high rocks beyond the bedroom window. Steamy summer heat lay trapped in the craggy rocks. The ranch finally felt like home, and I hated to leave it each week.

After a hurried breakfast, I rolled the Datsun out the driveway beneath the rocky shadows, fought my way up the roller-coaster grade, bounced across the cattle guards, and slipped out the hard-packed dirt road onto gravel, entering a world of yellow and brown. A herd of deer, blending into the scenery, paused to watch the dust chasing me along the road.

At the pavement I headed west toward Moro, then south on Highway 97, turning at Grass Valley toward Mount Jefferson and the Cascades. I wove my way slowly down the grade from the high wheat lands of south Sherman County to the rushing Deschutes River Valley below.

Reds and greens and grays of early rising drift boaters moved slowly in the morning, preparing to ford that section of the river too white with rapids, too dangerous to take a raft across, known as Sherars Falls, now owned by the Confederated Tribes of Warm Springs.

The Datsun and I did not cross at Sherars Falls but drove along the river of rapids to Maupin, then climbed out and traveled west through forests of junipers, then pines.

We entered the reservation of the Confederated Tribes of Warm Springs from the north, then continued through the old village of Simnasho, watching for spotted Indian ponies running wild.

Morning shadows marked red rocks that peered out like monuments from scrubby, thin-skinned hills on either side.

Finally, two hours and ten minutes after I left home, I snaked around a sharp turn, crossed a flat, and dropped down into the tiny town of Warm Springs and its native Indian people. I pulled into the parking lot in front of the community center and the Head Start offices, and walked inside to warm, round faces and the most interesting work I can remember—a long-distance blessing.

All my life I'd dreamed of one day working with Indian people. Knowing that fulfilling that dream would not be likely once we moved to Starvation Point, I'd told Jerry that leaving that longing behind meant grieving what would never be. "Maybe your writing will be the new longing," he'd said.

My going back to work in mental health had not been part of our plan. But it hadn't taken much accounting to know that our dream had cost much more than we had calculated.

In fateful Murphy's March, I had written a check for the Sheetrock, then checked and double-checked the account balance. "We'll never make it," I told Jerry, alarmed. The house-sale proceeds and the retirement savings I'd drawn out—the money that we'd planned to live on until the farm produced—had all been spent just on building.

After that, we had spent more than one night lying in the trailer's twin bed, hands folded across our chests, discussing options.

I felt disloyal going back to work, as though we'd been poor stewards of what God had provided. But as I thought about farm families, I knew few could make it without an outside job. My mom had worked for years as a nurse, her income helping to repair a tractor and to purchase a new dairy cow or two for the farm. My sister's family ran Hurtley's Pony Express, a horse transport business, in addition to their ranching enterprise. Diaries I'd read of pioneering women always commented on their husband's travel for shipping wool, for example, while they and the children tended the farmstead.

Jerry understood the language of the land better than I; he could fix machines and make them work. Finding work for me meant leaving.

Reality spoke louder than dreams, so still hoping to write full-time someday, I dusted off my résumé and sent it to the local college, then called some colleagues in mental health, thinking a project might come up. There must be something I could do a few months each year when the road was good and I could get out.

"If worse comes to worst," I suggested timidly, "we could sell the plane."

But Jerry assured me we could get the runway built during the fall, "to help us get out when the road is bad," ruling out that option.

I nagged Jerry and worried aloud, even though I knew it made him feel worse for not having predicted all the expenses and problems we'd had.

Then, wandering into a bookstore in The Dalles one day, feeling sorry for myself, fingering books I couldn't afford, I listened to *Chapel of the Air,* a radio program playing in the background. A woman was being interviewed about some subject I can't even remember.

But her final words stuck with me. "I learned," she said, "not to cry about what I can't do, to do what I can, and to trust the Creator for the rest."

It was as if she were speaking to me.

We'd done what we could do, tried to trust and obey, and if we were supposed to stay on the land, then something would work out. It was as simple as that.

I drove home feeling more confident than I had for months, stopping at the barrel Sherrie and I had hung beneath the mailbox, looking for UPS deliveries or oversize cartons. Nothing.

But inside the mailbox—among junk mail and bills—was a letter from a man who shared my profession and now worked for the Confederated

Tribes of Warm Springs. He would be embarrassed to think he was an answer to my prayer, but I had no doubt that he was.

Jim Quaid had housesat for us in Bend when we'd flown the Rallye back East several years earlier. Jim made things happen—as he did with the letter that awaited me that day in the mailbox. It described a job with the tribes. "I know you can do it," his letter said. "One day a week. If they hire you, they'll pay your mileage, too. It's working with little kids with special needs, and their parents, setting up the Early Intervention Program. Call me to schedule an interview."

Jerry read Jim's scrawling handwriting on the yellow-lined legal pad, delighted at what we knew was a heaven-sent gift. We set up the interview, and a week later I began working and learning one day a week on the reservation.

From the beginning, Warm Springs was more than a job. It was a place to challenge my mind in ways that fencing or clearing land did not. It met my higher needs to interact with people and to discover things about myself as I listened and talked with others. It was a place willing to use my skills in counseling, setting up programs, and working with parents and children. Each day I was reminded that the way I saw the world was not the only way to see it, and I loved the insights and stories that the people shared.

They tolerated my cultural ignorance well, teaching me, overlooking my blunders, and sharing with me their view of history and change.

I especially loved the days of the mini powwows, when the young children dressed in full regalia and danced on light, buckskin-clad feet around the circle, toe-heel, toe-heel, stepping gently to the drummers while the singers sang their flutelike native songs and the parents beamed with pride. Watching, I marveled at the perseverance of the people, preserving pieces of their tradition despite the overwhelming, uncompromising culture of the whites. My parents often drove up for the powwows, my dad especially loving the music and the dances.

Those three tribes combined the cultures as few tribes had. The three separate groups of root gatherers and fishers—the Wascos, Warm Springs, and Paiute tribes—formed a corporation that employed well over six hundred people. They ran a lumbermill, a power plant, a resort, a radio station, and all governmental services for the reservation's twenty-three-hundred-person population. Like any corporation, they employed a cadre of lawyers and lobbyists who knew their way around the state legislature and Washington DC.

The reservation was another country, with different laws and goals. It moved at a different pace, change coming on a grandmother's moccasined feet: softly, slowly, with accumulated wisdom.

The people I worked with liked to tease and laugh at themselves, with one another, and eventually at me. Once, during an open house for the program, they mischievously allowed me to wear a nametag one whole day that read "EI Person" for the Early Intervention Program.

I seemed to make all the grandmothers giggle as they sat there along the wall in their bright-colored dresses and moccasins. Scarves were wrapped around their heads, and they carried worn, beaded purses.

"What are they laughing at?" I finally whispered to Geneva, a teacher and a traditional Native American who encouraged me to learn.

"It's your EI tag," she said, smiling. "In our language, *ee-i* is how we say *pregnant.*"

The giggles just grew louder as I added my own.

The parents I met were like parents everywhere: wanting to do the best they could for their children, though less confident than most that they were their children's best and most important teachers. Somehow that tradition had not been so easily preserved.

I spent part of each day in the company of teachers and colleagues I liked and admired for their commitment to Native American families and programs. The rest of the time I spent with babies, toddlers, and their families.

The children were refreshing, all curious and smiling. Daily, they kept me looking at the world through new eyes. Once the daughter of the woman I worked for asked, "Are you an Indian?" I told her no, that I was Caucasian, something having to do with the color of one's skin. I held my hand out in front of me, turning it this way and that, and said, "I don't know why they say we're white, though. It looks more…I don't know…more like…"

"More like ham," Natalie answered confidently. And she was right. I looked much more like ham.

I had no children of my own, had been frightened of them for years. They seemed so fragile, yet demanding. And then the decision to have any of our own was made with an emergency hysterectomy two weeks after Jerry and I were married.

Warm Springs shared its children with me, if only for a day or two a week, preparing me, it seemed, for a time just three years later when a baby would enter our lives. The children gave me wonderful perspectives to take home to Jerry, perspectives like the one I learned from five-year-old Wynter the day I had the hiccups. These weren't ordinary hiccups; they were hard, body-wrenching jerks that everyone in the office heard and tried to cure. Scaring me, giving me mustard, having me drink water while standing on one foot—nothing worked, and I finally bumped my way to the parking lot and left for my scheduled home visit, still hounded by hiccups.

The home housed a young woman, who was barely thirty years old, and her five children. Her son was enrolled in our special program, and I worked with him weekly and with her, too, on activities she could do to encourage him each day.

She was bright, quick, and pretty, despite her broken teeth and her struggle simply to survive as a single mom. Some days she'd say, "It's not a good time. Can you come back tomorrow?" I'd always honor her request.

That day, as I sat on the arm of her couch, I apologized for *my* bad day, the hiccups interrupting our conversation.

Wynter, the woman's daughter, watched me from where she stood, half-hidden behind her mother on the couch. Since she usually lived with her father, I'd only seen her once before.

"Can we get you something for them?" the mother offered.

"No thanks," I said. "Let's just (hic) ignore them."

And so we talked in between the hiccups, unable to ignore them, until suddenly, without warning, Wynter stepped across the space and cultural restraint, wrapped her thin brown arms around me, leaned her head against my chest, and squeezed.

A perfect hug.

My hiccups stopped!

As she stepped back across the space, a smile filled her small, round face, and a sparkle lit her brown eyes.

"You've cured them!" I said. "How smart you are! I never knew that hugs could cure hiccups!"

Her smile grew bigger, as did mine. She had touched me, literally, with her spontaneity and care, just as Warm Springs people did each day with their rare gift dropped so graciously into our lives.

At the end of that August day, I retraced my steps, looking forward to sharing experiences with Jerry and smiling as the dogs bounded out of the house to meet me at the gate. I watched the shadows move slowly across the rocks and yellow fields, saw the deer stop browsing as I passed, and thought, *If only once I can touch someone as deeply as Wynter touched my heart, it will well be worth the time away from Jerry and our homestead.*

The phone made survival on Starvation Point so much easier. That fall, friends called, planned visits, and received a road report before starting out; or we could ring them up and warn them it might be best to stay away that day. With the phone, we were connected not only to friends but to the world at large. I could contact Warm Springs if needed. By modem, we were part of a Bonneville Power Administration study that kept us energy-efficient: once a month we read a computer on the wall in my office and sent the information to Bend as part of another research project about electrical heating costs.

Best of all, we discovered the perfection of Jerry's design: the house was both comfortable and functional. Sunglasses, books, hunting vests, and fishing poles, plopped for easy retrieval on the tile-covered island in the kitchen, gave the house a vacation-home appeal. The blue-winged teal watercolor and the ancient Chinese partridge print hung over the flowered couch as if they'd always belonged there. Jerry's guns and animal mounts fit perfectly in the loft above the kitchen.

Sometimes we could look up from the leather chairs in the great room, gaze through the window at the top of the vaulted ceiling, and smile at equine eyes staring down on us, as Blue or Henry stood curiously at the very edge of the rocky ledge beside the house watching us. The dogs' toenails clip-clipped gently as they padded across the wood and tile floors.

Life on the homestead was private and temporarily serene. We needed no drapes.

Our pace moved more slowly. Somehow, as the earth prepared to rest and hibernate, we found that we, too, could hibernate and find respite for our spirits, bodies, and minds.

We sat on the deck on the warm days, watching, reading, setting little goals, taking stock of what we'd accomplished our first year: water, power, a home, and a phone. Meaningful work. We could appreciate now how much better our site was than if we had built on the ashes of Con's cabin, as we'd first hoped to do. Together, listening to a Bonnie Raitt tape or to the crickets and frogs, we watched stars come out during nights cooled by soothing rains, and we inhaled the scent of sagebrush and wet earth.

Jerry hunted birds and fished the John Day for steelhead that fall, just as he had dreamed he would. We canned the pink fish in tiny jars and later served it with cream cheese on crackers as hors d'oeuvres before a pheasant feast with friends. We felt we had been gifted beyond measure with the bounty of our land.

Fall was Jerry's favorite time of year, and he took the dogs and his friends hunting for pheasant, chukar, and doves. They walked the rocky hills, enjoying the clear air and the still river below with reflections of deer drinking peacefully beneath the tall red rocks. He savored the time with his friends, even when they saw no birds.

It was Josie who helped bring home pheasants for dinner. She retrieved the birds well. Hansel, though he instinctively hunted and pointed well, held and honored other dogs' points, and even located the dead or wounded birds without problem, hated the taste of feathers, and wouldn't bring the game back. It irritated Jerry to have to crawl over the rocky ledges or walk out into the water to retrieve his own birds. But considering the taste and texture of feathers, I thought Hansel's opinion was another sign of his intelligence.

When deer season opened, we packed our freezer with venison for our winter's supply, although after I filled my doe tag and field-dressed the warm animal on a cool pink morning with geese flying overhead, I decided I was better at watching deer than killing them. Jerry assured me that the one I'd chosen was old and barren and would never have survived the winter, and that we needed the meat.

We had gotten to know our four-legged neighbors and looked for them after the season: Floppy Ear the doe, or the Lame One, or the Brassy Little Buck that tore the petunias next to the house and wouldn't budge even when we jumped up and down, waving our arms on the deck. He must have thought we were amazing windsocks flapping in the breeze while he lazily munched.

Happily, even after hunting season, the Brassy Buck and all the does were still around.

We had the luxury of sharing our home with other friends for extended stays, not just quick visits as we'd had in Bend. The relationships were different—deeper—on the homestead. Perhaps it was because people had to travel so far to see us, or maybe it was because the pace permitted rest and intimacy not easily fostered over a hurried lunch.

Blair and David Fredstrom, their dog Daisy, and their children, Annie and Erie, risked the road to visit, and as they basked in the hot tub, they discovered our homestead life had certain amenities. "I wondered if you even had indoor plumbing," Blair laughed. Their presence brought us pleasure beyond measure.

Seven-year-old Annie crawled into our bed in the morning, *Cricket* magazine in hand. "Let's read," she said.

We did, enjoying story after story of ghosts and volcanoes and subjects I didn't remember caring about when I was seven. Three-year-old Eric soon joined us, ending the quiet reading time. Eric was a roly-poly live wire; we knew why his parents were sleeping in.

Getting up, he took Jerry's hand, and they waddled off together, giving me a fleeting glimpse of what there might have been for Jerry and me.

Then blue-eyed Annie pulled me from my reverie with childish arms around my neck. "I love you, Aunt Jane," she said before hurrying off to explore the homestead.

Another child formed in our lives that fall too: Ken and Nancy Tedder, who had helped lay the second phone line, called to tell us Nancy was pregnant. We laughed, figuring out that the baby's roots were on Starvation Point, and wondering how they'd had the energy to start new life with the phone-line project taking up so much of theirs. "Must have been the water," Jerry jested.

When Jerry left in November for three weeks of elk hunting, the dogs were my only companions on the ranch. I missed Jerry, but I liked the idea of being on the homestead alone, liked knowing I could manage the weather and road. I read and wrote at my own pace and spoiled the dogs, though letting them in and out a dozen times a day took time.

With Jerry gone, I kept them in the house at night, even let them curl at the bend of my knees in the bed. In the morning after breakfast, Hansel followed me up the steps and stopped at my office door. If he heard the beep of the computer turning on, he would throw his head back in a woof-woof howl and stomp disgustedly down the steps, sure I'd be there far too long for him. Later, lusting for his walk, he'd come back and crouch beneath my feet. That failing, he'd lean against me, drop his slightly graying whiskers to the keyboard, roll his eyes at me, and finally win me over. We would walk.

That first fall seemed to soften Jerry's dislike of cats, and returning from his successful elk hunt, he helped replace the ones we'd lost to coyotes. He brought home from his hunting buddy Dave Larson another cat, a tabby we named O.D.C. (for Outdoor Cat). We kept him closer to the house, hoping to avoid the coyotes. The Moores nursed back to health a seagull with a broken wing I found on the road that fall. Millie and her niece, a Portland emergency-room nurse, operated on it, and when it was healed—with David feeding it raw fish three times a day—we set it loose on the river, but we never saw it fly again.

We weren't flying much that fall, either, and without the airstrip or plane close by, and with things getting tighter financially, we decided to let the hull insurance lapse. The liability insurance, we decided, would cover passengers, if by some quirk we had an accident.

We lost Ricky again that fall, finding him ourselves, eleven miles *upriver* this time, at the Cottonwood Ranch of the Murtha brothers. Mike (handsome, standoffish, built solid as a pork roast) and his brother, Jimmy (friendly and as lean as a bacon strip), didn't mind the extra mouth to feed, throwing scraps of meat to their cattle dogs and to Ricky, who visited for the week it took us to find him just before the first snow.

We were ready for winter, a time we remember fondly as the calm before the storm.

21

Battle Plan

THE INCIDENT WITH THE RATTLESNAKE should have been a sign.

Jerry had been hunting next to the river during those first two weeks pheasant season opened. Crossing a barbed-wire fence, he squatted down, pushed his leg through, and had begun to swing his head and shoulders between the wires. Just as he lowered his face between the barbs, he heard the telltale rattle, sounding like a snare drum in his ear. He froze, chills racing up his spine.

The green diamonds of the snake lay unmoving, but the coiled reptile's tail vibrated loudly in the stillness, and the triangular head was frozen barely a foot from Jerry's face.

Jerry froze too, paralyzed in the awkward position, not a muscle twitching, aware only of the buzzing, the cold sweat moving down his back, and his heart thundering in his chest.

Minutes dragged by like hours.

Deciding Jerry was too large for prey, the snake finally, with great caution, uncoiled its thick body and slithered away in the tall grass as Jerry's held-breath escaped in a gasp of grateful thanks. A close call, but no real damage.

Winter came like a guest who first delights but quickly wears out his welcome by the demands he makes.

Whipped-cream snowdrifts collected in the ravines, covered the craggy outcroppings of rocks, and blew across the river, swirling and freezing into hard chunks of dirty ice that outlined the thin, black current of water not frozen over.

In the shallow, narrow sections, the river froze completely.

New snow fell on old snow, the temperature seldom rising above freezing. Thick-coated coyotes padded quietly in the falling snow, seeking white rabbits, well hidden. Scruffy-haired deer, pelted with clumps of wet snow by the sage they brushed against, browsed along the flat. The resident Canada geese were quiet black sentinels on small islands of ground blown clear by the wind.

The mules stood with their backs to the gusts, their long tail-hairs separated in the icy wind, nostrils blowing puffs of air out ice-shrouded noses. We lost Cissy that year, her obstinacy having kept her from coming in for shelter closer to the barn. We walked the ravines, calling, never finding even the leather halter to mark her old bones.

The dogs ran on ice-caked paws, which we thawed between our hands after our walks through drifted snows. They moved back into the house for the winter.

The neighbors said it was one of the snowiest winters on record. A solid slate-gray sky hovered constantly over the canyon, preventing us from seeing the tops of the rimrocks.

In December, when chains on our four-wheel-drive vehicle could no longer pull us up and out of the canyon, Jerry worked Deere John up the icy, drifted road, pushing and plowing. Keeping the road open became our lot, since the county plowed it once in the spring and once in the fall, whether the road needed it or not.

I rescued Jerry each day after a few hours of road-clearing, taking him home and gently settling him into the warm, rotating water of the hot tub, which we called the "plunge."

When we could stay home, we basked in our homestead, sometimes sinfully staying in bed all day. I read novels aloud to Jerry. He fixed cheese and crackers and a rare glass of wine and brought them to bed for snacks between reading. We appreciated this special time as a luxury few could afford. On Sundays we drove twenty-five miles to church in Moro. We'd attended some services in Wasco when Dennis and Sherrie had been with us, and we were welcomed by friendly people. But the Community Presbyterian Church in Moro had immediately felt like home when we entered its century-old foyer, seeing Nell, Bruce, Edna, Curly, and Vada, and Millie at the organ, all neighbors who had shared our building year.

We'd drive to Moro in a freezing fog that made the land and sky the same slate gray for days and iced the fences and trees into ghostly etchings across the barren landscape.

The trip to church in winter, crossing the drifted fields, plunging through snow on the seven miles of dirt road, was an exercise in prayer each Sunday morning, prayer answered by the welcoming faces of our extended church family.

After church, we'd drive back to Coelsches' and Spencers' gate behind Bruce's barn. There Jerry would don insulated coveralls, pull arctic boots onto his feet, and begin the three-mile trudge down the snowy ravines to home. I'd turn around the four-wheel-drive, slide down the shortcut to the gravel road, and drive three hours to Prineville to spend the night with Jerry's parents before leaving Monday morning for my day at Warm Springs. An evening phone call assured each of us the other was safe.

Coming home from Warm Springs meant a night drive and a stop at Bob and Marion's to check on the road. "Did it thaw at all?" I'd ask Jerry, so thankful for the phone.

"Some," he'd say, and that usually would mean I'd spend the night at the Boyntons', not attempting the steep, icy grade when the almost-frozen moisture over packed snow promised skids along the curvy road.

The Boyntons' guest room became my second home that winter. A half-dozen others were offered by people all along the highway, but it was Bob and Marion's where I felt best.

In the morning, the frozen-solid road would be safer, if it hadn't snowed more in the night or drifted. If it had, I'd approach the great unknown with a promise from the Boyntons that if I hadn't called within an hour, they'd start out to find me, and a promise from Jerry that if I didn't arrive, he'd start up Deere John for my rescue.

Sometimes, so Jerry would have the four-wheel-drive, we left the red Datsun on top, near the mailbox. Jerry would bring me up in the pickup in the morning, scrape the windows and shovel the accumulated snow, and see me off. At night he'd make the icy trip to the top to pick me up.

I had respect for the road, but I tried not to let it intimidate me any-more. Once, as I crept around the top of the ravine at night, staying close to the inside edge, I suddenly found I couldn't go any farther. *There must be something wrong with the four-wheel-drive!* I thought desperately, contem-plating a long, cold, dark walk home.

But I backed up, turned the wheel slightly, and inched on home, amazed and grateful, as I was each time I got there alive. Jerry had watched my head-lights against the snow, nine hundred feet above the ravine, wondering why I backed up. The next time we went out we solved the mystery by looking at my tracks in the snow: In my effort to avoid the drop-off, I'd driven too close to the *inside* bank, inching partway up a slim ledge on the side of the hill! A foot farther and I'd have tipped the truck and tumbled over the very ravine I was trying to avoid. Our guardian angels worked overtime that year.

Still, the trip reminded me that I was coming to terms with the road. In fact, just a few winters later, I was brave enough to risk the road after a drift-ing east-wind snowfall when the temperature hovered at minus-eleven degrees. Marion had urged me to spend the night, and a visiting neighbor had said the drifts were awfully deep. But I wanted to be home. So I left, with the Boyntons promising to start out if I didn't call within the hour. I hit the drifts on the gravel road just before dusk and got stuck once as I entered the field; but I managed to rock and roll the vehicle and finally break through the deep drift without chaining up.

I left the road soon after, plunging through the drifts piled on Melzers' stubble field, returning to the reptile road only when the field disappeared into sagebrush or a steep bank. Then I followed the road, keeping sight of it by the tops of sagebrush sticking through the drifts and outlining its edge.

It amazed me that once I had hyperventilated regularly on the dry, bare road, and now I plunged through three-foot-high drifts, alone, at dusk in minus-eleven-degree weather. People really could change.

As I rounded one of the last bends before the cattle guards, my confidence vanished. There was no road. No sagebrush marked the way. The world was a sea of white with no distinction between the land and sky. Everything was drifted shut.

I felt the engine grind down, and at the same moment that panic entered my throat, I knew that I was stuck. It was too cold. I'd been stupid to try this. I had only thin boots; we'd taken out the sleeping bag the week before. Jerry couldn't meet me because the diesel in Deere John was frozen. My breath came in short, cold gasps as I stomped around the front of the tires, knowing that I still had one more way out: I could put on chains and not drag Bob and Marion into this snowy night. "Please, God, you know how I hate to put on chains," I said aloud as I stomped around the vehicle.

I wondered if that phrase reflected pioneering spirit—of people hating to put on the chains of routine and tradition, liking instead to strike out, unencumbered, to make new paths through uncharted territory.

I had little time for philosophical thinking as I rocked the four-wheel-drive and breathed a sigh of gratefulness as the drift released me and I headed on, aiming for where I thought the road should be and finding it just before a drop-off.

The rest of the trip was uneventful, since the east wind had piled the drifts on the outside of the grade, allowing me to creep down close to the inside edge. But remembering my adventures during that first snowy winter, I stayed on the road this time and didn't crawl partway up the steep side. Soon I was happily welcomed by the dogs, who met me in the driveway; I called Marion before the hour was up.

Coming and going took most of our energy that first snowy winter, though we did still gather up supplies. Just after Christmas we edged our way out to Rancho Rajneeshpuram, the city south along the river that had stung Oregon like a band of angry hornets shortly before we bought our land. Now that city was disbanding, the followers of the Bhagwan disappearing to points around the world.

Kay and I had visited the city just before our first trip together to Starvation Point. By a strange set of circumstances, we'd learned that one of the cult's leaders had been a Girl Scout counselor with Kay years earlier, and I'd attended workshops in mental health the woman had led.

The cult had purchased the Big Muddy Ranch and brought in thousands of followers, who covered the dusty land with a hotel, restaurants, shops, homes, barns, a lake, an airport, a massive greenhouse, and a community center. They'd made enormous progress in the few years they'd been there, though Jerry reminded me they'd had thousands of free laborers working six and a half days every week. Kay and I had lunched with the followers and marveled at the vineyards they'd planted and the lush gardens of broccoli and cauliflower that grew beside the John Day River.

But in the winter of 1985, despite all their money and free labor, they were disbanding. The ranch would be sold, along with much of their equipment. In their effort—their mission, as Kay's friend described it—to build a city, and another city underground, gathering up great books of knowledge onto microfilm in preparation for a terrible catastrophic event, they had disregarded laws and people and had alienated their neighbors and best allies. Now they were selling pumps and tools, plants and parts, to the highest bidders before moving out of Oregon, chastised by a string of indictments and jail terms for many of their leaders.

We bought an irrigation pump for the alfalfa and watermelons we hoped to plant in the spring, two long rugs to protect the oak floor by the living-room door, tire chains, and some odds and ends at the late December sale, where we shared peanut brittle with the red-clad followers who loaded the pumps in our truck.

We drove out past the stone guardhouse, smiling at their road sign: "Essentially a One-Lane Road." We would have bought it if it had been for sale.

As we drove the icy roads that looked remarkably like ours, I wondered why we were still surviving on our inhospitable point, while with ten times the help and money, the Bhagwan's followers retreated.

Nineteen eighty-six began as a disaster. First there was a national one, the *Challenger* explosion. Then there were our own disasters. It snowed more that January, then thawed. Even in the night we could hear the pop-pop, crack-crack of the ice breaking, pushing up against the shore of the frozen river. As the river began to rise with the melting snow, we knew the dikes would be well tested.

On January 26 I wrote in my journal that I felt we should *Prepare for a battle* of sorts. The phrase had come to me as clearly as the urging *Go to the land* had stuck in my mind some years earlier.

I couldn't imagine how to prepare for an unknown battle. I read the book of Hebrews, about people of great faith. They had simply trusted in God. "We've survived this far," Jerry noted when I told him of the phrase.

By mid-February most of the snow had melted, and based on the previous year, we thought the high water was probably over and the dikes had proved themselves again.

Jerry's daughter in Florida called, deliciously describing warm sunshine and sandy beaches and growing grandchildren Jerry hadn't seen for six years. "Come on down for a week," she said. "You need a break." The relationships were worth the expense, and I'd sold a story to *Mother Earth News* about laying the phone line and some other stories to the *Oregonian,* making it financially feasible.

No battles there.

We rested in Florida, despite the reports of late, heavy snowfalls in the Northwest and flooding on many of Oregon's rivers. Our time with Kathleen was special for father and daughter and grandchildren and the fiancé, Joe, whom we met and admired.

No battles, really, even when my parents called, saying Bob had reported the dikes had broken and the flat had flooded. The river approached the pump house and trailers.

We flew home to a road rutted and gouged with the runoff of heavy snow. From the top we saw a section sliced through the dikes, as though some cookie monster had taken his bite. The water had receded, but it still swirled around the electrical transformers next to the river, drawing back from the trailer and pump house. Tops of sagebrush floated above the water like lily pads in a still pond.

"Highest water since the big flood of '64," Bob said as we evaluated the damage and considered the costs—and the merit—of repairing the dikes.

Still, we didn't feel defeated. The dikes could be fixed. The water would recede. The pump house and trailers hadn't flooded. We'd had a wonderful break in the Florida sun. We had water and power and phone service.

We were living our dream.

Meadowlarks and red-winged blackbirds chirped, announcing the arrival of spring. The sun burned warm on our faces, chasing away the fog. Nancy and Ken came to visit, and we thought all the big battles were behind us.

"She said I have to gain weight!" Nancy said, repeating her doctor's instructions and patting the baby masquerading as a basketball beneath her maternity top. "I guess I'm too active teaching five gym classes each day."

"Not bad to be *told* to gain weight by your doctor while you're pregnant," I said.

"I guess," Nancy sighed, picking the book up off her stomach. "But I have to go to half-time at school until the baby comes in May. I hate that. I like to keep busy."

We were sitting on the deck on lounge chairs enjoying the unusually warm March day. Yellow bells had come and gone; wild purple phlox now dotted the dirt that would someday be lawn. Up on top, tumbleweeds rolled like bowling balls across freshly sprouted spring wheat. The month was almost over, and I was relieved. Hansel, lying on his belly at my feet, had escaped any more seizures. So far, the spring work had gone well.

We'd hired a neighbor to rebuild the dikes with Deere John. Jerry then turned the flat into a rat maze of ditches, readying it for irrigation pipe. Ken and Jerry were carefully burning grass and sagebrush they'd uprooted the past few days. If all went well, we'd have water on the flat next month, using the Rajneesh pump, and seed it with alfalfa. Then we'd clear the benches for the vineyard.

But tomorrow the four of us would go flying.

"Are you sure it's okay with your doctor for you to fly?" Jerry asked Nancy over supper.

"Oh sure," she answered. "I asked her. She said do anything I want to relax. We're really looking forward to it."

"Thought we'd fly to Dave and Sharon Larson's," I said, giving her the itinerary. "Jerry and I can meet an instructor there and complete our biennials. It's pretty country, near La Grande."

"Sounds great," she said, patting her mouth with the napkin.

They'd been with us for four days, Ken helping Jerry during the day, Nancy and I relaxing and reading, the four of us playing The Farming Game at night until one of us went bankrupt or owned all there was. We reminisced about the past summer's hard labor and their plans for the baby so soon to arrive.

Tomorrow we'd fly. On Wednesday they'd drive back to the coast, I'd leave for Warm Springs, and Jerry would return to battling the sagebrush—the only battle in our future, we thought.

After all, we'd weathered rattlesnakes and other battles, and Murphy's March was almost over.

22

Cluttering Up the Streets of Wasco

LATER, AFTER THE AMBULANCES, the x-rays, and the emergency surgeries, after the hazy world of white uniforms and pain, we could still recall each detail.

In the early morning hours, we two pilots began the next day in our hospital beds, reliving those few seconds, wondering what signs we'd missed that might have warned us, what things we might have done to keep us and our friends from plunging to the earth.

Silently, years later, I still thank God it was the cool head of my husband—and not me—piloting the day we crashed the Rallye and cluttered up the streets of Wasco.

On that calm, high-overcast March morning, we lifted our four-seater Rallye 220 from the strip in Wasco, rising easily above the wheat-stubbled fields and the early green growth.

Wasco, rich with rural traditions and wheat lands, sits slightly off Highway 97, nine miles south of the Columbia River. Its narrow paved strip runs east and west, uphill and down. The town's tall trees stand like the dot of an exclamation point at the end of the 2,750-foot runway. Ranchers and spray pilots primarily land there, where talk had grown about moving the strip so no one would have to fly in over the trees and town, or land uphill or downhill on the 3 percent–grade runway.

The picture window of a pretty green home looks out onto the paved strip of Wasco.

With Ken and Nancy, we flew east over the Blue Mountains to the Larsons, chattering for hours about aircraft, as only aviation lovers do. Later we kept the appointment with an instructor, and both Jerry and I completed our biennials before flying back west, toward home.

To Wasco.

From the backseats, Ken and Nancy Tedder took turns pointing out the black dots of elk grazing in the clearings that separated the timber of the Blues.

The weather suited Nancy and her unborn baby just fine—no turbulence, no thunderstorms, no rain, no fluffy clouds, or spiking thermals. Just steady westerly winds, which, if they held, would have us landing west, downhill at Wasco, toward the house with the picture window, instead of uphill and over it.

Far south, virga—streaks of rain released from clouds that never quite touch the ground—danced across the landscape stage. Miles away, Mount Hood stood partially obscured, perhaps by a spring rain or rising dust. But all was clear within our world.

From several miles out, the windsock seemed to be confirming a western final approach; but as we neared the airstrip around 4:00 p.m., we both could see the ground wind was from the east, full sock, straight down the runway. *Well, good,* I thought. *If we have to land over the town, at least there are no crosswinds.*

We watched a spray pilot refueling at the upper end of the strip.

I knew that if Jerry had been alone, he'd have landed as the spray pilots sometimes do there: flying a short pattern from the side, avoiding the town, straightening out, and pulling power just before setting down. But Jerry seemed to know I'd grumble if he did, especially with the wind right down the runway. So he flew the standard pattern.

From my copilot seat I noted all the positive signs of safe landing: a full twenty-knot headwind rushing right down the runway, eighty-five-miles-per-hour airspeed, one notch of flaps.

The Rallye was designed for short fields. Its performance in the past at Wasco had been solid, usually setting us down with three-quarters of the strip to spare, even at our usual touchdown point well beyond the threshold *X*'s at the end.

We came in higher to compensate for having to land uphill, over the town. At 400 feet of altitude, we were 850 feet from the end of the runway.

If anything goes wrong now, I thought, relieved, thinking of an engine loss, *we could glide into the airport.*

From past experience, I turned and told our friends, "When we come in over these trees, there'll be a little drop. But we'll go right on through it." Ken and Nancy smiled, and I turned without alarm to face a safe and certain landing. I couldn't have been more wrong.

An eerie silence followed.

Then the nose ballooned up. The engine roared, but no wind sounds swirled around the cockpit. We seemed suspended, briefly, like a spider hanging from a single strand of web.

Jerry gave the plane full power, dropping the nose as much as he could to gain airspeed. I wondered why we didn't move ahead. Beyond his concentrated face, the tall pine trees still below us gave me momentary relief; I thought we were still okay.

Then we drifted right—too close—to bare branches of the walnut and locust trees. I said, "Jerry, the trees...?" as if he would give an explanation of why the branches, like gripping fingers, were reaching toward us.

We heard the locusts scrape against the fuselage of the plane like lake reeds scratching the bottom of a metal boat.

I held my breath, still believing for one brief second that we'd fly on through and land safely, well beyond the trees and power lines and houses perched on the runway's edge.

And then the jolt!

The plane banked sharply to the right, and I knew we were going down.

So it's to be like this, I thought. The pilot had done all I could think to do, and so I prepared to die. Without panic, really, I wondered if the propeller would come swirling back to quickly end us all once we struck the ground. I thought of blood. I didn't even pray. I braced one arm above my head, my right foot forward as if to brake. I thought it odd that the sky had suddenly turned a brilliant, blinding white. I felt no fear, just surprise that this was really happening.

Another jolt, another tree, and then the impact, propeller first.

Amid shattering sounds, the four of us seemed to perform a dreamlike dance in slow motion, limbs thrust forward, air forced from our lungs. A flood of pain washed over me as if a thousand bees had stung me all at once.

The fuselage settled, then plunged to pavement. This time our bodies pounded back against the seats. I saw my elbow hit the sheepskin seat cover; then I watched the bone between my elbow and wrist wrench forward and separate, leaving my wrist hostage, like a sausage, held only by the casing of my skin.

And then, in the stillness, I asked the bloody face beside me if he was alive. Jerry answered yes, and I remember, then, thanking God and thinking: *This is the battle. You know, God, we can't get through this on our own.*

Behind us, Ken frantically called out Nancy's name, his words forcing my head around. Nancy gasped, choking, her head thrown back, arms flailing about. *Head injury!* I thought, though my mind couldn't figure what her head might have hit.

We were all alive. Then followed the awful stomach-punch of knowing there was damage to our friend, perhaps her baby, to our bodies, and our plane. Fumes of gasoline broke now into my prayers and thoughts. A fire siren wailed. *Get out! Get out!* But I couldn't make my one good hand release my belt.

Jerry saw my struggle and reached across to unfasten my seat belt. I felt so sad for him, seeing his eyes pinched with pain. I saw the throttle pulled way back and bent, so at some time in the falling he had pulled the power, hoping still to set us down safely.

With seat belt free, I stood straight up—through the broken windshield. The bee stings came again as I stepped, then fell into the street, my leg failing to hold me up.

Men in coveralls came running up the hill. Jerry crawled on hands and knees behind me, blood dripping from his face. "I can't believe it. I can't believe it," he repeated.

His back! I thought, *Oh no! His back!*

From my crumpled position, I could see that we had crashed just beyond—and south of—the picture window of the green house, 450 feet short of the runway, between three houses, in the middle of the paved street. In Wasco.

The coveralled men carried us to the grass. People ran inside the green house, though no one was home, bringing out blankets. I felt suddenly cold, and my teeth chattered as I prayed, *Please, God. Help Nancy and the baby. Please, God!*

We had clipped four-inch walnut branches with the right wing and tail, then dropped through several locust trees and one blue spruce that finally stopped us, pitched the nose straight down, and tossed us to the street. All pieces had stayed attached until the final impact, when the pavement ripped the right wing from the fuselage. The main wheels held. There was no fire, despite the broken wing tank dripping gas.

The EMTs tended Nancy first. She refused the oxygen and yelled in an uncharacteristic way to be left alone. Ken hovered over her as she lay on the grass; occasionally he looked back, trying to reassure me.

"Can we call someone for you?" a voice above me asked.

I tried to think. Someone would need to feed the dogs until we got back home, maybe tomorrow. "Maybe Bob and Marion," I offered weakly. They arrived within fifteen minutes.

I felt sick when I lay down. A woman's voice behind me said, "Lean on my knees," and I sat, gratefully leaning against legs I didn't know.

A dog came sniffing. They called him off, but he returned, finally resting his collie body at the base of my painful foot, protecting me, it seemed. They called him off again, but he persisted in lying near me.

The ambulance took Ken and Nancy and Jerry, whom I had not seen since he crawled from the plane. I waited for another.

Bob and Marion hustled through the crowd, looked down at me with worried faces, and reached for my good hand. Then I lost it, crying as if I were an infant. "I'm so sorry, Marion, so sorry for this trouble." I was embarrassed to have caused disruption for these people and this little town.

"We'll take care of everything—the dogs, your coats, whatever else is in the plane. Who can I call?" she asked.

I could think of no one. My parents were back East. Jerry's would just worry; it was too soon to call them.

"What about your sister? Let me call her," Marion urged, though I resisted, not wanting to bother her either, then finally struggling to remember her number.

The EMTs did something to my arm and foot with air and plastic, then loaded me into an ambulance, and we raced away, winding along the Columbia River in the growing dusk.

Ken leaned over me at the hospital. "I suppose this means I'll have to cook dinner tonight," he joked. His face was ghostly white, his voice high-pitched and scratchy.

"How's Nancy?"

"She's resting. She's going to be just fine," he said, blinking his eyes.

I didn't believe him.

Marion had ridden in the ambulance with the EMT and our pastor, who was the driver.

Rushed into the emergency room, I kept conscious as doctors touched and probed. I assured them nothing internal was wrong—just my arm and foot. *I'll need to tell Warm Springs I can't be there until next week,* I thought.

Into x-ray. The technicians used gentle hands. A chaplain entered and asked if he could pray with me. They stopped all work, and as he read a psalm and asked a guardian angel to "encamp around us," I lay still, relaxed at last, comforted by the picture that came to mind: an Indian village, buckskin tepees set on green grass, wisps of smoke drifting upward, dogs barking in the distance. Imagining the peaceful village, I knew, somehow, we'd be all right.

I asked the chaplain to call Jerry's parents, to assure them that we were fine. They'd be upset to find it out some other way.

Jerry's hip was broken, both ankles, too, plus sprained fingers and wrists, and cuts and abrasions on his face. The engine block had broken on top of my right foot, shattering all the bones inside and setting off the thousand bees stings. My wrist and arm were splintered several ways.

They let Jerry and me talk, rolling our gurneys together in the bright tiled hall before taking me to surgery and Jerry to his room.

"I'm so sorry," Jerry said, gently reaching, touching my fingers. "You know what happened, don't you?" I shook my head. "The spray pilot on the ground saw it. He watched us coming in, even though our approach was high, then saw us drop almost straight down and heard the windsock whip around, still at twenty knots, but west, now on our tail." When I still looked confused, he said, "Wind shear."

There had been no room to dip the nose and gather airspeed, with trees too close and our drop too swift. And so our eighty-five miles per hour became just forty-five.

The Rallye stalled at fifty-eight.

A freak, once-in-a-million accident, I thought as they rolled me off to dreamless anesthesia.

Jack and Carol, Ken's parents, were in the room I shared with Jerry when

I returned from surgery at 2:00 a.m. Jerry's mother had called them, and they had raced up Interstate 5.

From the other bed, two cast-encased legs and a purple, blotchy face with a dozen tiny stitches greeted me. "You look terrible," I mumbled.

"You don't look so hot yourself," Jerry answered with a tender smile.

A nurse entered. "Do you remember me?" She looked familiar. "Jullie Mikkalo," she said. "From across the river. I saw your names and just couldn't believe it was really you. I'll pray for you," she added, gently touching my arm.

It was an offer we happily accepted.

Jack and Carol asked if there was anything we needed, looking warily at my casted foot, my arm held together with seven metal pins and something resembling a *Star Wars* Tinkertoy. My arm wound oozed onto the pillow. The darkened room smelled of disinfectant. Jack and Carol told us their daughter-in-law and unborn baby would be just fine.

I didn't believe them.

I drifted off while men and women wearing white placed pillows under my heavy arm and leg that I thought must belong to someone else.

There'd be new battles in the morning.

23

Passing It On

Dawn came like a baby's breath: soft and sweet and warm. From our window, the first blush of pink spread across the cherry blossoms covering the hills around The Dalles like a fresh bouquet. It was Easter week.

We would miss the sunrise service.

The days passed in a haze of pain and medication, broken by unwanted shifts of pillows to support our legs and arms and hips and hands. Then came lessons on using strange crutches for me and maneuvering a walker for Jerry.

At night, falling nightmares tore at me, and I awoke, screaming.

Jerry couldn't reach me through the railings of his bed until one night a thoughtful nurse simply pushed the beds together. The hospital staff worked around the awkward placement of the beds after that, tending to their patients' needs rather than their own convenience.

We agonized about the accident, struggling with the unanswerable "Why?" but were forced by reality to focus on the future. "What will we do now?" I'd ask Jerry. "How can we possibly go home, do all the work? Pay for all this?"

At Jerry's instigation, we made a pact that for a few days we would only think about healing, regaining our strength from the trauma, pain, and shock. We'd consider only the basics, like how to sit up in bed by ourselves, or trying to sleep through the nights. "We'll figure out the rest later," he said.

When I cried for no explained reason, Jerry reached through the railings to rub my hardware-reinforced arm to reassure me. "It's going to be all right," he'd say. "We're alive."

After two days and my insistence, they brought Nancy down in a wheelchair to convince me that she was recovering well. "I don't remember anything after you said, 'Jerry, the trees…?'" she said. "I remember nothing about the crash. And they say the baby is fine. I went into labor, I guess, but they stopped it, and except for my neck being a little sore, I'm fine. We're going home tomorrow, though I won't work for a while."

I blinked back tears as Ken wheeled Nancy out the door. "We'll keep in touch. Honest," Ken said.

But I wondered how the breath of death blowing on a relationship would change it, especially if the baby were born not quite fine.

A second surgery was scheduled to straighten the bones in my arm and wrist. At midweek I saw the x-ray of my shattered foot—a white cloud of broken bones puffed in the space between my toes and my ankle. Mom was with me when the doctor told me I might walk on it again but never run. Metal bolts and screws were holding it together.

Jerry would need a hip replacement, though he decided to wait. Somehow, despite the distance, word reached our friends and former colleagues, who, along with half of Sherman County, filled our room with flowers and cards and balloons, candy and calls. Their kindness went beyond the usual duties of friendship.

The Wasco Variety Store owner found Jerry's glasses in the wreckage, located the popped-out lens, and brought them to the hospital, along with books to read "when you feel up to it." Friends loaded what was left of the plane and hauled it out to the ranch, where one of the cats took over the cockpit. As we limped by it some months later, with cats' eyes watching us through the broken windshield, Jerry remarked, "It's a rather expensive cat house."

Between the Moores and the Boyntons, the dogs were tended daily.

Sandy drove up, loaded with sweatpants and shirts we could cut the arms out of to go over our casts and my metal frame. She shaved off Jerry's beard, clearing up the moth-eaten look made by so many stitches patched all over his face. We appreciated the comfort of a friend just sitting quietly beside our beds as we moved in and out of restless sleep.

My friend Blair called, just two weeks home from the hospital herself, recovering from spinal surgery. "I had the most terrible nightmare," she told me, "and I realize it's because I almost lost you."

Jim Crislip, our pastor, and his wife were two who didn't grimace when they entered the room; they brought me a hot-pink nightgown that perfectly matched my bruises. Our bodies wore a changing array of color: deep purples, then reds and greens, as the bruises on our arms and legs and faces slowly healed. We looked remarkably like eggplants rotting in the sun.

On Easter, Julie, my friend and boss at Warm Springs, drove two hours to see us. I still believed that maybe not next week, but the one after that I'd be back at work.

Later Julie told us the word that best described us was *pathetic*. All casts and arms and legs propped up, like a cartoon drawing of an accident. "And you thought you could come back to work in a week!" she scoffed good-naturedly.

But like the concrete worker with his open-heart surgery scar, I needed to work, to believe that I could.

At the beginning of the second week, we were released to the horrors of the real world. Dad drove the van to the hospital entrance, and after more than an hour of maneuvering us out of wheelchairs into the van, with almost no use of our legs and limited use of our arms, we started home, heady with the fragrance of mums and azaleas covering the floor, and balloons bobbing as we drove the bumpy reptile road home.

Already exhausted, I couldn't imagine how we'd get into the house.

Bob and Marion followed us down the grade, helped unload, arranged a bed on the couch for me and a bed in the guest room downstairs for Jerry.

Then they unloaded us.

While I watched from the van, Bob and Dad stood on either side of Jerry and his walker as he slowly inched up the hill. He looked so unprotected in the gray sweat suit, his bare heels exposed from the casts to the cool March winds as he staggered uneasily up the steep bank. Finally, seeing his exhaustion, the men lifted him up the steps and carried him into the house. The lump in my throat as I watched almost choked me. "Oh, Mom," I said, swallowing tears, "I don't think we can make it."

A private person, not overtly religious, my mom surprised me with her response as she held my cold hand in hers. "We'll just have to trust in Jesus," she said. In the next few months, we would find that trust was easier said than done.

Dad rose early, peering over the balcony to see how I'd survived the night on the flowered couch. Then he helped Jerry to the living-room recliner for the day. Mom, the light sleeper, helped meet our nursing needs, padding softly down the oak stairs to help me stand and wobble to the bathroom, getting into toilet training once again. With peroxide, we cleaned around the seven metal pins in my arms twice a day.

Each morning we watched the sun come up above the green ravines while listening to scratchy versions of *Morning Edition* on a radio set close to the window. We watched the Mikkalos' cows move up and down the breaks, guessing at how long their trip to water might take.

We waited for the dogs to overcome their hesitation at how strange we looked and how different we must have smelled, with pain and sweat, disinfectant, and the white plaster dust of the casts sprinkling the air when we moved.

Finally, Josie pushed her nose under Jerry's swollen fingers for a pat, and Hansel rested his head on my chest, his eyes pleading for the walk that never came. Sparky curled up at my foot. Ricky had gone touring again.

At the end of the day, we listened to *All Things Considered,* ate a light supper, and laughed over the Patrick McManus books like *They Shoot Canoes, Don't They?* delivered by David Moore. At dark, Dad would open the door and call out, "Kennel up! Come on, Hunzie Bunzie!" Then the barking dogs rushed happily down the steps and into their kennel for the night.

He released them from their kennel each morning, wondering once how during the night they managed to eat the bits of dog food that they'd pushed outside the chain-link fence with their noses. Later in the week we moved the dogs into the house day and night when we realized coyotes were eating the dogs' food next to their kennel, harassing them right under their noses.

We had energy for nothing but solving such simple puzzles and lying there, healing, watching others do our work.

When we thought it was safe to sleep in the same bed without injuring each other with our plaster and metal, Mom helped us into the guest-room bed, tucked in our three casted legs, pink toes pointing upward, settled a pillow under my arm, and kissed us good-night. I was embarrassed to need such basic care yet so grateful she would give it.

Dad laughingly called us hostages, but they were hostages too, to our needs and their decision to drop everything to care for us that spring and early summer.

Jerry spoke of flying again.

My palms got sweaty just thinking about it.

Friends who came to relieve Mom and Dad that spring planted our garden and watered the dozens of trees and the roses we had planted. My brother and his wife sent movie videos. Friends brought *Fletch* and *Amadeus* to expose us to the ridiculous and the sublime, while they planted rows of azaleas below the deck.

Charlie the Wasco barber and his wife drove out with the Sunday paper and scissors to cut our hair on the deck. Our dentist friend in Bend delivered the trailer load of PVC irrigation pipe that had been waiting, loaded, on the day after the accident. People from Moro brought groceries and made sure we had dog food and milk.

Jerry's dad shared two walking canes from his collection, for future reference.

As we healed and the throbbing pain lessened, we moved past the gratitude of surviving and into the wonder of why we had been spared. What purpose was in all this?

We were frustrated by our limitations, often angry, growling, even though our outrage was with what had happened, not with each other.

We had more time to worry.

Were we being punished for some terrible thing? I found I couldn't pray for healing for myself. Nothing for myself, but I could pray for others, so I did.

"Time and chance happen to all men," Jerry's mother paraphrased kindly from Ecclesiastes 9:11.

Still, it was difficult not to wonder if the accident was God's way of telling us we should move.

Reading 2 Chronicles one morning, we found the words that told us we should stay—if we could—when I happened on the fifteenth verse in chapter 20: "Do not be afraid nor dismayed…for the battle is not yours, but God's." He knew of this battle, had forewarned us, really. We simply had to trust He'd control the outcome.

On a day when we became the contraption attractions, laboriously arranging ourselves on chairs in our little church, we found an encouraging quotation by theologian Paul Tournier across from the morning's first hymn. "To seek the meaning of things and God's will does not spare us either from error or from doubt; nor does it solve all the mysteries of our destiny, all the insoluble problems which are set us by any event of Nature or in our lives; nevertheless, it does give a new meaning to our lives."

In the months ahead we'd discover those new meanings. Once, we watched a doe and fawn on porcelain legs hurriedly crossing the river to the island. The river rushed swiftly through the place they'd picked to cross, but they were almost to safety when the fawn stopped and stood, shaking in the middle of the river. The doe turned back, nudged him from behind. Too scared, he wouldn't budge. So she met his need, however odd the timing, and nursed her fawn right in the middle of the river. Nourished, he quickly followed her to safety on the other side.

"I've never seen that before," Jerry said as we watched from the window. I hadn't either, but the scenario reminded me of how God had sent His tender care to us in the middle of our fear, giving us strength to continue on.

We tried to find the humor in it, like a day when Jerry and I met for an awkward kiss in the hall, but first had to decide what to do with our metal and plaster. Or the day I made it up the stairs alone only to fall in slow motion on the landing. I lay stranded like a turtle on its back until Mom could come and help me up.

We also laugh now, thinking about the first afternoon we were anxiously left alone to fix our own lunch while Mom and Dad shopped in town. Jerry was more mobile with his walker than I was, but he wasn't able to carry anything. I could hold a dish but couldn't move easily with it. We stationed ourselves between the microwave and the table and managed to survive on our soup and sandwich. But the difficulty in accomplishing such little things frightened me as I thought about the future.

Still, we kept saying, "It could have been worse!"

Besides our concern for Nancy, our greatest worry was the flat, still scarred with open ditches waiting for pipe. Without the irrigation, we'd have no crops; then we'd have trouble making payments and perhaps, like the Rajneeshees, would have to leave the land.

We should have remembered our neighbors and friends, and the completeness of God's provision.

Few moments in our experience of homesteading on Starvation Point equal the gratitude we felt on a hot, muggy day in late April when assorted cars and trucks began winding their way down the steep ravine, slowly weaving along the reptile road, arriving six minutes from when we first spied them on the grade, carrying men with shovels and gloves.

Vehicles were parked every which way on the narrow drive as the men surveyed the work that needed doing and then spent that day—and others later—digging and carrying and gluing the PVC pipe, fighting off rattlesnakes, dirt, and sweat to bury the lines in the ditches we'd dug.

From the deck we could hear their deep tones as they called to one another, the breeze picking up their voices; we could hear their laughter of camaraderie next to the river.

I had to ask Marion, who orchestrated the event, who some of the people were, wondering why strangers would help us.

Women from the church and others we didn't even know covered my grandmother's harvest table with casseroles and fried chicken and salads and home-baked pies, then sat around talking, catching up with one another.

Armchair supervisors, we watched Dennis Gant, Steve Pederson (of our gold-panning days), our pastor Jim Crislip, and Chuck Kloos (Jerry's fishing and hunting friend) and his son Tracy dig and bury the smaller irrigation pipes that would one day water a lawn and protect the house from fire.

Chukars chattered in the red rocks next to the house. A warm breeze rustled the weeds below the deck.

It was a social occasion, like a barn raising might have been half a century earlier.

Jerry and I sat on the deck helplessly watching, nervously twitching in our chairs, sharing the strangest mixture of joy and despair. What a wonderful thing they were doing for us! But how could we ever repay it? How could we ever pass on what they gave?

I said something about that to Keith, a rancher, and his artist wife, Carole. "We love doing it! Don't take it away by trying to repay it," he said.

"It's a gift," Carole noted. "You pass on the pleasure of gifts by enjoying them!"

"Just pass it on," Keith said. "That's how we get along here."

The best gift of all came later in April, with a phone call from Ken.

"Hello, *Aunt Jane*," he said with emphasis into my ear.

"Oh, Nancy had the baby!" I whispered, afraid to say anything more.

"Yup! It's a girl," he said proudly. "Lisa Leigh." Then he gave the weight and the length and the details of the delivery, adding that Nancy and Lisa were both resting and that both were fine. He sounded delighted.

Everything must have gone well.

"Is the baby really okay?" I asked. "There's not even a teeny, tiny seat-belt mark on her forehead or belly?"

"She's perfect," Ken said grandly. "Not a thing out of place—has all her fingers and toes. Everything is where it's supposed to be."

I handed Jerry the phone, unable then to hold back the tears of fear I'd been saving all these weeks, waiting to be released from any more guilt or anguish. Jerry held me with one arm as he talked with Ken and I cried with relief on his shoulder.

There was much to do. We'd lose a year in our homesteading efforts. What progress we made in the future would be painfully slow.

But with that baby's breath, relief and fresh new life had sweetly joined us. Older lives could now move on.

24

Milestones

To us, MILESTONES OF MAJOR IMPORTANCE marked that summer and fall. They told us many people were holding our hands in their thoughts.

We eventually exchanged our crutches and walker for walking casts, so we could move among the rows of cantaloupes, watermelons, peas, and carrots planted by our friends. Some rows, each containing corn and tomatoes and peas, reminded us of how many different people had raked and hoed in the dirt, not always sure where one row began and another left off, creating a salad of each row.

For Jerry's birthday in late June, Mom fixed an apple cobbler. But before we could eat it on the deck, we discovered Coelsches' cows tromping through the garden. We were alone for the afternoon and hated calling Krista and Leo, who lived twenty-five miles away. But we couldn't chase them out ourselves.

The Coelsches arrived with healthy teenagers and dogs, who quickly rounded up the cows and then joined us for Jerry's birthday dessert. "We brought you a present," Krista said, her dark eyes flashing with a smile as she handed him a seed package of corn and peas. "Since the cows seemed to like those best," she added apologetically. We would plant them the next year.

The Warm Springs kids found my *Star Wars* arm intriguing when I returned to work. Mom and Dad drove me to and from the reservation for a month, since my walking cast wouldn't work well for driving. On weeks when I worked two days, I stayed with my sister, who wrapped my cast and arm in plastic each morning and helped me slip into the shower, teaching me to wash my hair with one hand.

The mules chose that summer to fall in love with Murthas' gelding across the river and left their untended fence. Henry found the river ford, walking out into the water until it got too deep. He backed up and moved over, going forward again until the water hit his chest, then backed up again, his harem close behind him at his heels. Eventually they joined the horses on the other side. The Murthas had no phone, so we couldn't tell them they were feeding our mules.

But in a few days, Jimmy drove down the steep grade with his stock truck full of mules. It was a fifty-mile round trip for him to pick them up and deliver them. Fortunately, he closed the padlock gate as he drove through it toward the house, for when he began to unload the sassy mules, they revolted at being deprived of their beloved gelding and decided to run.

Henry kicked up his heels, lowered his neck, and brayed in delight, then raced below the house toward the hangar and shop, with Blue and Miss Em kicking up dirt close behind him, their roached manes bobbing in the wind.

Jerry's dad walked the road after them, shouting and waving his cane. Jimmy's good nature kept him sashaying back and forth, too, as the mules waited until he almost touched them, then bolted, heels kicking up to the hot summer sky, racing out toward the gate and their gelding.

It went on far too long as we agonized, unable to do anything but watch.

Finally the mules tired, allowed Jimmy to catch Blue and lead her, with the others happily following, through the gate into their pasture, where they munched as though nothing had happened.

We thanked Jimmy profusely. What else could we do? He just smiled, choosing to comment on the flowers rather than mules. "Never thought I'd ever see roses on Con's place," he said, tipping his hat as he said his good-byes.

Eventually, Jerry's casts came off, and the metal screws were backed out of my arm. The doctor said I could do this without anesthetic. I'd asked because I wanted to be alert later, when Jerry and I planned an outing into Portland, alone, to celebrate the parole of our legs. My parents were skeptical.

To divert me from the pain as the doctor unscrewed the pins, backing each one slowly out of my arm and then across the back of my fingers, each turn an agonizing wrench, the doctor asked where we lived. "On the John Day," I panted in pain. "Where Hay Canyon comes in."

"Not that new house, in that deep ravine, on the Sherman County side?" He looked up from his torture, into my eyes.

"That's it," I said, grimacing.

"Shouldn't we give her something?" said the nurse whose hand I was slowly breaking. "The anesthesiologist is standing by…"

The doctor shook his head. "I always wondered who lived there," he mused, now holding the drill in midair. "I've floated that section, fishing. Figured they must be hardy folks," he said, returning to his task.

"If I live," I said, "I'll invite you to come steelhead fishing. Does your mother know what you do for a living?" I asked as he tortured the pins from my arm.

He grinned happily as he handed me the seven pins as souvenirs, then plastered my arm in a cast.

In Portland, even without leg casts, we learned we were not as nimble as we'd been. It took us forty-five minutes to get from the van to the motel. We still needed our crutches and walker; I now had my arm in a cast. Jerry finally gave up trying to help me put on pantyhose while dressing for dinner, a job requiring two hands on one body, or the skills of a contortionist. I resembled a beetle stuck on its back. It was not an event for the faint-hearted. Neither of us even considered dancing that night.

The trip did prove we could be independent again, and soon my parents began weaning us, leaving us alone for the weekend, then for a whole week, and finally they left us the van so we'd have an automatic vehicle to drive through the summer.

Then they set us free.

I was frightened again as they left, wondering if we had the stamina to climb the hills to hand-water the trees each day, to work on the irrigation, to keep clearing the ground.

"There's a lot left to do here," Dad said, surveying the ranch just before they left. "But it's a good purpose."

The day the washing machine finally died, Jerry and I drove all by ourselves to pick up a new one. We brought it home and up the hill not designed for handicapped people, and then by brute force and awkwardness, we pushed it inch by heavy inch up the oak stairs (because the dolly wouldn't work). On that day, not even Sir Edmund Hillary standing high atop Mount Everest could have been as proud or as jubilant as we were, realizing what we'd accomplished together. Like Hillary, we had conquered the shining white mountain, though the flag on ours read "Sears."

In hot July, the Millers, their ten-year-old son, Drew, and their black Lab puppy, Champ, visited us. The lab bounded into the house, heading for the nearest water supply, and found it in the hot tub "plunge," startling himself and the rest of us as he splashed into the water and lunged back out, shaking himself all over the house.

But he looked cooler, and, foolishly, we decided we'd be cooler, too, floating the John Day River from the Murtha ranch down to our homestead, using the boat and pulling a small one-person raft behind us for Drew. It was foolish because the river water was low, and we ended up having to walk long sections, sloshing along the slippery rocks, pulling the boat, with neither Jerry nor I that well retrained in our walking.

The river meandered eleven miles through steep canyons inhabited only by deer, badgers, porcupines, rattlesnakes, and occasionally Bob's or Murthas' cattle. If we had fallen or had trouble, getting help would have been many long, difficult hours away.

But while we walked more than we wanted and our legs ached and I slipped once, scraping my good leg on a boulder, there was only one brief incident when our hearts beat a little faster. In a deeper section, we picked up some speed with the current and Drew, lighter in his plastic raft, passed us by, only to lodge ahead on a sharp rock, punching a hole in his raft.

We watched as his little craft deflated and filled with water while he frantically tried to bail it out. His dad yelled, "Stand up!" and we joined in the chorus as Drew's hands futilely scooped: "STAND UP!"

When he did, his pale face broke into a grin, for he was standing barely knee deep in the rapid current.

We laughed about it later, thinking that all of us had done that too, frantically tried to solve a problem in a cumbersome way, when what we needed was to just stop bailing, stand up, and gain a new perspective.

We began to look for the good in the plane crash.

The liability insurance we carried on the plane paid the hospital bills for Ken and Nancy and what my major medical had not. Exactly. No more and no less.

We'd had special time with friends and family not likely to have occurred otherwise. Our prayers for little Lisa's safe delivery were answered. I'd been able to return to work. Jerry's back hadn't been reinjured. The irrigation pipes got buried. We had kept up with our bills. Lloyd's county road crew had generously put gravel on bad spots in the road. We had a lovely place to recuperate. Our freezer was full.

We could carry on.

Slowly, Jerry began putting valves into pipes lining the ditches. Slowly, we returned to some parts of our routine.

In the classified ads, Jerry learned of a ranch in Bend that was going out of business. If we'd take their giant wheel-line irrigation apparatus apart, we could buy it for a good price. Jerry located Matt and his new wife, Melissa, in a dark apartment they shared with two men in Bend. They'd gotten married the year before, and both had sworn they were clean and would stay that way. But they'd failed to show up for Thanksgiving the year before the accident, then had driven to the ranch once late at night, asking for tuition for

Melissa to start college. We had paid it, but were never quite sure where to find them after that. We heard Melissa dropped out of school. We received a letter asking for a month's rent, followed by a call now and then, pleading for food money.

Jerry's parents tried to check on them, and we did too, bringing them meat for their freezer, adding to the money for food we'd already sent. Jerry's brother and his wife offered support too. His ex-wife, Lelah, called to see if we knew how they were. But Matt and Melissa moved around frequently.

Jerry found him between jobs, so Matt was free to help unscrew all the nuts and bolts of the irrigation wheels that summer in return for a used washer and dryer we bought them.

He worked well, and despite my initial reservations, I enjoyed his quick sense of humor. We appreciated his help.

We also acquired the satellite dish from the same ranch and had it delivered to Starvation Point. At last, connected back to the world in a visual way, we could see the moving face of the man named Gorbachev in the midst of newspaper stories. We could finally feel a sense of immediacy with the world we'd almost forgotten was there.

The irrigation work went slowly, even with the good help of Matt and my nephew, Chad. Painstakingly, the younger men tore the big lines apart, stacking them onto trailers. Then Jerry drove the equipment slowly to the ranch. We gave up any thought of planting alfalfa that year, or of having a lawn. "Maybe in the spring," we told each other, "when we're stronger."

My brother and his wife and new baby joined us for a few days that summer. Jack and Carol brought strawberry and raspberry runners, which we planted below the dog kennel; they also helped us expand our little orchard with a pear tree or two.

Ken, Nancy, and baby Lisa visited in the brilliant heat of July. The baby seemed a miracle as she watched us hover above her, her alert eyes following our lumbering moves.

"She had the best seat in the plane," Jerry said.

Nancy's first view of the wreckage made her queasy. "I just don't remember a thing," she said in wonder. I thanked God again that her mind had just shut down in her shock, announcing "false alarm" to her baby.

We learned to walk with canes. The dogs adjusted to the pace we both developed: Jerry swinging his hip like John Wayne; me, thump-dragging my foot like Igor. Jerry returned for more x-rays and tests, which confirmed his need for a new hip. "When I can't walk a quarter-mile without pain, I'll get it," he said. I suspected he wouldn't have the surgery even then, since he already set his jaw tight in pain going up and down the stairs.

That fall, Jerry went elk hunting just to prove he could, I think. It was a hard trip on the mules, and he never fired a shot; but to have done it at all was accomplishment enough. I walked around the house while he was gone, squeezing clay to strengthen my hand. I kept my foot elevated whenever I sat, and from the ache in my bones, I predicted rain within twenty-four hours. I held Jerry close when he returned home.

Fortunately, the winter was mild. Rain came on the weekends and didn't interfere with the road. The river flowed smoothly, unencumbered by ice. Snow fell and melted quickly, leaving shallow puddles in the dogs' footprints. The deer looked healthy and sleek. The fog made only short pink visits in the morning, then slithered on up the river.

We both felt fortunate that the really hard winter, with the heavy snows and broken dikes and overnights at Marion's, had been the year before the accident.

Driving to Prineville for Christmas in 1986, we had little trouble winding up the reptile road. "Maybe we've had our trials now," Jerry said hopefully as we turned onto the pavement.

But we'd just been tempered for the real test of our tolerance. A genuine milestone, and perhaps the real reason we survived at all on Starvation Point, lay just ahead.

25

Chaos Like a Fragrance

THEY WORE CHAOS like a fragrance.

It swirled around Matt and Melissa in their dark, cluttered apartment in Bend, in the clothes tossed in corners of the living rooms they shared with longhaired men and women who lounged about watching science-fiction videos while cats crunched from bowls on the table. Though they moved frequently, their residences always looked the same.

I didn't like the fragrance of their chaos. But they were family, and Matt was Jerry's only living son. That Christmas, when Matt and Melissa disappeared, we were worried.

A roommate called to tell us they'd taken some of her things, not paid their share of the rent or utilities, left two of their animals—a cat and a pit bull terrier named Taboo—and taken off.

"I'm being evicted," she said. "And their stuff has to be moved out."

We drove to their trailer the day after Christmas, facing a bare, frozen yard filled with trash. The hungry young pit bull looked pregnant, and the cat badly emaciated.

Jerry wore a hard expression as we went inside and tried to overlook their drug paraphernalia—pipes and bongs. We packed their clothes into boxes—Melissa's wedding dress of the spring before, a furry pair of boots we'd given Matt one Christmas that Hansel barked at, some photographs.

I knew Jerry was thinking of another time and another child whose belongings we'd packed after his death. I was furious that Matt would put his father through the pain of this uncertainty again.

We loaded the washer and dryer we'd given them, a few other pieces of furniture that seemed worth saving, and fed the pit bull and cat, who then both willingly came with us.

Taboo, the dog, licked my face happily as she sat between Jerry and me in the truck. We headed out of Bend to the ranch, wondering if and when we'd hear from Matt and Melissa again.

Taboo was pregnant, probably by Dylan, Matt's malamute-and-Airedale dog that apparently had gone along when they left. There were spats with Hansel and Josie until the territories were established. Still, Taboo was a happy dog, her thin tail wagging against the chair legs as she stirred through the house. Her pretty brown face sliced by white often gazed out from behind the flower barrel on the deck, the two cats overlooking her fondly as they walked around the railing.

In early January, Taboo died while giving birth. The conditions of her death still lingered in the air when we heard from Matt and Melissa a few days later.

"Yes, we'll accept a collect call from Matt," I said, handing the phone to his dad.

"In California? What are you doing there?" Jerry asked. I watched the color drain from his face as he pulled a stool up to the phone and sat down. "What for?" he asked. A long pause. "When will you ever learn?" He spoke sadly, knowing there was no answer. "Well, keep us posted." Another pause and then, "I love you, too."

He hung up the receiver and cleared his throat before turning to tell me.

They were in jail. Both of them. Not for drug violations, but for transporting stolen property, driving with a suspended driver's license, and violating a probation imposed when Matt had disagreed with a landlord and trashed an apartment. We could guess that drug use was the cause.

"We're not bailing them out," I said firmly.

"No, he didn't ask for that, just to be able to call us collect until they transport them back to Oregon," he said, an event now just days away.

Jerry's mother called when she learned of their situation and said, "Well, they'll just have to live with you. What else will they do?"

"They're not coming here," I said, terrified at the thought. "We didn't do well parenting him the first time; I'm not sure how we'd be any better now."

My mother-in-law backed off, but I knew she was frightened for them. And for us.

I softened. "Maybe just while they wait to go to court, but that's all."

Melissa was released first, with just a misdemeanor on her record. She stayed with "clean" friends in Bend to be closer to Matt, who remained in jail another four weeks.

Jerry visited Matt weekly and talked by phone with Melissa. We often drove the 160 miles in silence, and I worried that the old feelings and walls built up when Matt was a teen would come between us again.

I visited Matt once. He peered out from behind the thick glass in a space not unlike a phone booth. His thin face looked pale against the jailhouse blues. But for the first time, he didn't blame anyone else. "I know what got me in here," he said. "And if I get out, if they don't send me up for probation violation, it will be different."

Familiar words from those confined, but he said them with a conviction I hadn't heard before. "This could be the best thing that ever happened to me," he volunteered once, and I began to think he might be right.

They came to stay with us for three weeks while we waited for Matt's hearing.

"We've lots of work for you to do," Jerry said. "You can clear sagebrush, feed stock. Earn your keep until the hearing. And no drugs or you're out."

They were both agreeable and swore they'd never touch another thing.

My professional training made me wonder if it were possible for two people to simply give up marijuana and cocaine, though their forced detoxification for six weeks in jail had taken them through the first, worst part.

While they worked, they talked of seasonal jobs that had been promised to them in California where their huge dog, Dylan, still stayed. I breathed easier, believing their stay was temporary—relieved, uncharitably, that they had a place to go far away from Starvation Point.

They worked hard, pulling sagebrush, helping clean, fixing meals on days I worked. Melissa talked about the horrors of being in jail, the addicting nature of crack. "Once you've had it," she said, "you'd sell everything you have to get more."

Sharing experiences of their turbulent lives of drug use, they told of a time when a dealer wouldn't take their money for crack "until we paid our rent and had food in the refrigerator." I was surprised any drug dealer would care.

They left Bend, they said, to get away, to start over, free from drugs, living in their car. But then came the vagrancy arrest. Problem solving wasn't one of their strong suits. They seemed so incredibly young, in need of so much.

I found their presence intrusive. They were messy people, without meaning to be. They discarded hairbrushes sporting blond hair on the kitchen table, left wet towels heaped on the floor. We had to state simple rules, like asking before using, or knocking first on closed doors. Coordination was difficult. When I was at Warm Springs, decisions were made without me, and sometimes Jerry forgot to fill me in.

Jerry and I had little time to talk privately, and unlike other houseguests, Matt and Melissa put us on edge. Half the time we worried that something we said would send them back into their old lifestyle; the other half, I worried that they'd stay at Starvation Point forever.

They were frightened people too. Once the power went out, and they imagined that someone had found them, cut the lines, and planned to hurt them. They spoke of threats and of choosing friends because they were big and could defend them. "No one has ever been as kind to me as Matt," Melissa told me once. "And now you folks, of course," she added.

I fought back tears, ashamed, since all we'd really done was what we had done for Taboo. We had only fed, sheltered, and clothed them. I, at least, needed to try love.

They began putting on weight. "We never ate so much before," Melissa noted once as we were fixing a third meal of the day. "But then we've never worked outside like this."

They seemed interested in our lives, asked questions about Jerry's resuming flying again, my work at Warm Springs, the vintner book beside Jerry's chair, the quality of fishing on the river, our plans for the ranch, the delay in work caused by our accident.

But despite the relative smoothness of their stay, I was apprehensive that if Matt were incarcerated for the duration of his probation, Melissa might want to remain with us; or worse, they would *both* not want to leave. I wasn't ready for any long-term commitment to their care.

The Sunday before the hearing began as a particularly difficult morning. The memory of what exactly caused my distress escapes me now, but I was angry, and I blamed the kids. I knew I wanted them to go. Soon.

But during the church service, surrounded by friends, I felt as though a weight were lifted when Jerry held my hand. I felt protected and secure.

The four of us drove home, enjoying the windless sunshine, talking about fishing in the river and other ways we'd spend the day. It was a surprisingly pleasant time, like being with good friends.

After lunch, Matt and Melissa went fishing at the river, and Jerry called me into the bedroom. He was lying down. I stood, waiting for him to tell me what he wanted.

"I've got to talk to you about something," he said, patting the side of the bed, motioning me to sit. "And I'm afraid to." His voice broke.

Even with all we'd been through, I'd never seen him so distraught. "It's okay," I said. "You can say what you want to me." I sat beside him on the bed.

"I know you want the kids to go. And I did too," he began. "But this morning, I saw this picture in my mind. The vineyard was finished, and they were working in it." He picked up my cool hand, gently rubbing his thumb across the back of my fingers as he talked. "And I prayed about what we should do about them, and this voice inside of me, as clear as anything I've ever known, said 'I've already shown you what you should do.' "

With his other hand, he thumbed the moisture from his eyes. I was moved by his love for his children, his great faith, and that what I thought mattered so much to him. I was surprised that my heart didn't pound.

Perhaps this was the way we would pass it all on.

"They won't come between us," he said, anticipating my fears. "I promise you. We'll figure out a way to have separate living quarters for them. We'll have some privacy." He paused to wipe the corners of his eyes with his wrist. "I don't know if they are even interested in staying. But I want to ask them to consider it, and if they agree, to offer it as their plan at the hearing next week."

I was thoughtful. "If it's what you think we should do," I said finally, "then we'll find a way to manage."

Anxieties about how we'd support them hadn't even begun.

They were interested. "We talked about it ourselves," Matt said happily. "We wondered how you'd ever do all the work here in the shape you're both in."

Over supper, the four of us explored the worst things that might happen, which to me weren't accidents or rattlesnake bites, but miscommunications and hurt feelings. "We'll all need to speak up, express things before they explode," I cautioned, hoping to avoid destroying our network of family and work. We agreed to use family meetings to work out differences we knew would occur.

Those issues decided, my parents drove Matt and Melissa to California to pick up and return the stolen property and to recover Dylan, their dog.

Then they drove them back to Bend to pay fines so that finally, on the day of the hearing, their lives were in order. They told the judge and Matt's probation officer with some assurance that they had a safe place to live and would be starting a new, drug-free life on a homestead at Starvation Point. The judge agreed to their arrangement as long as Matt continued on probation until he paid full restitution for his previous offense.

After the hearing, they were like teenagers spilling out of the van on the ranch, the late February wind catching Melissa's long blond hair in strands across her happy face, Matt holding her tightly, pleased to be starting over.

Even Dylan strutted confidently around the vehicles, marking every spot where Hansel might have been, claiming his territory.

Watching them smiling and chatting, scratching the dogs' ears, I couldn't foresee all the turmoil these boomerang children would bring us. Nor did I imagine how they'd touch us. And I never dreamed of the joys we would share.

26

A Family Affair

EVERY COUNSELING AND TEACHING SKILL I could muster, every bit of courage and parenting experience Jerry could enlist, we called upon when Matt and Melissa moved into our lives at Starvation Point. We dealt with the difficult, painful times of confrontation over little things, sharing feelings better left unsaid, noticing strengths and building on them, coping with disappointments, frustrations, and change.

Just when we needed it, during Murphy's month, I sold some articles and was offered three separate short-term jobs that, along with Warm Springs, took me away from the ranch five days a week for the month. I regretted that the work kept me from home. But it allowed us to secure housing for Matt and Melissa in a separate fifth-wheel trailer we purchased and were permitted to put in a septic system down by the shop (legal for agricultural help). The jobs helped us feed them and Dylan, buy shoes and boots for them, set up their household, and pay them a small salary.

They worked hard on the ranch, clearing ground, stirring up rattlesnakes in the hot sand. Once Matt yelled "Snake!" and Jerry headed down to the flat with the Special loaded with shot shells.

We heard two shots echo back from the field.

"Must have been two snakes," Melissa observed wryly, sitting with me in the house. "Jerry never misses." And he hadn't.

Matt skinned the snakes and tanned the hides for a hatband he planned to make. He had fourteen at the end of the summer.

While Jerry and Matt worked to clear the flat, fighting the wind and the snakes, Melissa and I planted pine trees on the hill behind the house and roses along the driveway. Together, the four of us planted a garden, though Matt was disappointed later, when the flowers they'd planted to surprise me didn't grow. And on days when Jerry's back was especially bad, progress still went forward because Matt caught on quickly.

He seemed to like farming, and together we decided to plant ten acres of the flat in watermelons to be sold commercially. I liked watching Matt and his dad talking by the barn or over supper, sharing fishing stories. I heard Jerry say "I love you" to his son, even when he lost his temper in irritation over something Matt might have done carelessly by not following directions.

For example, one day Jerry looked up from setting pumps by the river and saw Matt racing across the field to the shop. The small tractor Matt had been running next to the river was nowhere in sight.

Jerry ran, too, limping, meeting his wet, dripping son returning to the river with Deere John.

The little tractor sat submerged in the river. Swirling rushing water rolled over all but the tops of the wheels. The tractor and Matt had plunged into the water when a twelve-foot-high section of the bank split away, weakened by the rushing, high river. The muddy water swirled around him, but Matt was a strong swimmer and he had headed, drenched, to the shore.

Shaken, he then ran for Deere John.

Jerry had warned him about the high water and the weakened banks, had urged him to stay well back from the edge because the river undercut them in ways not easily seen from on top.

We'll never know why Matt didn't die in the river, with the tractor tumbling over his head, or why the river didn't take the tractor on downstream. Nor would we know why the little 1946 Ferguson we'd bought from the Larsons continued to work once Deere John hauled it from the water and the men took it apart but dried only the important pieces with my blow dryer. We were simply grateful for those miracles in the water and sand.

Ours was a family affair, sharing entertainment those first months, playing The Farming Game together some nights, watching videos on others. We found our way around the satellite system. Matt and Melissa joined us in Moro for Barnstormers rehearsals, the local theater group I got to act in while Jerry helped build sets. We went to church together.

In our reparenting, we tried hard to be vigilant and consistent in our actions, to not repeat the mistakes of the past. We took time to explain our reasons, especially for the consequences of their behavior; we stressed the importance of thinking ahead.

Neither Jerry nor I was permitted to escape into ourselves or to avoid the discussions that sometimes concluded painfully. Often it was only Jerry's faith that kept us going, his belief that we were all doing the right thing.

One afternoon we had a long talk with Melissa when she found a job in The Dalles. It was part time, working four days a week in a group home for adults with handicaps; having a job meant she needed a car. "It's only for the summer," she said, a little indignant that we had reservations about her driving a hundred miles round-trip every day, leaving the men without a vehicle on the days I, too, was gone.

"The cost of gas will hardly have you earning anything on days they want you to work only an hour or two," Jerry pointed out.

With some assistance, she worked out alternate plans for those days with her employer.

We talked about the need for compromise and planning when people live and work together. At our family meetings—which we now opened with prayer—we worked out the arrangements we needed. I was frequently surprised that we would start those meetings faced with some difficult problem with no alternative in sight, then together we'd come up with something that pleased us all. It was the prayer, we guessed, that gave us the courage and solutions to continue.

As an early birthday present, we paid for summer tuition so Melissa could take nine college credits, since she was in town every day. She was the first high-school graduate in her family and was proud of her perseverance. We talked about health insurance and covered them until Melissa's job provided benefits.

Jerry and I had less time together and found we needed to work harder to let each other know we cared and still harbored the dream.

In April, Don and Kay, our Wisconsin friends, joined us for a week. I hoarded my time with Kay, who marveled at what we'd accomplished in such a short time. I didn't want to share my time with her by having to deal with Matt or Melissa.

But Melissa complained of a bad wisdom tooth. Because her pain tolerance was low, I wasn't too sure how bad it might really be. Through Marion, we located an emergency dentist, and Kay and I drove Melissa to The Dalles.

I was shocked by the dentist's first words after he examined her. "She'll need to have all four wisdom teeth pulled," he said. "But we've got to get this infection down first. She's a pretty sick girl." He gave her some medication and a prescription to fill, and then helped us schedule surgery in Portland for the next week.

Melissa looked awful. I felt pretty awful, myself, because I hadn't taken her pain very seriously. "I'm hungry," she said as we walked to the car. When Kay asked if she'd like a milkshake, Melissa nodded, and we drove to a little restaurant.

Before the soothing shake could arrive, though, Melissa paled.

"Do you want to lie down in the car?" I asked, and she nodded.

"But will you come with me? Help me get there?" Her voice quivered.

Did she feel she had to ask for such basic nurturing and care? Did she think I had so little concern for her? I *hadn't* given much of myself to her, now that I considered it. While I'd had easy, constant loving myself as I was growing up, Melissa had been reared by several stepmothers whom she remembered without fondness. But even knowing that, I had held back from her, unfairly, afraid that if I loved her, I'd be hurt.

As I walked with her out to the car, holding her close, I knew I had much to learn about passing love on.

The remainder of that week, while Melissa recovered from her infection, the rest of us worked in the wild spring wind to set the hand lines along the rows of watermelons.

Jerry and Don hovered over the pump, setting the huge suction hoses into the water, remaking a valve, manipulating and adjusting the valve. The watermelon seeds had already sprouted, but the windbreaks we'd planted had not. Five acres of plants already looked dead. Only water on the flat—soon—would save the other five acres from destruction by the gritty lava sand, blowing in the abrasive, whirling wind under the dry, hot sun.

Kay and Don stayed an extra day, just knowing that "Tomorrow, you'll have water, and we want to be here."

On a Friday in April, Jerry and I took turns inching up to our armpits in the cold, high river water, our tennis shoes squishing around our feet, the wind chilling us to the bone. Our spring swims set the hoses and pumps that would pour river water onto the land for the first time in almost thirty years.

Finally, at dusk, exhausted, Jerry turned on the noisy pump. We held our collective breaths and waited, cheering and hugging one another through grateful tears as water surged up through the suction lines, rushed through the pipes that our friends and neighbors had buried almost a year before, and emerged through the valves at the far end of the field.

We watched in admiration as each sprinkler in the line filled, then the next and the next, until two long lines sprayed their circle of life over the withering seedlings.

The wind howled around us, making one last effort to turn us aside, pushing mud and water into our faces as we cleared dirt from the sprinkler heads, staking and securing the lines so they could run all night.

When the wind died, as it usually did in the evening, the six of us sat quietly on the deck listening to the *cachunk-cachunk* of the sprinklers nourishing the watermelon seeds. We hoped the crop would see us through until the alfalfa grew and the grapes were planted and producing.

Hansel sprawled peacefully around the deck; Dylan snored at Matt's feet. Matt and Melissa's cat, Nikki, stalked a mouse in the driveway, while John II walked back and forth beneath Josie, tickling her belly with his tail.

In the fading light I photographed the irrigation lines making dark brown stripes along the sandy flat, bringing us one step closer to fulfilling the dream.

The land was changing, as was this family who worked it.

In the quiet evening, with the North Star twinkling above the rocks, Jerry reached for my callused hand, and we both wondered how we would ever have accomplished this work of our dream without the efforts of family and friends.

The next week Jerry drove Melissa to Portland for the oral surgery. She and Matt decided that Jerry would be a calmer companion at this ordeal than Matt, who was already agitated about Melissa's pain.

"She wore braces for five years," Matt told us. "And had her whole mouth restructured and rebuilt as a kid." Then he added with alarm, "How will she eat?"

They both had often worried aloud about food and about getting enough to eat, about their hunger. Kay noticed it too. I was reminded of psychologist Abraham Maslow's theory that before self-esteem and spiritual needs can be met and flourish in a person, life's basic needs of food, clothing, and shelter must be secured.

I debated then about asking Melissa if she wished to join Jeannie, my sister, and me for our scheduled women's retreat at the coast. The event fell at the end of her surgery week. I needed the break myself, and when I was honest, part of my wish was to go there without her. It would be a spiritual event that probably would not interest her, I thought, and decided not to ask her.

But then I did anyway.

"That would be nice," she said, surprising me.

The two of us met my sister and my friend Jeannie in Portland and carpooled the remaining two hours to the coast. The weather was good, the company fine, and we laughed together as Jeannie and I related stories from our first retreat. Hair dryers had blown fuses, leaving us stuck in dark shower rooms. I recalled again the eventful decision to homestead I'd made that weekend.

The retreat speakers encouraged and challenged us, with the evening and next morning's events proceeding as scheduled. Melissa spent some of the time meeting others and more time hovering close to us. Saturday's afternoon session ended early, and the next scheduled event was canceled. Then it began pouring rain, ruling out a leisurely shopping spree or a pleasant walk on the beach. Instead, with notebooks and Bibles held close to our breasts, we jumped over puddles and ran across the parking lot into the motel room the four of us shared, shaking wet jackets, running fingers through our damp hair, and laughing comfortably together.

We know now that it was not coincidence that we suddenly had spare time and that it was raining, forcing the four of us there together in that motel room. Since moving to the homestead, I no longer believed the dozens of details that affected our lives simply happened without some greater plan.

The remarkable event that followed didn't, either.

That afternoon in a motel room overlooking the ocean, Melissa somehow told us of her spiritual needs, and fumbling, we somehow responded.

We prayed a simple prayer together, and then with nervous fingers, Jeannie found the Scriptures and words that would bring comfort and new spirit to Melissa as she invited Jesus into her life.

Judy and I sat quietly on the bed, at first feeling awkward, as though we'd walked in on someone half-dressed, standing in her slip. But Melissa seemed unaware of our discomfort, absorbed only in the questions and answers of her need.

Then Melissa walked toward us, wiping her eyes, a quiet smile on her face. Jeannie stood behind her, teary-eyed, too. The four of us huddled on the bed, arms around one another's shoulders, not speaking, just moved by the peacefulness of the moment.

Suddenly, Melissa leaned back and turned to me, her eyes full and pleading. She began to sob, the deep, throaty sobs of someone profoundly affected, yet so vulnerable and exposed. "I love you," she said, reaching out her arms to me. "I just love you so much."

Even then, I hesitated briefly before putting my arms around her, holding her, crying now, for the child she was and for the privilege of sharing this moment. "I love you too," I whispered, stroking her long blond hair as she quieted. "I love you too."

In that moment, when love filled the tiny room and all of us were equal in our needs, I began to understand why we were all surviving on Starvation Point.

27

Raisin' Watermelons

WE KNEW THEY WERE THERE, moving in the dawn down steep paths that wound like loose braids around the rock outcroppings.

They passed slowly through the watermelon field, avoiding the rattlesnakes that found respite in the wet, leafy shade. But the deer didn't touch the tiny shoots that grew in rows, covering five acres of land marked on old Oregon maps as "Starvation Point."

Neither did they bother the plants when the shoots became vines, snarling between the weeds. Like calling cards, the deer simply left dark, pellet-shaped droppings among the rows as they wandered toward the river.

Even when the fruit, like fat, green thumbs, popped out from the blossoms, the creatures gingerly stepped around them, leaving only tiny hoofprints in the sandy soil. But when the striped green melons were ripe, the intruders on Starvation Point seemed to know it first! They bit holes in the tops, swallowed every speck of pulpy pink flesh, water, and seeds, leaving a trail of empty green gourds to greet us in the morning.

The deer were just one of the elements that made raisin' watermelons both exasperating and divine.

With water, the plants grew quickly in the steamy, sandy soil, promising a healthy, tasty crop, like the ones we'd grown in the garden the year before—juicy and fragrant. We'd delivered them to neighbors who had helped us so much that summer and received requests for many more.

With a machine, we could cultivate weeds between the rows. But within the rows—having chosen not to use pesticides and herbicides—we had to hoe and separate by hand.

Knapweed, a noxious import from Russia, was the most prolific weed. Pulling it, even while wearing leather gloves, left a metallic taste in one's mouth. Hoeing barely budged it.

There were other kinds of weeds, too. Hundreds of them thrived in the field. In fact, the soil conservation people estimated that on untilled soil like ours, there were probably five hundred pounds of weed seeds to the acre.

An even greater variety of intruders rode the irrigation water from the John Day and germinated into weeds more frequently seen in faraway places, such as Buttercup and Spray, which were not usually found in our area.

Leo Coelsch called and asked if he could bring his son down for his biology-class project. "He needs fifty varieties of weeds in bloom," Leo said cheerfully.

We didn't need to wonder why he thought Starvation Point could oblige.

We dug a pond beside the pump, hoping to keep some of the weeds from strangling the irrigation suction tube; it meant someone had to enter the river several times a day to clean it out. But the pond recovered too slowly, so it became a breeding ground for tadpoles. Matt watched their progress, planning a gourmet feast.

"Tomorrow's the day," he announced, licking his lips in anticipation of frog legs. But in the morning, instead of succulent frog legs, only raccoon tracks remained beside the pond.

Matt became the main watermelon weeder; Jerry and I helped as we could. The plants would have survived without all that tending. But as it is with children, those raised with care do better than those that just grow up on their own. Sandy visited one weekend and just shook her head. "Matt's dwarfed by all those weeds!" she said.

He did look like a speck of pepper in a bowl of pea soup. Matt seemed to like the work, though. His back tanned to a golden bronze in the sun, and his wavy blond hair bleached almost white.

He was always cheerful despite the sweat and dirt. "I guess I knew once that watermelons would come out of the blossoms, but it just surprised me," he said, delighted to show us the first evidence of fruit. "Sometimes I feel like my whole life has been a funnel of events all pouring into my being here on this place," he said one day as we stood leaning against the tractor. "I love it here."

And of course now, with Melissa's news, he had even more reason to find his place in life.

A few days after Mother's Day, when Melissa and Matt brought tears to my eyes with a lovely card and Melissa's remark that I was more like a mother to her than any she had ever known, she shyly, almost frightened, said, "I think I'm pregnant."

"Oh, probably not," Miss Pollyanna offered weakly. "Have you thought you were pregnant before?" I asked hopefully, knowing that starting a family when they were just launching their own marriage could be devastating.

"Only once," she said. "But we've never used anything. I just thought I couldn't have children."

They were healthy for the first time since they'd been together, and off drugs, which probably now accounted for their fortune—whether good or bad.

I pulled her to me, put my arm around her shoulder, and said something I didn't quite believe: "Whatever happens, it'll all work out." Even as I said the words, my mind wondered: *Five of us here on the Point? Could that really be part of a plan?*

Melissa *was* pregnant. She told us at the same time she informed us that the pickup she drove to work would be too bumpy for her, that the road would be too terrible for a pregnant woman to drive on. "And we'll need more space," she said, escalating her worry. "There's no room in that trailer for a crib."

"Have you thought about health care?" I asked.

"The nurse said if I didn't have insurance, I could just have my baby at the emergency room. For free."

My stomach knotted. "You can't just have your baby in the emergency room," I said. "It isn't free. You'll need prenatal care. What if you have complications?" My voice was more strident than I intended.

I also heard her saying we'd have to buy a different, gentler car for her, and buy them another house. Instead, I suggested, "Maybe you should consider living closer to town then, to have all these needs met."

She was silent.

I agonized over this baby. How would they support it? Would they want to stay here on the ranch? Jerry told me to stop worrying, that everything really would be all right.

But two days later, when Melissa came home with a St. Bernard puppy, neither of us was so sure.

It had been enough of an adjustment to accept Dylan, the epitome of the junkyard dog—wiry, tough, black, and brown. Hansel picked fights with him that he couldn't possibly win. While we were planting the watermelons, Dylan had been bitten in the throat by a coiled rattlesnake before anyone could get him away from it. He'd acted a little ill for a day, and the fur around the fang marks dropped off. But he lived to kill many more snakes, just as he had killed the one that bit him. The silver lining was that his barking in a special way alerted us all to a rattlesnake's presence.

Dylan was not the kind of dog for Hansel to take on; but he did, trying to protect his territory on more than one occasion. Hansel ended up with chunks out of his ears, puncture holes in his rear and neck, and long teeth-scrape scars on his head.

Finally, the dogs developed a truce of sorts. And now, into a trailer too small for a crib, with hardly money to feed themselves, let alone their dog, Melissa had invited a St. Bernard.

"I really don't like your having brought another dog here without first talking with all of us who are affected," I said, practicing my words at the house before walking to the trailer to speak to them.

"Well, it's over and done with," Melissa snapped. "The dog's here, and that's that!" She slammed the spoon into the frying pan where she'd been making Matt's supper and put her hands on her slim hips. She'd never been verbally angry with me before, although I'd seen it directed at others when she was upset.

"It's *not* over and done with," I said, feeling my neck breaking out in anxiety blotches. I caught my breath. "I didn't say you had to take the dog back. I said I was unhappy with the way you brought it here without thinking of the rest of us. It scares me that you are expecting a child that you can't even pay for and want a bigger place to live in. You can't even feed Dylan—and then you bring another dog home."

Matt stood behind her, quietly rubbing her shoulders while Jerry worked on plumbing in their bathroom. I wanted him with me, but he didn't see my signal, so I had to go on alone.

"Well!" she snapped. "You don't want us here anyway. You want me to have an abortion!"

Despite their distance from the truth, her words stung me.

"Whatever gave you that idea?" I said, totally surprised. I sat down.

"Isn't that why you told us we should look for somewhere else to live?" she said, calming a bit.

"I said that if the road was going to be a problem, then you'd have to think of being somewhere else, because we can't change the road. And we can't afford a different car right now. Or another house. But I also said we'd work it out."

The last thing in the world I wanted was for them to leave or to have an abortion. But we hadn't wanted to influence their decision. So we had avoided the subject, avoided trying to tell them what to do, which apparently had been taken as rejection of them and the baby.

"I thought you meant you didn't want us," she finished lamely, "and I wanted something to hold, something that would be mine, like Dylan is Matt's. So I got the dog."

We hadn't talked enough about how to get needs met, I guessed, hadn't said "I love you" enough. Maybe she'd come from a world where people kicked you out when they were unhappy, so you had to act first and fast.

"We'll hold you, Melissa," I said, taking her hand. "Just ask. We just want what's best for you." I hugged her, though I was still scared of the future. "But if you wonder what we're thinking, or if I say something that seems unkind, then tell me!"

"But it's hard to talk about that kind of stuff," Matt volunteered protectively.

"You think it's easy for us?" I asked.

They both nodded.

So far from the truth.

Jerry came out of the bathroom, and the four of us *did* talk then, trying to resolve the hard issues a baby would bring, trying to love them more as we talked.

The dog, named Shiloh, stayed. From their earnings, Matt and Melissa agreed to pay for their dogs' food. We explored options for expanding their space. Melissa negotiated a prenatal package with a physician, and life went on, though it was a difficult pregnancy.

Once the phone rang at 4:00 a.m. from the emergency room, telling us that a dog had jumped on Melissa while she worked the night shift at the group home and that she was in labor. Matt raced to the hospital, where he and the doctor spent the night keeping vigil near the small, pale body beneath the sheets. But things calmed, and Melissa came home in a day.

Later, while Ken and Nancy were visiting, Melissa came up to the house talking of bleeding and aching. We called the doctor, who told us softly that she might be having a miscarriage. He told us to keep her lying down, to withhold food, to give her water, and to bring her in later.

Amazingly, by noon, the pain and bleeding had stopped, and at her next checkup, all was announced well.

Melissa stayed out of the watermelon patch most of the summer, checking its progress from a distance. Sometimes she walked out to the river, taking Matt's lunch to him there. But that stopped, too, on a day he was working with Deere John. He saw her screaming, jumping up and down in the sand, her maternity dress ballooning about her. He thought her bare feet were too hot in the sand and laughed from a distance. But when she got up to the tractor, her eyes showed sheer terror.

"I stepped over a rattlesnake!" she screamed. "Back there, all coiled up."

It was a miracle it hadn't struck her. Matt killed it and added the skin to his hatband collection. The close call kept Melissa close to the house for the rest of her pregnancy.

In July an old childhood friend of Matt's came with her husband for a visit. The morning they were to leave, we could hardly believe what we saw in the watermelon field.

"Are those cows?" Marybeth asked, pointing.

And they were.

Coelsches' cows, come for a visit. This was before the deers' feast on the ripened melons. When the cows wandered into the watermelon patch, the watermelons had just begun to form striped green tubes. The cows' hooves grabbed at the vines, ripping them from the soil, until we could chase them out of the field. "We have insurance," Leo apologized.

Between the wind and the weeds, the cows, coyotes, and deer, we wondered if there would be any melons left.

But in August thousands of striped green melons almost tumbled over one another in the field of green. We all hovered over the tiny pigtail curl close to the melon's stem. "When it turns brown, we'll be ready to harvest," Jerry said.

"Do you have them sold?" I asked Jerry naively.

"Well," he said, clearing his throat, "the stores don't actually take contracts, and the brokers don't want to handle just five acres."

"What does that mean, exactly?" I said.

We would all soon find out.

Jerry took the dump bed off the dump truck, had a fifth-wheel plate attached for the trailer, ordered pallets and cardboard bins, and waited for the melons to ripen.

We weren't the only ones waiting for ripening fruit. The deer were better at finding the ripest ones first, their teeth leaving scars across the hides of melons not quite ready. "Maybe we could sell those with teeth marks as 'quality-checked by deer,'" I suggested to Jerry, who didn't approve.

Coyotes liked the melons too, leaving their scat on ones they apparently planned to return for. Rattlesnakes and black widow spiders also relished the damp, cool patch, so we learned to turn the melons with our boots, safely knocking off the spiders with orange hourglasses tattooed on their backs before we checked the curly brown tail that would tell us when to pick.

And if Dylan wasn't around to warn about snakes, and if Jerry and Matt couldn't find a rock to either kill or scare off rattlesnakes, they pulled unripened, softball-size watermelons, still hard as a rock, and stoned the reptiles into leaving, pelting them with their homegrown lethal weapons.

Raisin' watermelons had such fatal potential.

We knew the majority were ready at last when, on a hot August day, we broke into one rivaling the size of our Josie and found it juicy and cool, its center hot pink and sprinkled with black seeds.

We began the picking then. We pulled melons from the vine and tossed and caught the footballs of fruit to load the trailer while red-tailed hawks dipped down from the rock walls. The fragrance of sweet nectar hovered over the field, and brassy deer made their way down the steep rock outcroppings and then, in broad daylight, ate their own August watermelon brunch at the far end of the field.

28

Watermelon Whine

AUGUST 23, 1987

Dear Ken and Nancy,

This week the word is Safeway. We sold our melons to SAFEWAY! Or at least, this week's supply. We had them sold to a broker, but he said we were too small to handle after the wind took all but five acres. So since mid-July, Jerry has been madly trying to sell melons. To add to the chaos, Matt accidentally drove over a main irrigation valve and crushed about twenty feet of four-inch and six-inch mainline, which cost us two days and $120 just for pipe. Then Jerry drove to Sisters with the dump truck to get my Dad's trailer to haul melons out on, and two cylinder heads broke on the truck.

So he spent three days at his brother's, who, by the grace of God, had absolutely no repairs that week! Isn't that amazing! So he helped Jerry. The parts cost close to $300. Added to the axle we replaced the week before, it's getting a tad spendy. Anyway, Jerry drives it home and discovers it now has such improved compression that it is using a quart of oil about every fifty miles, and that it will need a new "short block" or something like that.

On Tuesday of last week, Jerry sells ten bins (about four tons) of melons to Safeway in The Dalles and Hood River. So we're trying to figure out how to get the melons out with a bad truck when my sister says they have their truck fixed that they're planning to sell and would we like to use it for a week to see how it will work and see if we want to buy it.

Well, it's a lovely truck. Air, stereo, turbo, diesel, four-wheel-drive, running boards, aluminum flatbed, double tanks, etc. Matt said it made us look like prosperous melon growers (which is the joke of *this* season).

So Jerry comes with me to Warm Springs Sunday, and he drives the truck home Monday. Goes to Hermiston to get the crates and bins on Tuesday while Matt begins pulling melons (using Blue, the white mule, with her packs on, which actually worked pretty good when only one person was there to pick).

Wednesday, we have two extra guys come down to pick, and they have ten crates full by noon. One says it would be easier to bus people in to eat the melons than to haul them out! We put the melons on the red trailer because it is lighter than my dad's. Only after they are on there, we realize it will be too low to back up to the loading bays at Safeway and allow the forklifts to work at the store.

We pull the trailer out Wednesday evening with Deere John. Matt and I follow behind in the pickup and watch in horror as two bins slide—in slow motion—off the trailer on the roller-coaster grade because it's so steep. We can't signal Jerry, who blithely chugs on up while watermelons roll under the pickup and congregate at the bottom of the hill like politicians at a convention. We have to reload the survivors and go back and get more to fill up the bins on top.

It rains during the night, and the bins are cardboard.

In the morning I'm awake at 4:00 a.m., praying. The sun comes out; I take a picture of Jerry, Matt, and Melissa in front of our first load; and we head down the road. The sun hits the bins of watermelons, and it looks like we're delivering a load of bald heads.

We go to the public scales to weigh in.

We arrive at the Safeway in The Dalles to try to figure out how to unload, since we're low. Jerry has this elaborate scheme to stack five four-inch blocks and get two ten-foot, four-by-twelve boards to back up onto these little stacks of boards that look to me like Mickey Mouse–engineered ski lifts. Well, Ken, as a mathematician, you will understand what he did wrong at the first place, as it didn't work.

We didn't get the trailer up high enough, so we had to unload six bins of eight hundred to nine hundred pounds of melons by hand. Of course, another trucker was waiting to deliver meat, to add to the pressure.

We go to the public scales to weigh in empty.

By the time we got to Hood River, Jerry had the angles and little pieces of boards figured out, and we backed in, moved the blocks, and rolled right up and unloaded, which was good because we got there at noon, and the produce man was all upset with our timing. Apparently, noon is not a good time to deliver.

Then we drive back to The Dalles to weigh empty and go to the store to give them the invoice, and we meet with the manager and produce man who say we have a problem because they are cutting into the melons and 50 percent are GREEN! My heart sinks. I can see the discarded melons in the garbage, their little pale faces looking up, and I see all the work and pain and money and don't understand because we've been pulling them, eating them, and they've been ripe, and the one he cut open when we delivered was just perfect. So he thinks it might have been just that bin, but will sell them as cut melons, (they won't move as fast, but Safeway won't get complaints and won't be mad at us) and we'll bill next week. They actually want more for next week (although we are now so terrified we don't know what a ripe melon is that who knows what will happen).

Anyway, we drive back to Hood River because we have to tell that produce manager about The Dalles problem, expecting we'll have to take the melons away with us, since he's already mad that we arrived at noon.

I know there is a God in heaven because somewhere between The Dalles and Hood River, those melons ripen.

The Hood River manager is a gem. Says he's been cutting like crazy, and they're perfect and would like six bins next week and each week we can deliver and approves our invoice so we can bill Safeway.

I say to Jerry, "Can we go somewhere where I can throw up?" The anxiety and uncertainty are absolutely wrenching. I know it will work, and I had the same feeling the day before we delivered the melons as I did when we left the road and started on the hill while doing the phone line. I just *knew* that dumb machine was going to make it. Not great, but make it to the end. And it did.

So I am not worrying now, exactly, but am absolutely amazed at what more can possibly go wrong next, trying to remember The Farming Game strategy of hanging in there. There are, however, thousands of more things to go wrong in a real farm than with that game! It is wonderful, of course, to have Safeway willing to buy, because next year, when we know what we're doing better, we'll have a good reputable buyer who is local, and we can sell to some other locals as well.

The next week we had extra bins, but Safeway couldn't use them all, and we were stuck with all these bins of ripe melons! Jerry sends me around to the smaller groceries with a melon in front of my stomach, pregnant with anxiety, begging the produce managers to buy our Crimson Sweets. None of them do. But later at home I call Sentry in Goldendale, Washington, and they say they'll buy at least two bins!

Wow! A sale! Maybe this is the high my brother, Craig, gets from being a salesman!

The smaller ripe melons that the stores don't want, I take to Warm Springs and sell for fifty cents or a dollar. One of the elders now calls me Watermelon Jane, but they all say they are the sweetest, juiciest, best tasting melons they have ever eaten.

I like pulling the melons with Matt. We take turns and signal like they do in football, deciding who will be up on the bucket of Deere John loading and who will pass from the ground. One bucket of John fills a bin, by the way, and Deere John doesn't bend over to eat like Blue does.

The other morning, just after sunrise, I noticed a shadow on the hill where the river bends, and I asked Matt what he thought it looked like, and we both agreed it was George Washington watching us turn melons with our toes. It was hot work. Steamy in the canyon even at 5:00 a.m. We always pick them fresh on the day we'll deliver.

The deer still think the watermelons belong to them. The game warden gave us some firecracker kind of shells to shoot out over their heads, to move them on, but they've figured out it's only the sound of our fury, and they just stand there, happily munching. Next year we will have to plant enough to make sure there is enough for them—and us.

Yesterday we watched an older couple walking across the Safeway parking lot, carrying one of the smallest melons Safeway accepts, and it was exciting to see something we'd grown from a seed, watered from the river, picked with the help of a mule, delivered through the efforts of family and friends, end up in the arms of that couple.

How lucky we are to be living in watermelon land!

Will write more later. Hope all is well with Baby Lisa.

Love,

Jane

29

The Dirty Dozen

FALL. MORNINGS IN THE CANYON are cut with sharp scissors. The rocks stand precise against blue sky. Geese cut the silence like a cheat-grass sliver. We hear them before spying them through the early morning river mist. We watch as suddenly they lift to flight, rising high above the rimrocks, bunch grass, and pale sage. They circle, gathering others like a magnet as they climb upward, moving on to stubble fields above the canyon rim.

It is a yellow-and-gold time of year, when friends come to visit for fishing and hunting, fellowship and food. It is a slowing-down time, as the land readies to sleep—a gathering-up time, of storing food and supplies for the winter.

Matt and Melissa flew to Florida for two weeks, using their savings and help from Matt's mother and us. It was partially a reward for staying drug-free and working so hard with the watermelons and Melissa's job. It was their first "real" vacation, and the first time Melissa had met Matt's grandparents and sister.

Watermelons still speckled the field well into October, though the market had dropped early in September. We passed along some of our good fortune, taking car trunk loads of watermelons to church with us each week and donating a couple of bins to the Future Farmers of America for their annual fair barbecue. Three times that fall, we loaded the dump truck full of ripe melons, forded the river, inched on up a reptile road on Neil's side, and provided his pigs with rich, fattening fruit. Once, on a return trip, with the moon already rising over the shallow river and our dump truck, we passed a fisherman as we entered the river. Fording requires driving downstream a ways before crossing on over, and as the truck rattled down the riverbed, Matt called out to the fisherman, standing now with mouth agape: "River's too shallow to float," he said, "so we thought we'd drive down it instead."

During deer and pheasant seasons, melons still dotted the field like eggs at an Easter egg hunt. Neil said there were watermelon plants growing all over his wheat field, sprouted from seeds left in droppings by wandering deer. Bob fenced off a plant by his pump. And Jack Tedder told us of the best-tasting melon he ever ate: the cool heart of one broken open on a hot October day next to the John Day River, where he'd found it growing.

Watermelons had been a success, a little fun, and a lot of hard work. I would have preferred growing something lighter, like rose petals, but melons were in the plan again for next year.

The alfalfa had not been seeded yet. We were waiting for the fall rains, since the wheel line had never gotten assembled to irrigate the remainder of the flat.

We decided to try just a few cattle, for the winter, to see how it went. We bought hay from Neil and brought the heavy bales across the river during the cool of October. Dylan panted happily atop load after load until the red trailer broke, right in the middle of the river.

Neil and his helper unloaded the heavy bales once again, transferred them to their truck, and stacked the seventy-pound rectangles where the refrigerator and washing machine once stood.

Surveying the stack, we decided we were ready for cattle—though nothing could have prepared us for the dirty dozen.

They arrived two days before Christmas, twelve feisty calves. While we can laugh about it now, their presence—or rather their absence—eventually brought more discouragement than the plane accident and months of healing, more frustration than laying seven miles of phone line twice, and more anxiety than traveling the slick road in winter.

It seemed a simple enough project: locate and purchase a dozen calves, feed them the hay we'd brought across the river, and sell them in the spring and make "big bucks." If it were that easy, of course, there would be many rich retired ranchers (of which we knew none).

We did locate twelve calves from a rancher not fifty miles away. He sold us a dozen healthy little adolescents, their little white faces hung on red hides, though one or two looked to have some Brahman blood in them. But they were seen for such fleeting moments and at such incredible speed, it is hard to make an accurate description of the dozen who came for Christmas, but didn't stay.

But I'm ahead of myself—when we should have been ahead of those calves.

The dirty dozen rode slowly down the winding, frozen ribbon of road in Bob's cattle truck. We considered unloading them into a corral for a few days, to get them accustomed to their new surroundings. But they'd been corralled and our field was small, so this seemed an unnecessary precaution, one we would later regret not taking.

"The gates are closed, aren't they, Matt?" Jerry asked as they watched Bob back up to the gate. Matt nodded yes. (Later it was determined that he had nodded yes to another question.)

Bob backed his truck through the gate, which was promptly closed behind him. A ramp lowered from the truck allowed the dirty dozen to push forward like teenagers waiting to move into a rock concert. They were not the least bit intimidated by their new surroundings. They marched down the ramp, then inspected the field by moving along the fence perimeter in a single line, looking for any indication of our dereliction of duty.

"The gate at the upper end is closed, isn't it?" Jerry said again. "You did walk the fence line and check." Anxiously, he watched the adolescents pick up speed and move closer to the upper gates.

Matt was silent, as if thinking to be sure.

But it was too late.

Like any adolescents worth their salt, they had found our weak link.

Jerry's heart sank as the dirty dozen scampered out through the open gate like leaves skittering across a frozen pond.

"I'll head them off!" Bob shouted on a run. It seemed certain that the five-strand barbed-wire fence beyond our field would stop them, turn them back toward the open gate.

They were moving now, globs of reds and browns, heading for the fence. But instead of respecting the pointed barbs and turning back, they jumped them. Some lifted their lean bodies easily to soar over the field definers; others pushed through them, leaving behind tufts of fur.

Spots of color spread through the acres of public land, up the ravines, toward the thousands of open acres of the neighbors' land. If they weren't stopped soon, they'd disappear, would never return to our ranch, since they'd never once been fed there. They were moving to areas bereft of water but blessed with fiercely blowing winds.

The cattle guards should hold them on top, Jerry thought desperately while limping in an awkward trot toward the truck. "Maybe they'll settle down, and we can move them back down the ravines with the mules," he said aloud.

Matt ran to catch Blue, throwing blanket and saddle on the surprised animal, who was usually only ridden during deer or elk season.

But at the hilltop, Jerry and Bob saw not a quieter, settled bunch, but the continued blur of colors. The dirty dozen had disregarded the cattle guards, jumped the metal strips across the dirt road, and disappeared in a tangle of sagebrush. They had no old cow along to tell them, "Don't jump the cattle guard," or, "See that wire? It hurts."

From atop Blue, Matt scanned the frozen ground for tracks. Bob and Jerry followed footprints, too, noting the group had split.

Both gangs were heading west, driven by some unseen desire. I secretly believed they knew I wanted a weekend at the coast and had decided to torture me by getting there first.

As evening fell, I met Bob on the gravel road heading for home.

"We've had a major disaster," he said, shaking his head sadly. He told me to keep an eye out for the calves. "We'll round up some folks and horses and look for them tomorrow—wildest bunch of calves I've ever seen," he mused as he drove away.

Jerry and I both awoke at 3:00 a.m.

It was Christmas Eve. Most people were hurriedly finishing their shopping, bustling about, wrapping gifts, making last-minute preparations, readying their homes for the arrival of family and friends. Our own family would arrive the next day to spend Christmas with us for the first time since we'd moved to the homestead. I had a million things I wanted to be ready.

Instead, we asked neighbors and friends to desert their holiday preparations and help us locate the dirty dozen in a vast expanse of land.

I was embarrassed, sad, and discouraged. It seemed everything we tried on the ranch, everything we did, ended in disaster, forcing us to ask others for help, making ourselves look naive. We had wanted to be so self-sufficient!

Instead, twelve calves roamed Sherman County, lost, with no information about where their next meal would come from. The ground was frozen; water was scarce. We could lose them all, including the money we'd invested, and what little ranching pride we had left.

Jerry and I dressed and watched the first pink sunbeams filter across the canyon. When it seemed light enough to see the tracks in the snow again, we drove up the frozen road to pick up tracks along the wheat stubble. Matt had left early, whispering good-bye to Melissa, who had been bedridden since Thanksgiving by toxins filling her very-pregnant body. He'd saddled Blue in the dark and headed up the ravine last visited by the fleeing calves.

We tracked in the silence while a clear blue sky covered us. It was cold and crisp and quiet, except for the occasional call of geese overhead, the crunch of Jerry's feet against packed snow, and the slow engine hum of the truck I drove, following him. He walked across the hard, uneven stubble, scanning the horizon for our lost treasures.

We changed places after a while, and I searched the ground, seeing pheasant and deer tracks as distractions instead of the pleasures they usually gave. There were tracks everywhere, but no calves. The dirty dozen had covered acres of ground in the night, apparently never resting.

As the hours passed, our task seemed more and more hopeless. I'd seen ominous ads in the classified sections of Bend's *Bulletin: Lost. Two Hereford calves. Last seen on Butler Market Road. Reward.* I'd chuckled at the time, thinking the ad resembled a Wanted poster from the Old West.

There was nothing funny about it now, though.

By midmorning Bob arrived with his horse, and Leo and Mark, owners of the wheat lands, arrived with four-wheel-drive ATVs. The latter covered miles quickly, and by 11:00 a.m. Mark had located seven of the adolescents far from any road. "They're moving north, and boy are they in a hurry!" he said.

But before we could move on a plan for rounding them up, Leo returned to say that the other five were trotting down the gravel road, now about seven miles from the ranch.

"Let's try to corner those five at the Fields' place," Bob suggested. "They have a corral. One of you drive down to let the renters know and to secure the corral, and I'll follow with the horse."

The renters, Evan and Sherrie Schneider, seemed delighted for the diversion. Grandparents and kids awaiting Christmas events bundled themselves up to fill in missing gaps in the corral. Evan drove his truck to plug a large hole, and his father moved his car to block a side road the calves might pick if they went past the corral; an inner fence was quickly fixed to hold them if they got that far.

We waited in our places, chatting back and forth until we saw the calves in the distance. They moved like wary adolescents. There was some delay in a thicket of sagebrush below the house. Eventually, four came out of the sage. They hesitated. We were quiet. I held my breath.

They moved along the driveway with Bob pushing gently on his horse. As they trotted through the gate and into the corral, we closed in behind them, rushing quickly to latch the gate.

Four were in detention!

We took a moment to catch our breaths, and Matt said he didn't understand why the critters were being so difficult. "All we want to do is give them feed and water."

"It's what you plan to do after that, I think, that bothers them," Sherrie said. "Apparently, they want to renegotiate their contract."

A fifth calf remained in the sagebrush. "He was exhausted," Leo said. "But we could rope him and drag him into the corral. He just collapsed back there from his all-nighter."

The experienced ranchers scratched their cowboy-hatted heads, with Bob finally noting that dragging a tired calf like that could kill it. We stood around, grandparents, renters, kids, and ranchers, deciding, finally, not to risk a calf's death, but to hope it would move into the corral on its own to be with its mates.

It seemed the humane thing to do.

"Let's check on him," Leo said, and we walked back to where the desperate, exhausted calf had collapsed.

He was gone!

"So much for mercy!" I said.

His tracks headed east, but we decided to focus on the other seven spotted an hour before, seven miles back. Mark located that group again with the ATV, and we dropped off Matt, along with Evan (who had deserted the holiday preparations) to walk a mile or so behind the seven, moving them into a ravine toward another old corral on Elsie Drinkard's old place.

They were within mere feet of the opening of that pen when they bolted and split up again, two disappearing down another gravel road and three heading back up the ravine they had just trotted down.

Leo roped one of the calves running down the road, and we lifted it onto the back of the truck and delivered it to the corral holding four of its buddies.

The calves in the ravine were so scattered now, so much wilder, we decided to let them be, bring feed up to them, and hope in a few days they'd settle down enough that we could try to round them up again.

The ranchers left, but Matt and Jerry and I decided to track the "exhausted" calf we had so compassionately not roped earlier. The tracks disappeared into a scab patch of sagebrush, rock, and ravine that sliced two wheat fields. Matt and I walked on either side, looking for a blotch of red.

"He's here!" Matt yelped. "He's lying down in the sagebrush."

Jerry came from behind with the pickup, threw Matt a rope with a caution to be careful. The next sound I heard was *"Umph!"* and a mournful wail, and I just knew Matt was dead or brain-injured.

I rushed through the thick sage to see Matt picking himself up from the frozen ground, rubbing his neck and shoulder. "I was just gonna put the rope on, and he ran right over me!" he said, astonished.

We watched the "exhausted" calf bound easily up the hill.

The calf headed toward the renters' corral, at least a mile away. By now, Jerry's back was killing him, and Matt had a very sore head. My bad foot hurt too, but I was in the best shape to follow the calf on foot over the stubble fields and fences that he jumped with ease.

Jerry and Matt rushed back to the holiday preparers to let them know we were heading their way once again. People and cars were cheerfully moved into place.

The calf stayed ahead of me, stopping just short of the corral. Jerry, Matt, the holiday gatherers, and I formed a circle as best we could to slowly move in on him. He looked at us. Then at the corral. Then at us. Then at me.

He must have known I was the weak link. He made one mad rush toward me. I couldn't head him off. He disappeared again down the sage-brush ravine.

Dusk sank into our world, bringing fatigue and cold. We had less than half of our five-thousand-dollar investment rounded up. We'd need to bring up water and feed to the captured ones, and maybe the renegades, too. We would need to start the process all over again the next day. Christmas Day.

A sad Matt headed back with Blue, while Jerry and I took another drive to see if the other six were anywhere within sight. We saw nothing. But they were there. We knew it. Plotting, as only adolescents can.

We drove home in the dark. Silently. I didn't think I could feel worse. It seemed time to sell everything we had and do something excruciatingly predictable for the rest of our lives.

We talked of calling everyone planning to join us for Christmas to tell them not to come, that we'd need to track calves instead of host a Christmas feast. I'd had no time to clean or bake. Dog hair filled the cracks in the floor, which was waiting to be vacuumed.

But before we could decide, we met Matt and Melissa in their car on the driveway.

"Melissa's water broke," Matt said excitedly through the car window. "We're going to have a baby!"

A month early.

Matt called an hour later to say the baby was breach and they would have to drive to Yakima, an hour farther away, for a Cesarean section.

30

Miracles in the Midst of Mayhem

ONCE AGAIN, IN THE MIDST of disaster, we were blessed beyond measure.

Despite the catastrophe of Christmas Eve, we didn't uninvite the family. On Christmas Day, we took food and water to the five adolescents, left hay in the ravine for the six still on the lam, and wondered where the "exhausted" twelfth calf might end up. Our family accepted a less-than-clean house and shared stories they'd heard of people losing calves, letting us know we were not alone.

Jerry's parents made the trip with mine. My sister's whole family—minus a married son—had driven down the frozen road. Sandy made it. Bob and Marion joined us for part of the day. Even Matt made it back from Yakima in time for leftover turkey.

He called before midnight on Christmas Eve, announcing that a five-pound baby girl had arrived safely into the world. "Melissa and Mariah Nicole are doing fine, Grandma," he said proudly, washing away the pain of the day. They'd chosen an old pioneer name to honor the wind that always seemed to blow across the Point.

All had gone well.

Melissa never went into labor, never had to deal with exceptional pain. Matt was with her for the surgery and birth.

Melissa hadn't had to drive the road to work during the worst of the winter; the delivery, though early, had come on a day without blizzard or ice. Melissa planned to take six weeks off from her "summer job" that had expanded so she wouldn't have to drive with the baby, even if the weather got worse.

They arrived home two days after Christmas—mother, baby, and dad. When Matt handed me the bundle as light as flower petals, I thought it must be the diaper bag. Instead, it was Mariah, with auburn hair and blue eyes. She had lost a few ounces and now weighed less than five pounds.

Jerry held her, not his first grandchild, but the youngest and the only girl. She wrapped her hand around his stubby finger, snuggled her little body back and forth in the blanket, and like Cupid's arrow, pierced the hearts of those around her.

"The doctor said my uterus is damaged, and that's why she's so small and never turned around," Melissa said, hovering over the bundle. "He was surprised I could even get pregnant!"

"We have to take her in and have her bilirubin checked," Matt said. "Her count isn't right."

But other than that, she was the perfect Christmas present, another miracle in the midst of mayhem.

The dogs were wild with excitement, never seeing such a tiny moving doll before. They sprawled in front of the couch, welcoming the newest addition.

Jerry celebrated New Year's by catching prize fish, two huge steelheads, both of them nearly thirty-six inches long. He could barely hold them both up for the picture he had me take of him and the fish in front of the Christmas tree.

"How about a picture of the two of us?" I suggested. But Jerry was anxious to drive the steelhead up to Bob's for review. "Guess I know where I stand, below two dead fish," I chided him as he kissed my forehead hurriedly, rushing out the door with his catch.

Though Matt would have loved to go fishing, his new family kept him occupied, away from the river. They spent the next week in the guest room getting acquainted. Hansel sniffed and whistled impatiently when either Jerry or I held Mariah and didn't seem the least disturbed when the family of three moved into their expanded living space next to the shop.

We'd invested in another used trailer and converted it into living room, laundry room, bath, and bedroom, leaving the fifth wheel to serve as kitchen, bath, dining room, and nursery.

The work of leveling, connecting, skirting, and insulating had taken several weeks in the fall. The arrival of Mariah pushed the project's completion.

For the first week of her life, Mariah made daily hundred-mile round trips to The Dalles for blood checks until we suggested Matt and Melissa tell the doctor how far out they lived, and he said, "Oh, just come once a week, then."

On one of the trips, even though they had driven the four-wheel-drive pickup out, it had snowed and then thawed before they drove back in. The truck slid on the ridge above the house, stopping just at the edge of the nine-hundred-foot ravine. Matt had cautiously stepped out into the darkness, his heart thumping, then he lay on his back in wet snow and pulled chains onto the tires before inching the truck home with Melissa holding the baby.

Melissa still shook when they got to the house. I held her trembling body, knowing how that road could swallow one's courage.

Melissa worked the night shifts again, and they'd purchased their own used car in the fall. So when she readied herself to return to work, Matt could watch Mariah in the evenings until Melissa drove home around nine in the morning. On days I was home, and Melissa needed to sleep or had late meetings, I watched Mariah, bringing her up to my book-lined office, rocking her cradle with my foot as I wrote.

When she was awake, there was little writing time, and my admiration for busy mothers grew!

A little chair I'd bought at a sale when Jerry was buying up siding and tools all those years before sat next to my desk. "It'll be yours some day, Mariah," I told her, the closest thing to a granddaughter I'd ever have.

In January we had word about another miracle—another of the dirty dozen survived.

A rancher on the paved highway thirteen miles away called to say he had a stray calf he thought was ours. Jerry and Matt picked him up and, along with the other five, moved them home, to a corral this time, built inside a closed fence.

They settled down slowly and once broke through a closed gate and hustled upriver, but Matt was able to coax them back with the promise of a steady meal.

In February, while we were clearing sagebrush from the benches, the renters at the Fields' place called to say two calves were hanging around their corral. Jerry and Matt managed to crowd them inside with the help of the renters (minus their holiday visitors), and eventually those two were loaded into the trailer and brought home.

We only lacked four.

Watermelons replaced our interest in prodigal calves as March approached. Matt planted the five acres on the flat with a hardy wheat designed to be a windbreak. The watermelons would be planted later, in the middle, in rows, with grain on either side to protect the seedlings as they grew.

The greenhouse came next, designed and built by Jerry and Matt with plans to start cantaloupe plants and other varieties of watermelons there. "We'll plant them below the bench, closer to the house, so maybe the deer will leave them alone," Jerry explained.

The alfalfa and oats planted the preceding fall sprouted, a whisker of green across the flat toward the river.

Hansel hounded me for walks, especially in the spring. Chukars cackled in the rocks, pairing up, finding mates. Pheasants, too. I watched the dogs carefully then, making sure they didn't start hunting, since birds were mating and setting on eggs. Lupine bloomed blue in scattered patches on the hillsides. A lone blue heron perched on the roof of the house, sometimes on the rock ledge, driving the dogs crazy. Eventually, he moved to the shop, swooping out to startle us as he headed for the river and a mate.

The spring runoff proved higher than usual, challenging the dikes with its abundance.

It was March, and the dogs and I walked by the river, careful to avoid the soft, high banks that broke off easily in spring, as they had with Matt and the tractor.

Josie drank from the river's edge; Hansel stepped in and back out, shaking water from his wiry back. Sections of logs and roots, and piles of tumbleweeds and grassy trash bobbed along on the high water, making me dizzy as I watched.

"Let's get away from this section," I said to the dogs, talking as though they knew what I meant. "Come on, Josie, Hansel," I yelled, noticing the wind picking up. "We'll go down by the pumps. It's not so steep there."

Josie turned and came immediately, her speckled body trotting to my side. Hansel turned too, but then stopped, slowing, sliding backward, the river seeming to pull at his back legs, drawing him into the water.

Why doesn't he swim? I wondered. *The current's not that swift.*

And then, with dread, I saw his eyes just as his head disappeared under the water, and I knew: he was having a seizure!

I ran toward the river, screaming for Matt as I jumped into the water, oblivious to its depth or speed or temperature. I grabbed at Hansel, yanking his muscular body up on the side. But his convulsions were so violent, the bank so rocky and steep, that he tossed himself back into the river, his head sinking under, dirty water pouring over his convulsing brown frame.

Jerry was gone. Into the wind, I screamed for Matt.

Again I plunged into the water, losing my footing on the slimy moss of the rocks, not able to see the bottom through the muddy turbulence. I pulled at Hansel, crying at the heavy, wet, jerking dog, panting, and dragging him onto the bank, praying in gasps, *Please don't die! Please don't die.*

Again his violent convulsions pitched him back into the swirling, swift river.

This time he lay on his side, and his whole body went under as I helplessly watched my dog float out into the speed of the current, now boiling with wind-whipped whitecaps.

Since the plane crash, I no longer marveled at how thoughts could rush so quickly through my head. *He's dead!* I thought, watching through eyes blurred with tears. *He's dead and will just go on out to the ocean!*

I sloshed out of the water toward the shore, half turning my back on him, crying. Wet jeans cooled against my legs in the March breeze. My feet squished in wet shoes.

I looked back to say good-bye.

Just then, Hansel's neck caught up on a rock, giving me a few seconds to consider dragging him in, before he was taken on to the Columbia and out to sea. He was farther out, but he had stopped drifting momentarily. I didn't want him to just feed some vulture or coyote pups in his death. Disregarding the sense of it, I plunged back into the river to pull in my dead friend.

To get to him, and behind him, I had to go deeper, grab and tug harder. But it didn't matter. I knew he was dead, and I didn't need to be gentle.

The current pushed stronger against my legs. I surged deeper, in water up to my chest. I tried not to look at the water racing by almost at eye level, bumping the sagebrush along.

Reaching Hansel, I sloshed behind him and his rock, using most of my energy just to stay upright. Then with extra adrenaline, I unhooked his neck from the rock and pushed him toward the shore, pulling, then dragging, finally heaving and hauling his heavy, wet body up on the bank. I gasped for breath.

He was dead. Just like that. It was March. I should have remembered.

Grief's icy fingers clamped my heart as I knelt, pulling tiny rocks and twigs from his still beard, patting his wet body, wondering if CPR might have helped.

Then the miracle. Hansel started to breathe!

He wasn't dead!

He gasped and spit and suddenly, breathing his fast, panting breath, he gulped into the phase that last time preceded his snarling and growling at me! I grabbed a sagebrush root and held it tightly like a weapon, backing up. I yelled again for Matt at the top of my lungs, hoping he'd hear me, though he was inside their trailer and the wind hadn't stopped.

Hansel's fast breathing slowed. His eyes opened. Menacing stillness. He sat up, pulling his lips back, lowered his head, bobbing, turning to me. I raised the sagebrush root in protection…but then he turned, moving away from me this time, limping, wobbling from the bank, away from the river, up toward the house.

Matt had heard my last scream and already headed down to the river in his car. He picked up Josie and me, and we roared back to the house, following the direction Hansel headed.

"I thought you'd been bitten by a snake," Matt said as we sped up the hill, "and had panicked and picked it up." He pointed to my sagebrush root I still held.

We reached the house without finding Hansel, then looked down across the flat and saw a brown spot standing not far from the barn. He came when I called, looking sheepish again, but whole and alive. I put him into the kennel, still cautious. He jumped the chain-link fence, something he'd never done before or since, and stood on the deck, looking in through the living-room window with his pleading eyes until I opened the door and let him in.

He sat beside me while I called the vet.

Before we could get him to his scheduled appointment, he had another seizure, just two days later. Dennis and Sherrie and Matt's mother (visiting her new granddaughter) were all there. They had been enlisted to plant cantaloupe and watermelon seeds in hundreds of tiny trays housed in the greenhouse.

Hansel had his seizure by the shop this time, where everyone could see it.

"My mom's dog has diabetic seizures," Sherrie said, watching Hansel's spasms, "and she gives it Karo syrup when that happens." Matt ran into the trailer and grabbed pancake syrup. Jerry tried to pour some into Hansel's mouth as he panted, but more covered the dog's beard than went in.

As he came out of it, I warned the others.

We stood far back, and Dennis talked easily to him. Hansel looked warily around, sought out Josie, then sniffed at her, covering her with the syrup as well. Then he wobbled over to Jerry and finally to me, sheepish again, but not growling or mad, nuzzling my hand.

I took him into the upstairs double shower with me, lathering him up with shampoo.

That afternoon Sherrie and I drove him to Goldendale for the tests that diagnosed the problem: not a brain tumor, not diabetes, not an allergy, not leftover pain from an injury, not hypoglycemia, but epilepsy, as simple as that.

"He doesn't have that many seizures, so medication wouldn't be worth it," the veterinarian said. "Just put him in a safe place when they happen. Let him come out on his own. I doubt he'll ever hurt you. It's just like a seizure a person would have."

We drove home, relieved. He would have others, I knew. I would have to be wary, especially in March, when the river was high.

The dog meant too much to me, I supposed. He'd shared each part of our dream, was such an important piece of my life. But I'd been foolhardy to jump into the river, though Jerry never said it aloud when I told him. Hansel was almost family, and I was appreciative once again, despite the mayhem and disasters, that he'd survived his river ravage.

"With careful tending," I told him, patting his body as he slept next to my side of the bed, "you'll be around for the big event this year, the final chapter, when we plant the vineyard on Starvation Point."

And he was.

31

Grape Expectations

IT WAS THE FIRST THING NOAH DID, though he must have had the vision long before he left.

We wondered. Did he snip the cuttings from a family vineyard, then wrap the tender shoots in wet wood shavings left scattered on the ground around his finished ark? Did he keep them cool, maybe in a manger beneath his mules' hay? When he stepped off the rolling ship to a slowly drying land, did he stand with his wife, rest his arm on her shoulder, and talk with his sons while surveying the earth and the soil? Did he hover over the pruning and planting? That spring, in March 1988, we felt a kinship with Noah.

Thunderclouds rolled along the canyon ridges. The air smelled fresh, cool. A meadowlark warbled from the windshield of the plane wreckage, saw the cat inside, and hopped to a sagebrush top near the pump house. Other birds chattered and cheeped, their calls echoing within the still canyon walls. Cats curled on the haystack top.

Jerry reached into the sawdust and pulled out a bundle of plants. He broke open the tie, tossing aside the Cabernet Sauvignon label. A damp scent, like the woods after a rain, exhaled from the tangle of roots.

We each grasped a plant eight inches below the woody stem and cut the tangled roots with pruning shears.

It was a drastic step that made us wonder if we'd cut too much.

When the roots were trimmed, we turned to the slender stems, looked for the healthiest one, and cut the others off. Then, on the single stem, we cut the tops to just above two tiny nubs of buds—another drastic step.

What if we cut the branch that would have grown the most? What if the buds we pruned off were stronger than most? Can cutting these plants back really be healthy?

We snipped and clipped for hours in the March coolness, eventually trusting that as it is with living, pruning back is sometimes what's supposed to happen.

Arrow, Matt and Melissa's new pup, rolled on the cuttings we discarded, snuggling his malamute fur into sawdust and roots. Hansel lay with front feet crossed in a perfect *X.* Dylan, jealous of the attention focused on Mariah, had run off just three weeks before, and Hansel was content lying there, watching us snip. Josie stayed warm in the house.

When the bundle was finished, we sank the plants into a tank of water settled on the flat bed of the truck. In the morning we'd take the tank and the three hundred or so water-fat plants and nestle them securely into the newly cleared land.

The pruning became soothing work, with a rhythm and flow that sweetened the soul. My mind drifted. *It will be at least five years from planting to first harvest. A long time. Mariah will be in kindergarten before the grapes glisten in the hot sun, ready for harvest.*

Then it was time to plant.

David Moore helped us decide to start the vineyard at last. He and Millie had been our carpool partners on that first vineyard tour eight years before, sharing our enthusiasm for the grapes.

But in the spring of 1988, David was dying. He'd visited us the previous fall, looking "off his feed"; a few weeks later the cancer was diagnosed. He was younger than Jerry.

The bird's-beaks he loved bloomed, and this year David couldn't get to them. So we dug some, placed them in a pot, and took them to him after church. We'd started visiting him and Millie every Sunday, just to be there with them for a while.

"Do you feel up to driving out to the top of the Point," I asked him one Sunday in March, "to see the grapes on the benches?"

"I don't know," he'd answered hoarsely. "We'll have to wait and see."

David died before the week was out. One morning, at dawn, his soft hand patted Millie's head as she rested it on his chest in the parlor of their century-old home—and then he was gone.

We had not known David long or well, but he had epitomized neighborliness to us, a man kind and generous, always giving of his time. He loved animals and wildflowers, too, and no spring would ever bring the bird's-beaks with their rich but fleeting color without the memory of David—and the fleetingness of life—falling gently on our minds.

The grapes were the biggest investment of all and, it seemed, the greatest decision of faith. We knew now that capturing a dream took all the room in one's heart that could be given, took all the energy, sacrifice, and sweat a body could gather. But it was what we'd set out to do, as part of our homesteading dream that led to a life we both loved.

With help from a well-known Oregon vineyard in the Willamette Valley, we began. Years earlier we'd visited the vineyard, met the winemaker, and watched as field hands tended the vines.

I remembered the June visit as sultry green. Rows of broad-leaved vines spread out as far as the eye could see, furled across the black hills like emerald ribbons on a brunette's head.

Over the phone, their vineyard manager ordered plants and cuttings for us from a nursery they used; he also negotiated with a neighboring vineyard for other starts that would work best in our soil.

"Do you think we'll need the mule trailer?" I wondered aloud as we readied to leave, having no sense of how much room twenty-five hundred one-year-old plants and twenty-six hundred grape cuttings might take.

"Better bring it to be safe," Jerry had said.

We'd left on the five-hour trip just after dawn with the bird's-beaks splashed purple across the hills. We drove up the reptile road, out along the Columbia River, bypassing Portland, then headed south to the heart of the Willamette Valley and the gently rolling hills of Dundee.

The vineyard manager, younger than I imagined he would be, greeted us with an open smile that took up most of his tanned face. His hands looked like Jerry's: wide and callused, with rich black soil buried in the lines of his palms. "Glad you could make it," he said, touching his hat in greeting. "We've been waiting for you."

A small tractor and trailer pulled up next to ours, and in less than thirty minutes the plants were loaded into the back, stacked halfway up to the ceiling, covering half the floor that usually housed four mules. A tangle of roots, like a sleepy child's hair, flowed out from each tight bundle, making the groupings as long as blooming gladioli. A tiny label attached to each bundle read Cabernet Sauvignon, naming the variety.

"We usually pull and bundle these year-old plants in packs of fifty," the manager said. "But these were so big and hardy, we packed them in bunches of twenty-five instead."

I wondered how he knew that all that grew needed extra stamina to survive on Starvation Point.

The cuttings—resembling grocery-size bunches of asparagus without the buds—were stacked like cordwood in the other two mule stalls. Their little tags read Sauvignon Blanc. "There's a sawdust place down the road," the manager told us as I shakily handed him the check that emptied our savings account.

"Shovel your trailer full, bury the plants, and keep the sawdust moist. It'll keep the plants healthy until you're ready to put them into the ground."

He gave Jerry more specific suggestions for pruning and preparing the earth and promised us help in any way we might need; advice or suggestions could be had with a call.

I was still reeling from having made the decision. We had nothing now to bail us out if things went wrong—no money in the bank, no plane to sell for extra funds. I also worried that our bodies were weaker than they'd been when we'd begun almost ten years before. Still, we'd survived, even when the odds should have sent us away.

As we drove out past the rows of vines dotted by the red and black hats of the workers, I wondered how I could feel so delighted about something so expensive that was going to take so many years of hard work.

Farther down the road, we filled the trailer with the rusty red shavings and drove farther south to pick up a posthole digger and a packer Jerry had located in the classified ads.

Our twenty-hour day ended back at the ranch, with the dogs barking in greeting, and the new day already beginning.

Before we left to pick up the grapes, we had readied the land. With the little Ferguson, now known as the "swimming tractor," Matt had plowed the fingers of the bench, slowly turning deep black earth, plowing under the wildflowers and grasses. Few rocks interfered with his work.

In the ravines between the fingers of bench land, sagebrush, rabbit brush, and bunch grasses grew as they had for a hundred years, untouched by human hands. But the bench fields had never been tilled, never nourished a crop. Somehow, the knowledge that we were cutting into virgin soil created a greater responsibility to be good stewards. Such changing of the soil had to be done with reverence and care.

When the ground was ready, we planted grass seed (given to us by a friend) that would grow between the rows and protect the young leaves from the abrasive sand and wind. Matt packed the grass seed firmly with the roller pulled behind the tractor, preventing the ever-present spring winds from blowing the seed away.

When the land was ready, he drove across the thin driveway, which ran like a lifeline through the palm of a hand, to clear another section nearer the house, the piece that had burned black just three years before. With Deere John, we dug up the rocks that peppered the acres below the rimrocks like puddles on the meandering road.

"Over there!" Jerry—the rock warden—would yell above Deere John's steady diesel hum, pointing to some rock that Matt and I couldn't see.

The little rocks seemed to have rolled from the top of the rimrock ledges. But other, larger ones, were embedded deep beneath the soil. I remembered stories of early settlers believing that the devil planted rocks that always sprouted in the spring. As we maneuvered Deere John's bucket to pull and wrench them from their resting places, I decided the pioneers must have been right. Some boulders took a steel bar pushed beneath them, with Matt's already-tanned arms and back pulling and pushing to loosen their holds in the ground. Some we left, vowing to work around them, as they were merely the tops of huge *rock*bergs buried in the clinging earth.

We loaded all sizes of rocks into the tractor's bucket and slowly walked the tractor to a spot below the house path, dumping the rocks into a rocky ravine. Deere John had certainly proven his versatility.

Then, with the arrival of the cuttings, we were ready for the truly hard work!

Each day Matt and Jerry stretched a wire that had a red marker every six feet. We wanted those lines to be as straight as we could make them, because we'd be looking at those rows for the next hundred years!

At each red mark on the wire, Matt stopped the little tractor and lowered the attached posthole digger so Jerry or I could guide the giant corkscrew two feet into the ground. We dug as many holes as we thought we could plant in a day, usually three or four hundred.

On days I was at Warm Springs, Jerry crossed the river in the boat to pick up Jullie Mikkalo, who helped plant, again leaving her baby with Grandma. When I was home, Matt and I planted together, with Jerry dropping the vines next to the holes.

Matt could sink two plants a minute into the deep holes, spread the roots, pull the dirt around, pat, pat with his knuckles, pull more dirt, and leave the buds above the ground level. Then he'd pat, pat again, pulling moist dirt up over the top of the vine, then pat, pat the top into a little anthill shape over the buds, keeping moisture inside for as long as we could.

I could do a plant every forty-five seconds or so. My knuckles bled, even wearing gloves. My knees soon had scabs. I tried sitting and sinking the plants, walking on my gluteus maximus between the rows, but by the second day I could hardly sit down anywhere and walked strangely bowlegged.

The weekend before we were expecting friends to visit, Jerry knelt beside me as I finished up a plant. "Look," he said pointing toward the river and the end of the row, where Matt bent to his work. A bald eagle cleared the ridge above the river and soared easily over the vineyard. Matt noticed and waved at us, a smile on his face. *He's a good man,* I thought, *like his dad.*

The hills across the water were a velvet green running to the river, which was just beginning to clear itself of the spring mud. The huge wheel line stood ready to irrigate the alfalfa field on the flat below. Water had poured through it, testing, and despite having fifty different men helping glue the pipes together after our airplane accident, there had been no leaks.

In two weeks water would be coming to the benches as well, to nourish the grapes and the hill around the house.

The eagle soared out over the melon field where the windbreaks were coming on strong, then it swooped back over us. My Warm Springs friends always said the presence of an eagle was a good omen. The dogs sat up from their sleep in the sun. We heard a pheasant call; geese honked so loudly as they nested in the high rocks that we laughed, not able to hear each other talk. The sun was a soft caress across our arms and faces.

Jerry took my hand, looking at the chipped, short nails. I truly didn't miss my manicurist.

We didn't need to say what each of us felt at that moment, hand in hand, awed by the luxury of our lives and the privilege of living in this place. Having changed and worked together, with family and friends, the way our ancestors might have done years and years before, we now basked in a wonderful glow of peace.

We had almost finished pruning and planting by the weekend, when Blair and David Fredstrom visited, bringing their Suburban loaded with Daisy, children, fishing poles, and Blair's trusty walking crutches.

They joined us and Mariah, while Matt and Melissa spent an anniversary weekend alone in Washington State.

Blair was a special friend. Together we'd been through my divorce, my meeting Jerry, and our subsequent marriage, and together we'd also survived her spinal tumor and celebrated the birth of her beautiful children. We had worked side by side at the clinic in Bend and then made the adjustment from being coworkers, to colleague and boss and, finally, to the important relationship of best friends.

Our moving had been the hardest for Blair, who was disabled by her body's limitations and unable to visit much or help. We wrote often, though, and called at least weekly once the phone was in. She'd been the most skeptical about our remoteness.

On this visit Blair wanted to help. "I always sit and watch everyone else do things," she'd said, her blue eyes flashing irritation at her slender, immobile legs.

So while her husband, David, walked along the river with five-year-old Eric, occasionally throwing in a line, hoping to catch a chinook salmon, Annie entertained Mariah in the truck, and Blair made her way slowly down the steep hill using her crutches. She then maneuvered herself into the little red car for the short drive to the grape plants waiting near the pump house.

There, she, Jerry, and I snipped and clipped, pruning and plunging plants into the tank.

"You love it here, don't you," Blair said later, almost in wonder, as I limped a bit, fixing supper. Hansel sniffed into the refrigerator when the door opened; Josie lay sprawled on her back before the stove.

I nodded. "It's so incredible to me sometimes that we've been allowed so much pleasure in one lifetime."

"But it's been so much work!" She agonized for us.

"I read this diary, once," I said, turning to her, a spoon half raised in my hand, "in the book *Covered Wagon Women,* of a homesteader named Margaret Frink who came across the Oregon Trail in 1850. One sentence really stuck out. She said, 'I think none of us have realized until now the perils of this undertaking.' It was like that for Jerry and me, too. We had no idea that it would be so hard. And halfway through, when we knew it, like Margaret, it was really too late to turn back.

"And if we had, we'd have missed all this. Jerry and I are here together. We can see changes in ourselves and in Matt and Melissa, and even in our friends. You'd never have spent weekends with us living in Bend," I reminded her.

She nodded, her arms crossed, resting on the island counter.

"That much time together changes people—either kills them or brings them closer," I said.

I knew she understood.

We finished our evening meal, and while Eric plunked tunelessly on the piano, Annie opened her belated birthday present from us, oohing and aahing at The Chronicles of Narnia in her delightful eleven-year-old way.

Then Blair handed me my belated gift, a long, hard package the size of a portrait. But before I could open it, the phone rang. It was Ken and Nancy Tedder, checking on the grape progress.

"Jerry cut the phone line with the posthole digger when he was planting vines," I told Ken, laughing, "right where he made us cut across the field to avoid a splice."

I absently began unwrapping the present while I talked, but Blair signaled me to stop. She didn't want me to open it until I could give it my full attention.

Returning to the table, I knew why.

She'd given a gift she'd made herself, one that spoke of the richness of this place, of all we'd accomplished—but none of it alone.

As I walked around the table to hug her and thank her for her generous, thoughtful gift, through the dining-room window I caught a glimpse of the vineyard, now just dark ground with whispers of grass beginning to sprout.

Some day, it would be different, in a future I could now begin to see as Jerry had envisioned all along: there would be stakes and trellises and vines inching their way across the fields toward the river; we'd compromise with the deer, deal with the weather, and survive the hard work; friends would come to share the beauty, maybe even to help harvest; Mariah would walk with the dogs through the leafy rows, then stroll beside the river while white-faced cattle paused to watch her pass; Jerry would eventually have another plane to fly over the fields and land on the flat.

A double rainbow rose from Mikkalos' hill, ending in the vineyard. There'd be other strange and wonderful events. Other people would enter our lives, fulfilling the picture we'd once had of a refuge with a year-round water supply, a long growing season, and room for family and friends—family and friends who had been there to help us accomplish our dream and taste such a sweetness to the soul.

I hugged Blair. We both blinked back tears. Then I turned the gift around for Jerry to see. He smiled when he saw the gift that said it all: "A true friend," Blair had cross-stitched, "is the rarest of all blessings."

Struggling through the joys and heartaches of homesteading, we'd had the luxury of finding that out.

Journal Entry, December 1, 1988

On the craggy rimrocks outside my window perch two blue herons, their slender necks sucked in against the winter winds. They quietly survey our ranch, where many changes have occurred in the past year—changes we hope denote some progress.

The tall sagebrush that once entangled walkers to the river is gone. Instead, a field of green alfalfa spreads across the flat to John Day's banks. From the haystack of our first harvest, we now feed Jerry's mules and eventually, again, some calves.

If the herons looked a little north, they'd see the field where watermelons *didn't* grow this year. First the wild winds blew away the windbreak we planted. Then they blew a hundred trays of melon seeds to nothingness, just two days after planting. But melons will grow there next year—we have faith they will!

And a little closer to the barn stands a new corral and loading chute, where just before Christmas last year, the twelve frisky calves arrived—and then disappeared through the open gate. We tracked down eight by Easter. The last four miraculously arrived home in August, putting a new meaning to the phrase, "Wait till the cows come home!"

The two trailers, attached together, sit beside the barn, available for visitors. This fall, Matt, Melissa, and Mariah moved into Wasco to be closer to civilization and to Melissa's job. Matt will spend days working here again in the spring.

The lawn our friends the Tedders planted around the house grew and replaced the volunteer watermelon plants that sprouted after family and friends spit seeds from the deck as we gorged ourselves with tasty melons. Irrigation water from the river flows up around the house, forming a circle of green to protect us from range fires we might face in the future. A few more trees sprouted leaves. We beat the deer to three peaches, five pears, and some apples in the little orchard we began. The roses that line the driveway bloomed until our first frost this week.

But the biggest change is the five acres of grapes. Another twenty-six hundred cuttings will cover an additional five acres next spring, in fields yet to be cleared behind the barn, below the house and where the garden used to be.

Our first harvest (if we outwit the birds and deer, who both find the grapes quite intriguing) is expected in the fall of '93.

As we survey the year, we realize once again that God has blessed us beyond what we deserve. I have a job I enjoy, now working three days a week at the Warm Springs Indian Reservation. Jerry and I completed some photographic/writing projects *together* (and lived to tell about it!). I sold a few stories to magazines I admire. Friends and family braved our primitive road to visit. Despite Jerry's bad back and hip, we filled all our deer tags; he also went elk hunting and took the dogs pheasant hunting, and he still fishes quite a bit. Our freezer is full.

We have worked hard and endured much. Still, I sometimes gaze out over this homestead and wonder what we have done to inherit such beauty, such love, such bounty as we have experienced here at the river.

On old Oregon maps, it says we live on Starvation Point. We could call it Harvest Point, instead. For we have not starved during our grand adventure in homesteading. We have feasted beyond measure.

Part IV

THE HARVEST OF STARVATION POINT

Again foul weather shall not change my mind,
but in the shade I will believe what in the sun I loved.

—HENRY DAVID THOREAU,
Explorations

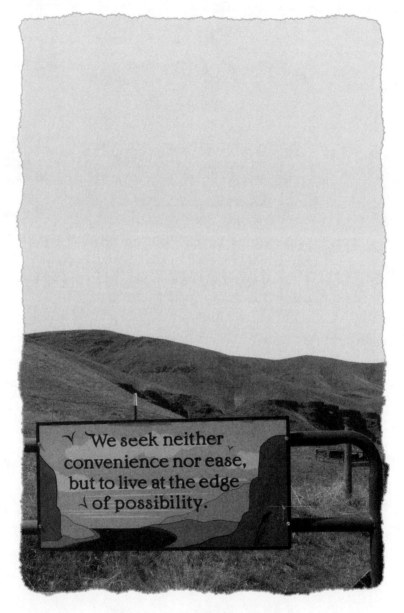

The sign on our "gated community."

32

Harvest

"WHEN WE GET YOUR LETTERS," Nancy Tedder of the airplane crash wrote, "we don't read them right away. We wait until after supper. Then we turn off the TV, and someone reads them aloud, because they're like chapters in a book."

Her words sparked the idea that perhaps I could write a book, not a novel—I'd never written fiction—not even a how-to book, but a book about our story, of coming to this land, told to encourage others to seek their passion, to follow their dreams, to step out on that cloud of faith believing they wouldn't fall through.

I'd written essays and had a few published since we'd moved to the homestead. One even earned an award through the Willamette Writers group in 1988. But Nancy's words provided for me the first experience of what author Madeline L'Engle notes about the creative process, that when we create, "we cocreate." We cocreate with Spirit and we cocreate with readers. Nancy's words suggested I could create something of worth with my words. Perhaps writing our story would be the next step in my charge to "go to the land and write." Who knew how that might affect others? I didn't imagine how it would affect us.

So late in 1989, in the evening after work at Warm Springs, I'd open my heavy old Kaypro computer and try to tell the story of our coming to the land. The process helped provide meaning to the tragedies and disappointments, put the joys into new perspective. After ten chapters, I wrote a massive proposal, big as a college term paper. It was seventy pages long and included all sorts of reviews of other books in print, why I thought I could write an entire book, and who on earth I thought would ever read it. I sent the proposal off to "Editorial" with a prayer and a self-addressed stamped envelope. Six months later a call came from Word Inc., a publisher then in Texas, asking if the manuscript was still available. When I said yes, they offered me money to complete it.

The good news: I had convinced someone that our adventure might make a good story. The bad news: I had no idea if I could tell it. But I began, and with the editorial help of Sue Ann Jones, especially, I completed it.

In 1991, a day before my forty-fifth birthday, a package found me at Warm Springs at the Head Start offices. Inside the package was my first book, titled *Homestead*. I'd wanted to call it *A Sweetness to the Soul* from the Proverb that says desire realized is sweet to the soul, but I learned then that writers rarely get to choose their titles.

The book soon went into a second printing and was chosen as a selection for the Word Book Club, and before long, letters arrived from people saying the book brought joy to their lives. And more, that our journey encouraged their own journeys, journeys that had nothing to do with moving to a place similar to our rattlesnake-and-rock ranch. They wrote of journeys to start again after a fire, or to endure a difficult pregnancy, or to trust that good things could come from tragedy.

Homestead sold nearly thirty-five thousand copies, went out of print, came back, went out, kept going, like a long-distance runner taking a water break. The letters continued too. People asked about our grapes and watermelons, how our children were, how Jerry's back fared. Was I still at Warm Springs? Had I written anything else? Some asked if they could visit. They told of reading the book aloud to a wife or husband, of feeling too old to still pursue a dream until they read the book, of wanting a life with the challenge, even if it all didn't go well.

The letters warmed our lives. I continued to write, mostly features for newspapers and magazines, an occasional devotional for *Guideposts*. Our lives were filled with ranching, my commuting to Warm Springs, and staying in contact with Matt and Melissa and Mariah as they moved from Wasco to The Dalles to other towns in the mid-Columbia region. We saw them rarely, though occasionally Matt would ask for work. We always had work.

That fall, Sherrie Gant gave birth to a baby, and a day later, Jerry's daughter and son-in-law, Joe, adopted Joe's granddaughter, Madison. We had new babies to think of.

Evenings I felt tired, and writing didn't seem all that important to my days. After all, I'd written that one book I believed everyone had in them. Perhaps that was enough.

After an essay about Jerry teaching me how to fish appeared in a national magazine, I received calls and letters from men telling me they hoped their wives felt the same way about fishing, as part of the mosaic of their marriages. Their responses, and a fiction author (who said that if an essay touches people, then the nonfiction writer can cross over to fiction) suggested that maybe I could write a novel, though I didn't know if I could create a compelling story, and I had no story in mind at the time.

Eleven novels later—the most recent released in 2005—and twenty years after we began building, we are still here beside the river. Writing brought hope and healing into our lives. "Go to the land and write" was the inner voice that spoke to my heart. Writing became a harvest.

Since that first book, many readers have asked, "What happened next?" The stories that follow share other fruits of our land, what has come to us and through us, from our living at the edge of possibility. It is our yield, our harvest. But the word *yield* also means knowing where one is going but sometimes having to step aside, to wait for God's timing.

33

The Dream Catcher

IN MY SMALL OFFICE on the reservation, I eavesdropped. I've learned, since then, that such behavior is a common habit of writers, who snatch conversations at restaurants or bus stops, pulling images into the web of imagination, often transforming words that later appear in characters' mouths.

Carolyn's tone of hesitation drew me from my papers that day in 1994. "No, I don't have a reliable Lamaze partner," my office mate said. "The baby's father travels a lot. He works construction."

I'd shared the office with Carolyn Strong, a Warm Springs tribal member, for about three years. I knew a lot about this tall, attractive Paiute-and-Yakima woman: she had finished her college degree as a single mother, she had sisters and brothers and her mother close by, and she'd birthed three children already. She had plenty of people she could ask to be her birthing partner. Surely, she'd find someone she could call upon.

I was in a birthing process of my own, trying to write my first novel, which I called *A Sweetness to the Soul*. My Lummi tribal friend, Jewell Minnick, helped me contact a number of elders to interview about the historical Sherar family that had once lived as neighbors to the Wasco, Warm Springs, and Paiute people. Jewell's daughter, Sunmiet, gave me permission to use her lovely name for an important character in the book.

The story had grown from a little essay written by Donald von Borstel, a Sherman County man, now in his seventies, who as a boy had won a contest with his words about his ancestors. I'd fallen in love with the story. I couldn't write it, of course. It wasn't my family story. It had to be told as fiction, and I'd never written fiction and I wasn't a historian. But Jerry urged me to write it down. "If someone doesn't like your version, they can write their own," he said with the absolute power of assurance that floated like breath around whatever he imagined.

I decided the only time I had to write was between 4:00 and 7:00 a.m., when all I'd been doing was sleeping. Even though I wasn't a morning person, I determined that for the duration of the novel writing, I could get up at 4:00 a.m. and commit to being at the computer by 5:00, setting aside sore throats and the harpies of critics sitting behind me and asking me, *Who do you think you are to tell a story of someone not even in your family? Who do you think you are to be writing a story with Indians in it when you're not one? Who are you to be writing a story about a landscape you've barely moved to? Why, you're not even a writer,* the voices said, shrouded in black like those harpies in Greek plays that announce bad things.

But one morning I committed. Not to write the great American novel or to get Oprah to know my name, but to tell the story I'd been given the best way I knew how and to trust that I was not alone in the telling. I committed to "showing up, to assuming the position of a writer."

The next day Jerry and I had gone to a historical society meeting, and I sat beside a stranger. "What do you do?" he asked after the initial formalities of name and address were exchanged. "I'm a writer," I said and didn't flinch, didn't present disclaimers, for the very first time. Even though *Homestead* was published and I'd written for fifty magazine markets worldwide, I didn't consider myself a writer until that moment. "What are you working on?" he asked, and I said "I'm writing the story of Jane and Joseph Sherar and their lives with the Wasco, Warm Springs, and Paiute people." I had not yet written a sentence. But I'd done the hardest work. I'd made the commitment. "You should meet my cousin," the man said. When I asked why, he said, "Because she owns the property that their original homestead was on, before it went back to being a part of the reservation. I'm sure she'd let you walk there." And she did.

That day the hairs on my arm stood up. Only later did I find the quotation from Goethe that hangs in my office and keeps the harpies silent for a time:

> Until one is committed, there is hesitancy, the chance to draw back, always ineffectiveness, concerning all acts of initiative and creation. There is one elementary truth the ignorance of which kills countless ideas and splendid plans: that the moment one definitely commits oneself, then Providence moves too. All sorts of things occur to help one that would never otherwise have occurred.

Beginning that day, I'd set my alarm for 4:00 a.m. and give myself until 5:00 to show up or talk myself out of it. Often I had a sore throat, and I was sure it would be bronchitis by the end of the day, if I didn't stay in bed and take care of it. But that commitment got me up, that belief that I was to go to the land "and write," and I wouldn't be alone in this storytelling. Writer Carolyn Myss in her book *Anatomy of the Spirit* notes that the throat is the area of the body signaling *commitment,* a word that in ancient times referred to banking. A commitment was a promise, a deposit one made, against which one could later draw. For me, it became a reservoir to return to when I became lost or uncertain.

One result of showing up each morning that early was freedom from guilt about not helping Jerry. After all, at 4:00 a.m., he was still sleeping. It energized me, so when I began my day at Warm Springs, I'd already accomplished something I'd set my mind to do. Desire realized carries an amazing amount of fuel.

I'd nearly completed the manuscript I called *A Sweetness to the Soul* when I overheard Carolyn, my office mate. I'd found an agent willing to represent me, and she'd shown the proposal to an interested publisher. Now all I had to do was finish the book, which was teaching me some surprising things about myself.

Jane and Joseph Sherar, the historical couple whose story I fictionalized, posed real parallels to my own experience. Joseph Sherar, born in the 1830s, was a builder, as Jerry had been before his injury. The age difference between Joseph and his wife, Jane, was sixteen years, as it is for Jerry and me. They had a crazy dream, to build a hotel in a remote river canyon and to build a bridge across a raging stream that would open eastern Oregon to settlement. Jerry and I had been homesteading, so to speak, for ten years on our remote site where, like the Sherars, people thought we had stepped off the end of the world. The Sherars accomplished their dream by living with integrity with their neighbors—Wasco, Warm Springs, and Paiute, the very tribe I worked for. And finally, another parallel: Jane and Joseph had no children of their own.

Jerry and I would never have children together. As I mentioned before, I'd had a hysterectomy two weeks after we were married, the year I turned thirty. Years of pain and discomfort, of ovarian surgeries and embedded IUDs, preceded my meeting and marrying a man who already had three children and a vasectomy. Those factors made the irrevocable decision to have a hysterectomy easier when it finally came time to decide.

Helping raise Jerry's youngest son, who arrived as a bouncing fourteen-year-old brandishing his independence and teenage bravado, gave me the sense that I probably wasn't cut out to be a parent after all. I'd always felt a little nervous around younger children, never sure why. I wondered if Jane Sherar, the woman I fictionalized, had wanted children and been unable to have them, or if the loss of nearly all her siblings in one week had simply made her decide that parenting was not for her either.

But my nearly ten years of working at the Early Childhood Center on the reservation changed me. Children changed me with their wide eyes, their absolute honesty, their clamor for stories and laps. Some days I grieved again what would never be for me, the role children might have played in my life.

"I'll try to have someone by the first class," I heard Carolyn say before she hung up the phone.

I'd told my agent that I thought I could write three more stories set in the frontier, about couples who had a passion for something, but truthfully, I didn't know if I could even finish the first one in what I called my Dream-catcher Collection. Then a course Jerry and I took about goal setting asked us to name experiences in life we wished to have. "Naming desires increases the likelihood you'll reach for that," the instructor told us. I'd never have children, but at Warm Springs, I found I loved them. And the idea of being present at the birth of an infant was a desire I finally named. Something in Carolyn's voice told me she might be open to my claiming that desire.

"Would you consider having me as your Lamaze partner?" I asked her when she hung up the phone. "I know you have your mom and lots of sisters. And friends. But the classes are held the night I'm here. I think I could get to the hospital in time, even though I live two hours away. I'm not an Indian or anything…"

She didn't interrupt me. She'd never interrupt me; it wasn't her way. But she did start to smile. "I'd like that very much," she said, and she turned to call the instructor back, giving her my name as her birthing partner.

I loved the classes, taking in new information, seeing what I might be able to do to coach my friend. Some nights the baby's father joined us, and she had two coaches, and no one seemed to mind. The videos they showed of new life entering the world brought tears to my eyes, and I prayed for a healthy baby that would meet the desires of more than one heart.

Meanwhile, back at the ranch, the grapes weren't doing well. I'd begun to refer to them as the "wistful vineyard." We'd look out at the fields in the morning and wistfully wonder if we should invest in worms to improve the soil. Or maybe we should deer-fence the five acres, an expensive and awkward proposition, given that the fields were planted on fingers of hills with deep ravines in between. Except for the field nearest the house. That field ran along the driveway and, with effort, could be fenced.

But all the vines were being eaten to nubbins, and after six years we had not one harvest. We'd plastered the vines with combinations of bone and blood, assured by the advertisements in agricultural magazines that the deer would leave such putrid-smelling stuff alone, and we apologized to the deliverymen who brought them. The deer did ignore the vines until we irrigated and washed the scent away. We hung fragrant soap on the vines, and the wind wreaked havoc as it had with the watermelons, our windbreak trees having died despite our efforts at steady watering.

So we'd returned to the idea of fencing at least the field nearest the house and just letting the rest of the vines go.

We planned a "steak for stake" party, inviting people from the class we'd taken in Portland, along with family and friends from both Bend and Warm Springs, though Carolyn decided not to come. It was getting near her delivery time, and she didn't want to bring on labor by riding down our road.

It was a grand weekend! We'd asked Mike and Kathy who ran the Wasco Deli and Goose Pit Saloon to cater our affair. We promised people that if they'd pound grape stakes (and help build the fence), we'd feed them steak. We planned an early Saturday work time, with the steak served around 2:00 p.m. Six hours of work from fifty or so people would mean a great deal, and we hoped to make it fun.

Jack and Carol Tedder of the *first* phone line came a few days early to prepare for the work crews. I worried over having enough tasks that people could actually help with and marveled that some places are entirely run by volunteers. Several helpers planned to spend the weekend in their tents and bring their kids and dogs, so we readied a Sunday-morning breakfast for maybe thirty as well. My parents came and did what parents do when their children come up with these unusual schemes: they cleaned, cooked, ran equipment, shook their heads in wonder. We'd be setting eight-foot posts and using Deere John to run the high wire along them. Inside the fence, we'd pound stakes at every plant. We needed to extend the irrigation system to the far end, so some helpers would be dispatched with shovels to do the hard work of digging. We'd done all the planning we could do. With our history of disaster, I could just imagine what might happen on our steak-for-stake day.

The morning broke balmy and beautiful, as gorgeous a May morning as we'd ever known. No wind, all still as a grape growing. People pushed out of their tents or arrived down the dusty road. Neighbors showed up, too, to stake a plant or two, to watch the babies, to keep the dogs from interfering. Bob and Marion Boynton came, from whom we'd bought our homestead, and the caterers arrived, saying this was just the best party they'd catered in a very long time.

One of Jerry's hunting friends, who'd first learned of us by reading *Homestead*, arrived with his shorthair dog, Duchess. He noticed our dog, Gus-Gus, looked thin. "He has lost some weight," I said. "I thought maybe it was because it was spring and he was finally free to be out and to run. He's only eighteen months old. Still just a pup."

"Just looks to me like he's struggling a bit," Chuck said. His shorthair dog was a constant companion for him and for the people in nursing homes he took her to visit. He knew his dogs.

"I'll take him to the vet next week," I said. "Just to check and see."

Meanwhile, Gus-Gus with his white whiskers sniffed at every new car, new knee, new arrival.

We made our volunteers stop working at 2:00 p.m. and told them they'd earned their steaks. We still had quite a bit left to do to finish pulling the wire around the posts, but we'd made a tremendous start, and with some hired help, Jerry thought we'd be able to finish the fence in a week or two.

But after a lunch of steak and salad and watermelon and jugs of iced tea and dessert, people put their plates down and headed back to work! They trimmed my roses, cut weeds along the fence, reshaped a birch tree that needed TLC. The men worked together to roll wire and lift it, working out their strategies, standing around talking, pointing, then pitching in to work. Women dug irrigation ditches beneath the wings of red-tailed hawks. Golden eagles wound their way through high winds, nestling on the rocks above the river, seemingly amazed at this activity on Starvation Point.

People worked until dusk, until Jerry nearly dropped with fatigue. They would have kept on if we'd had lights, the men from Portland saying it was the most fun they'd had in a long time; others suggested we should charge them for this activity. These hardworking people spent most of their days at desks, on phones where deals were sealed over dinner, not pushing with their shoulders to steady a post or "play" with the handles of a backhoe, getting Deere John to perform at his best.

The next morning several people stayed to finish the fencing. Oh, we still had the gates to set. We'd have wires to string so we could begin trellising the vines. Black plastic purchased from the former Rancho Rajneeshpuram upriver would get placed for irrigation, but for the first time since we'd set all those plants in the ground seven years before, it looked like a real vineyard and not just a wistful one.

By the time the last person packed up camp (with only one sprained ankle and no bee stings or rattlesnake sightings at all), I was ready to drop, secretly hopeful that everyone would just leave so I could fall into bed. Never mind that the sun wouldn't set for another four hours.

Instead, a phone call came from Carolyn's teenage daughter. "Mom's gone into labor. We'll meet you at the hospital in Madras."

I'd driven that road between Starvation Point and Madras each week for nine years. I knew it took me two hours and ten minutes to the reservation, though Madras was a little closer. Still, if I could make it in less than two hours, it would be a miracle. I just wanted to make it in time to be useful.

I pulled into the emergency room parking lot at Mountain View Hospital and rushed into the birthing ward. I met Carolyn in the hall.

"What are you doing out here?" I asked. "Shouldn't you be…somewhere?"

"False alarm," she said. "It's just as well," she added. "I want to have this baby when Dr. Nakamura is on duty. He's my favorite."

"I'm not sure that can be planned," I said.

She smiled. "We'll see," she told me, then apologized I'd had to drive so far for nothing.

"It's not for nothing. Now we know. I can be here. Especially if you call early like you did this time."

Two weeks later, while working at Warm Springs on a Friday, something I rarely did, I was called and told that Carolyn had gone into labor. I was asked to meet her at Mountain View Hospital. "Who's the doctor on call?" I asked.

"Dr. Nakamura."

I remembered what I was supposed to: when to breathe, what to think about, how to make Carolyn comfortable. The baby's father said he was on his way, but Carolyn hadn't seen him for several days, so she wasn't sure. Her mother came by and talked for a time, in between Carolyn's sharp bursts of breath mixed with pain. A sister-in-law, some friends, all added their support, until it was nearly 7:00 p.m. and Carolyn wondered if this baby would ever arrive; we wondered if the change in nurses would mean a change in the on-call doctor as well.

In the closet of the birthing room we found a poster showing positions that might ease labor pains, and we tried them all (Carolyn did, I should say!), finding one where she squatted to be best at releasing pain. I'd read somewhere that this was the position used by women delivering in wilderness places, women without the privilege of a birthing bed. It helped. Carolyn never cried out. I held cool washcloths to her head, gave her ice to chew, and every now and then, the doctor came by to check progress. We heard birthing pains in the next room, waved at family and friends of another Warm Springs woman groaning on the other side of Carolyn's wall.

Then, too late for the spinal block that Carolyn thought she was ready for, the doctor said, "It's happening."

In the catch of a breath, Carolyn delivered the small dark head crowning out into the world, so slippery I was sure the doctor would drop her as he said, "It's a girl!" But he didn't. I remembered to pray at that moment, to pray her from that watery world into our own, to welcome her into a life filled with family, tradition, laughter, and love. Tears welled, and I found myself speechless, even as Carolyn asked, "Is she all right? Let me see my baby."

Dr. Nakamura laid the baby on her mother's belly. Nurses oohed and aahed and commented on the dark thatch of hair. The doctor congratulated Carolyn, and then he said he'd cut the cord.

"Jane can," Carolyn told him, offering me an honor kept for the baby's father, had he been there.

And so I cut the cord, that length of lifeline, trusting that this infant would breathe now on her own, fill her body with nutrients brought from her mother's breast, not from this slender thread. The placenta followed, and for a moment I didn't know what the doctor lifted, a mass as round as the fry bread that had nurtured this infant for nine months.

Carolyn named the baby Lorissa. Then the nurses lifted her from Carolyn, cleaned and swaddled her, prepared to return her to Carolyn's arms. "Would you like to hold her?" Carolyn asked.

I would and did, marveling at the fullness of my heart.

I drove home at midnight beneath a full moon. It was June 4. I'd had an experience I thought I'd never have, but I did, just for the asking, for naming the desire and making the commitment. It was a desire realized, a sweetness to the soul.

I suppose, like many childless people, having dogs around met a nurturing need. Gus-Gus, the German wirehair pointer we'd purchased after Hansel died of old age, had never spent a day in a kennel. Driving to Idaho through a snowstorm to buy him from the breeder, he slept his first night on the pillow between Jerry and me. He often nibbled at Jerry's white beard, a patch of hair I thought might remind him of his mother's wiry fur. He was a bird dog, and Jerry, who often held back from falling in love with a dog, usually keeping them as working-only, spoiled Gus-Gus as much as I did, buying him toys. He even bought him a green frog toy that the dog would drop into his empty cowboy boots and then point, as though it was a chukar game bird or quail. Gus wanted the frog whenever we drove in the car and once startled our friend Blair in her wheelchair by dropping the frog wet and sloppy in her lap as she cooked.

For eight weeks while he and I attended obedience school, Gus went with me to Warm Springs. Once or twice I brought him in for the kids to meet. Whatever kind of tired I felt at day's end, this whiskered pup greeted me at the trailer door ready to run. He wouldn't be denied.

Today Gus-Gus panted in the seat next to me on the way to the vet in Goldendale, Washington, fifty miles away. It was the week after the steak-for-stake party. He did look thinner, and I'd caught him both coughing up and emptying another part of his anatomy after the steak-for-stake. But I thought maybe he'd just been eating scraps from too many plates.

The vet drew blood, x-rayed him, and brought my attention to his panting. "Does he do that all the time?" I had to confess that I didn't remember.

"I'm not a very good mother," I said. "I hadn't noticed."

The x-rays came back. "He's got a huge abscess in his lungs," the vet said. Even I could see it, like a series of shoestrings tangled together in a mass. "Might be a cheat grass he aspirated, and it's gotten infected. Could be something else. We'll send the blood work off to Pullman, Washington, to the vet school and see what they say. Meanwhile, let's get him on some antibiotics and see if we can break this thing down."

I drove Gus home from the vet, feeling guilty that I hadn't noticed his illness in all the ruckus of vineyards and births. The vet called on a Saturday to tell me the test results. I'd been working on the novel, hoping to have it finished before the Fourth of July. "It isn't cancer," the vet said. "But he's pretty sick. Bring him in again next week. We'll see how that growth is responding."

Gus lay on the couch in my office, and I knelt beside him. "You don't have cancer. Isn't that good?" He stared at me, and I fully expected him to talk. Instead, he put his paw over my arm to hold me there, if only for a moment longer. "I miss our walks," I told him. I didn't want to say anything about how wheezy he was. *Why hadn't I noticed it sooner?*

"Maybe you should leave him here," the vet said when I brought him in later that week.

"Why?" I asked. She didn't say anything. "Oh, in case he gets sicker, you mean. Well, I can always bring him back. It's only fifty miles," I said. Later I'd look at that interchange as an example of a time in my life when I chose not to tell myself the truth.

A week later, Carolyn, Baby Lorissa's mother, gave me a dreamcatcher she'd had made for me to hang in my car as a remembrance of Lorissa's arrival in the world. Dreamcatchers are placed above a child's bed and are meant to catch bad dreams in their weblike structure. Those dreams burn up in the morning sun, while good dreams soar on through the hole in the center for the child to race after into the future.

I'd chased the dream to write a novel, and I had. I finished *A Sweetness to the Soul* on July 3. It was to be the first in my Dreamcatcher Collection: much to my surprise, Multnomah Publishers had contracted with me for a collection of four books about frontier couples. Carolyn gave me permission to fictionalize a portion of Lorissa's birth that had become part of my first novel. Finishing the book, I felt like a mother giving birth myself.

July 3 fell on a Friday. I noticed that Gus hadn't eaten much for a couple of days. I called the vet and asked if I could bring him in.

The vet chatted amiably with me while he took more blood. He and his wife had read *Homestead* and loved it, he said. I'd mentioned the vet's office in it, but he commented on the part about our following our hearts, being willing to step out onto a cloud of faith, trusting we wouldn't fall through. "It's been a journey," I said. "My first novel will come out next year, and I actually have contracts to write more. Imagine that."

He x-rayed Gus, then performed some procedure to scope inside his lungs. When the vet pulled the swab out, the tiny end was reddish black. I knew that wasn't good. "We'll culture this and get back to you on Monday," he said. He held the door while I carried Gus-Gus out to the car. I laid the dog in the backseat. "If he gets worse, you can call me," he said. "I'm on call this weekend. They'll page me at the regular hospital."

"Vets are paged by the hospital?"

"In small towns, it works," he said.

I drove home chattering to Gus, and he actually stood up, paws on the console that separated the front seats. He panted, but not as hard as usual, and I offered him a small piece of cheese, which he ate. This was hopeful. At home, I carried him into the house and laid him on the couch, still not believing that this was anything more than just a little hiatus in his puppy development. He lifted his head when I came to sit beside him with a book in my hand, treating myself to a good read after finishing the birthing of "my baby." He laid his head in my lap, and I petted that rough beard that caught seeds when he ran through the grasses and held bits of cheese when I shared pieces with him. I had such hopes he would do those things again.

But within minutes, Gus thrust himself off my lap onto the floor in a massive seizure.

I shouted for Jerry, who ran in from the yard and knelt to hold the dog. Gus's right side now lay still as sunset, while his left legs flailed in the air.

I dialed the hospital, dialed it wrong, forgot to add the area code, couldn't remember the vet's name, tried to calm myself, asked the dispatcher to page the on-call vet, which they did. I hung up. Gus lay with his head in Jerry's lap. He'd had a stroke of some kind. He wouldn't want to live that way. The phone rang. I turned to answer it. Gus sighed his last sigh.

We drove him back to Goldendale for an autopsy. The vet wondered what Gus had died from. I couldn't watch, but Jerry did, talking softly with the vet as he worked. They found cancer in all his organs, his heart, lungs, liver, kidney, with only 10 percent of his lungs or heart even able to function. "He lived on love," the vet said. "That's all that kept him alive."

It was early evening when we finished with the autopsy. My eyes were puffy from crying, and we'd have to drive home and bury him yet. The vet said his wife would be pleased if we'd care to come to their home for a meal before heading back. We accepted the kind diversion of grief.

In less than a month, we'd seen a new baby girl brought into the world safe and healthy. The vineyard fence stood tight, the gates set in place. Good friends had graced our homestead. I'd finished my first novel, and now we were saying good-bye to a friend. Life was full of ups and downs, joys and disappointments. All that remained constant was family, friends, and faith.

"I don't want another dog," I told Jerry that night after we buried Gus-Gus in the bank behind the house. We put his water dish and green frog on top of the mound. "I can't believe how much I miss him. He was only a dog, I know. But…"

Losing Hansel had been painful enough. Jerry sought another hunting dog, and I'd thought maybe I could hold back so if something happened I wouldn't be affected. I knew people who lived with that protective philosophy. The price we paid for attaching was the grief we felt when those we loved left us.

"I miss him too," Jerry said. Even now, ten years later, I feel the ache for that dog, reminding me of the deaths of family members, making me wonder again how one survives the morass of loss.

"Every dream has shreds in it, I guess," I said. "Like old shattered silk."

"But think of the joy he gave you," my positive husband noted. "He had a good life, though it was only for eighteen months. But you took a risk, and what's the alternative? To never give your heart away, to live so you don't have to experience the pain? I don't think so," Jerry said. "We'll fall in love again," he said. "That's what life is about."

It was Mariah that following January, the month after she turned seven, who would bring the next dog into our days—and a new dream growing from the ashes of disaster.

34

Who Would Believe?

A SWEETNESS TO THE SOUL was accepted by the publisher, and the process of writing revisions began. I knew that the second book would be based on the story of Jerry's great-grandmother, who had been lost from a wagon train, found by native people, and raised by them until she was a teen. It was a story his mother had told me the first time I met her, and I loved the way it sang of God's faithfulness, even when we don't get all the answers in life that we're seeking. *Sweetness* was scheduled for release in June 1995.

In January of that year, a different kind of sweetness arrived in our lives, though it came in a cordial of bitter. The local sheriff called to tell us that Matt and Melissa had been arrested for running a marijuana operation in their home in Wasco about twenty-five miles from our homestead. The sheriff had Mariah with him and asked whether Jerry would like to come in and get her. She had just turned seven.

Jerry called me before I left Warm Springs to alert me to the change in our lives. We didn't know how long Mariah would be with us, how substantial the charges might be, or what we could expect. But one thing was clear: we would be there for Jerry's granddaughter and, as we could, for his son and his wife.

Since Mariah's parents had moved off the homestead in 1988, we'd had an on-again, off-again relationship with Matt and Melissa. Sometimes he'd want to work for us, and he would do well; then suddenly, for no reason, he'd stop coming to work. We'd eventually go to their house, try to figure out what was getting in the way, and try again, until the next episode of distance. We knew they were financially strapped. We worried about Mariah, especially when we'd go by to visit and she'd whisper to us behind a locked door that we couldn't come in, that her mom and dad were sleeping, and that she was cold. They didn't have any water or heat. We'd make a child-neglect report, but Matt and Melissa would quickly find resources, get fire-wood, visit the food bank, and pay their electric bills. They'd moved to The Dalles, and then places closer to Hood River, and then, when Mariah was about five years old, Matt's mother and stepfather purchased a double-wide mobile home on a lovely lot in Wasco for them. It kept a roof over their head. It kept them close, with Mariah in a good, small school. In January 1995 it also apparently housed a marijuana operation.

Even though we knew that half a million grandparents nationwide were raising a grandchild, we still felt isolated and alone. What had we done wrong in raising Matt? How had we missed seeing the deterioration in his and Melissa's lives? At one of our family meetings when Mariah was still a baby, I'd cried at the thought of their leaving and moving into town—Matt had seemed happy on the ranch, and we appreciated his work. Matt's eyes had teared too. "I just hope I can make it away from here," he said. I'd wondered how we'd fare without his good help, a thought that startled me, since I'd been reluctant in the beginning to have them even come to live with us.

But our dangerous access road troubled Melissa, as it certainly did me at times. Work for both of them could more easily be found living away from the ranch. And we hoped and prayed that we'd continue to be a close part of Mariah's life as she grew.

It was a roller-coaster relationship once they left the ranch.

Because of the condition of both their home and their daughter at the time of their arrest, our children were also charged with child neglect, a charge that could later be dropped if they completed treatment and three years of probation, which they began. We were not Mariah's foster parents, but Mariah was placed with us by the juvenile court, and our life with a second grader began.

While they were still in jail, Matt and Melissa asked us to get Mariah's clothes and their dogs. They had two: a big Husky mix, and a small black Lab that looked like he might have Newfoundland or Rottweiler kin. We found a home for the Husky (Carolyn took him to Warm Springs), and we kept the puppy. Matt had named him Brody. The dog had been getting around well, chewing and tearing as puppies do. But the night of the arrest something had happened, and when we picked him up along with Mariah's clothes, he could no longer stand up.

We made another trip to the vet for x-rays. "He looks okay. Lots of worms. Maybe during the arrest he was accidentally maced," the vet said. It's a small community; everyone knows everyone's business. "But everything works?"

"Yes," I said. "We feed him, take him outside, and stand him up. He does his thing, and we bring him back in and lay him on the pillow, and he never moves." The other dogs—a short-hair named Josie and a kelpie named Abby—didn't even notice him.

We converted the guest room into Mariah's room and filled it with stuffed toys and things she wanted from home. Brody (a word describing the black circles made by bikes on paved roads) slept on her bed. During the daily drive to school and back, we listened to Mariah and comforted her as we could. "Dad told me those plants he was growing were roses, Grandma," she said. "Sometimes I think he loved those plants more than me."

"I know it seems that way, but it was the drugs that made him act like that. He really does love you. You are the most important person in your parents' world; they just haven't shown you yet. They didn't go to jail; they are going to complete treatment and stay clean." Even while I said it, I wondered if I was telling her and myself the truth.

Except for Mariah and Brody's presence, it was not an easy six months.

Mariah missed her parents terribly, worried over them, as children in such households do. Jerry drove her every morning out the reptile road to catch the bus to school. We'd pick her up at night. Some days her mother would be waiting to drive her from the mailbox, where the bus stopped, to our place, a challenge to the visitation limits. Every contact was a struggle. I was gone three days a week working, and rising early every morning to write, an activity that offered healing in an unexpected way.

We had our own righteous indignation to contend with too, our own wishing we'd done something to prevent this, never certain if what we did *enabled*—the term of the decade—or showed mercy and compassion.

Jerry took the elk horns from all the elk he'd hunted and turned them into a light fixture so Mariah could do her homework at the dining-room table. She closed down at night, telling me that her prayers weren't answered. She wanted to go home, and God wasn't letting her.

Meanwhile, Brody began combat, crawling first with his front feet. Then the back legs began working, and one day he stood up and walked, much to the amazement of Josie and Abby.

I began work on another book, and once *A Sweetness to the Soul* came out, we had another life. Bookstores invited me to come not just to sign a book but to talk about our lives on the homestead and now this new direction as a novelist. I still kept up my work at Warm Springs and reminded myself of a television show of the 1950s called *I Led Three Lives,* though I thought of it as five: rancher, writer, social worker, grandmother, and wife.

In July 1995, though Matt and Melissa's treatment went well, the tension among the four of us around Mariah was as thick as river fog. Mariah returned home. Our relationship with her parents remained strained, and soon there were obstacles to our seeing her. They were busy. No, she didn't want to go to Sunday school with us. Others monitored Mariah's care, and Matt and Melissa continued in treatment. Jerry and I found solace with each other, in the homestead, watching grapevines grow at last behind the deer fence, making hay and selling it, buying up red Angus cows and a herd bull named Bug.

In October I was asked to speak at a Christian businessmen's conference to tell the story of our homestead journey. Jerry and I received as much from the other speakers as we gave that night.

One speaker used the words of Malachi in the Old Testament, reminding us that to make a commitment and not keep it was worse than not making one at all. "I tell people, if you have a need, you write it on that memo section of the tithe check," the speaker said. "And just see if God doesn't return it tenfold."

I wondered if that could really be scriptural. I'd received some money for *Sweetness* and had written the tithe checks but had yet to send them. As usual, money was tight, and it was hard to keep that commitment we'd made to tithe our earnings from writing and the ranch. But when we got home, I read the verse again and considered what we might really need. There was nothing we lacked financially, not really. The job at Warm Springs and Jerry's retirement kept us tended. But to be affirmed that writing fiction and telling stories were part of God's plan for my life would be a gift I'd like to claim. So I wrote "award" on the memo section of the checks when we got home. I guess I sought some affirmation that someone (besides my mother and those who loved me) liked the novels I wrote. Malachi said God wanted to be tested in His faithfulness. Asking for an award of some kind was my test. I mailed the checks off and forgot them.

While the grapes looked better than ever, the first small fruits we noticed that fall were quickly consumed, not by deer this time, but by birds. Every single one. "Next year," Jerry said. "Maybe we can get those air guns that shoot into the air every few seconds. Or better, we'll put up kites shaped like owls. I've heard that works to scare off birds." The acreage was simply too big to drape with a net.

At Christmastime, Matt and Melissa and Mariah joined us for a meal. Matt had found work with a mechanic in town, Melissa at a nursing home.

They all three looked healthy and well, and Matt said he really wasn't addicted to marijuana after all. He just liked to grow things. "Grow tomatoes, then," I said.

March of the following year found us busy preparing to irrigate our alfalfa field, hoping to recover whatever we could from another spring flood. We tended new calves from the red Angus bull. I researched and wrote, used the two-plus hours on the way to Warm Springs to plot and plan—I'd pull over to write something down before I forgot it and told people traveling Highway 97 that if they saw me at the roadside, not to worry, I'd be writing. We received occasional calls from Matt or Melissa asking for things: would we pay for a phone; could we take Mariah shopping for school clothes. Finally, one day they asked if Matt could come and work for us again.

We needed the help. We always needed the help. But we were cautious.

Matt did come back to work, but the pattern continued. Within a few months he stopped coming. We vowed it would be the last time.

On the way to church on a March morning in 1996, we stopped at the mailbox. A letter from the Western Heritage Center in Oklahoma City had my name on it. Inside it told about the organization, which has given awards to literature and films for thirty years, with names like James Michener, Larry McMurtry, James Stewart, and John Wayne on the list of Wrangler winners. Then came the paragraph that amazed me. "Your novel *A Sweetness to the Soul* has been named the Outstanding Western Novel of 1995." They wished to have us come to Oklahoma City to celebrate and pick up the bronze statue and award.

Award!

Who would have believed that a first-time novelist with a book from a small Christian publisher could receive such a gift? I remembered then the memo written on the tithe check. I might never again receive any outward recognition for my effort, but now I trusted that writing the stories was worthy work. The phrase "O ye of little faith" came to mind, and I understood now how the Israelites could have forgotten God's goodness to them over time. It was so easy to forget. I hoped that this award would always be a reminder of the importance of faithfulness to God's calling in things both large and small. Keeping those commitments to tithe, to write, and to be in service mattered.

That fall, a reader of *Homestead* wrote to tell me that when she'd moved to a new job and was waiting for her husband to join her, she'd come across the book. It had helped her adjust to the change in their lives, as they, too, pursued a dream that meant trusting and adapting. We began a correspondence, and later, when she read *A Sweetness to the Soul,* she also told me how that book had touched their lives. They so wanted a child and had been unable to conceive. But while they sought the help of a specialist, her husband's spiritual life had deepened, and he'd become her partner rather than a dissenter in attending church and trusting in God's guidance. She told me that the route of their spiritual journey was of greater value to them than even conceiving a child; in fact, they now realized that their growth might never have happened if she'd gotten pregnant. Like my character in the novel, she'd discovered strength in the disappointments, and now she thanked God for both. She shared this on a day when she drove nearly two hours to hear me speak at a local church.

Later she wrote to say that she was expecting and that she'd conceived the morning she drove to that retreat when she'd prayed with gratitude that her husband's spiritual life and their relationship was the most meaningful thing in her life, more meaningful than even having a child.

The meaning of the stories I wrote down went beyond me. As author Madeleine L'Engle wrote, when artists create, we cocreate, with Spirit and with readers.

That reader's words reminded me that disappointments can't be avoided; they can only be converted into lessons, gifts, if we allow. This time, a woman's dream to conceive was answered. (They now have two darling girls and a son and are living their dream to have a ranch business of their own.) Other readers told me they loved reading a book that had a happy ending without the character's bearing children.

In 1996 *Love to Water My Soul* was published, followed by *A Gathering of Finches,* which was later adapted for stage production. The following year, 1997, my older sister died of a rare and debilitating illness. She never got to read *Mystic Sweet Communion* that came out in 1998, nor did she read the book she inspired, *A Burden Shared,* released the same year. In 1999 I continued to research and to write in those early morning hours. I added another publisher, WaterBrook Press, a division of Random House. Since the year 2000, *All Together in One Place* and six other novels have been released. Readers still cocreate, one woman telling me at a signing, "When I moved to Oregon, the man I started dating gave me *A Sweetness to the Soul* and said, 'If you want to know what kind of man I am, you read this book.' I did, and I loved it, and I'm falling in love with him. So now I want him to read *A Name of Her Own* so he'll know what matters to me."

People write to say the stories have changed their lives, that they've found new direction through the words as they seek meaning. They say they've found healing, too, inside these stories. I've given the stories birth, but I'm not the one who reaches readers. Writers are riverbeds of spirit, perhaps in ways that parents are, the conduit through which God and guidance flow.

As we approached the new century, we still had Brody bounding around. He remained with us once Mariah returned home. On more than one occasion, when we were off traveling with the books, Melissa came out to clean the house as a surprise or to bake a pie for Jerry with apples from our little orchard. Matt found work as a boat builder in a nearby town. We began having Mariah for overnights, especially at Christmas Eve, her birthday. At last it seemed we'd found a truce of sorts with family.

You, sent out beyond your recall, / Go, to the limits of your longing. The poet Rilke wrote that God whispers these words as he walks beside us in the world, ending with, *Embody me.* I don't know if I embody God within my life, but I know that none of this writing and ranching and loving another woman's children and grandchildren could ever be without our having made that first commitment to step into the wilderness and dare to desire. There is no promise in a homestead adventure that everything will turn out fine. There is only what the writer Václav Havel says defines hope: "An orientation of the spirit, an orientation of the heart," and the absolute certainty that something is worth doing, regardless of how it turns out.

In but a few months, we'd find out about the challenge of certainty mixed with hope; and I'd learn that the word *family* came from the Latin word *famalus,* which means "servant."

35

Like a Lion

"It's a little like having a lion," Rylee J. told me. She was three years old, my great-niece who had turned three two days after I turned fifty-five and four days after the birth of her new baby sister, Dally Ray. (A *dally*, by the way, is the tight twist of a lariat taken twice around the saddle horn after a steer has been roped. My sister's youngest son, Chad Hurtley, and his wife, Shorty, like my sister, are horse people.) Anyway, Rylee J. and I walked across the tarmac, me limping, a residue from the accident. We were at High Lookee Lodge, where my parents lived on the reservation. My dad called it Nooky Nooky Lodge. In his later years Dad was a little "goofy," as my Florida niece would say, confusing me sometimes with other people, worrying over things none of us could see. But the reservation staff looked after him and gave my mom rest, so after my dad's head injury, my parents' transition from living independently to the tribal assisted-living facility went well.

On a Wednesday, after work, I stopped to visit them and found Rylee J. and her mom and baby sister visiting too. The sun warmed our faces, and the smell of April sage drifted across the parking lot as Rylee J. held my hand and chattered. I'd just asked my niece what it was like having a new baby sister at home, figuring that after two months she'd have a pretty good idea of how things were going to change.

"It's like having a lion," she said.

"A lion? Do you mean like a line, something you draw on a paper, or the animal?"

"The animal," she said.

"Tell me about that," I said, thoroughly confused.

"Well, it's kind of scary," she said. "It just lays there most of the time, but then they bring it into my room, and it makes those sounds in the night like a lion, and I don't know if she'll be staying there forever making that sound or what'll happen next. Like if a lion came into my room and woke up and roared." She caught her breath. "It's like that." Ah, out of the mouths of babes.

Change—even happy change—can be like having a lion in your bedroom.

We discovered that truth at the river. Our lion, this ranch, that brings us such joy, also growls often, and we wonder at times if it will ever be quiet and calm. During the summer, so much must happen at once: grape tending, weeding, irrigating, disking and seeding, moving the bull, vaccinating cows, rescuing the yard from the dogs. We've taken on the task of mowing the lawns of a vacation home built upriver. Jerry travels with me more often to places related to my writing, which I really like, but it means we get even further behind on the ranch work. Our seasonal helper plans to return to school, and Jerry is just too tired and hurting to run this ranch alone.

We've thought of leaving. One year we thought we had a grape harvest at last, checked the sugar content of the grapes, and then almost overnight, only tiny stems were left. At the far end of the vineyard, the culprits had yet to accomplish their theft, so we caught them, red-handed. Well, they don't have hands, but we caught them anyway, thousands and thousands of yellow jackets crawling on the fruit, consuming the Cabernet Sauvignon.

Our friends, the Kralls, visited that fall, and Kay suggested that we could at least make a wonderful jelly of the few grapes left. So we did, driving nearly forty miles to the Grass Valley market for paraffin and using a deer sack for our cheesecloth. We placed the pulp in the deer bag and let it hang over a bowl in the house overnight. The fruit produced a burgundy as rich as wine, that just happened to be jelly.

It was our first harvest of grapes.

We'd also survived a major flood that once again took out the dikes. On New Year's Day, Jerry used the rowboat to move cows, stranded near the main channel of the river, while floodwater worked its way around them through the night. Portland nearly flooded that year too. For us, it meant that every weed seed in the river system was once again deposited in silty soil upon our once-thriving alfalfa field, choking the good sprouts out.

We wondered if the message that we had to "go to the land and write" was somehow being changed to "now it's time to leave."

We'd made progress, then the black hole, as Jerry called the unexplained disasters, sucked us in again. We'd claimed a portion of the newly seeded oat field when the wind came roaring up the canyon and swirled the pumice dirt across the field before we could get the water on it. That happened after the seeder (an antique) broke down. Jerry spent the day welding before the oats could even hit the dirt. We wanted the oats up a few inches before seeding alfalfa—again—so the tiny shoots could be protected by the taller grain. But water had to be on it all, and that crop year—September to September— when we usually got eight inches of rain, recorded only four. The river runoff *that* year stayed within its banks, which was good for those of us who worry about flooding; bad for those dependent on rainfall to survive.

Then came our lion, the day before we were to leave for an event in Oklahoma.

On the upside, we discovered that the woman I'd been researching (for the book *A Name of Her Own*), Marie Dorion, belonged to the Iowa tribe whose headquarters happened to be ten miles down the road from Jerry's cousin in Ponca City, Oklahoma. We also learned that the homeland of her people two hundred years ago was along the Mississippi River near LaCrosse and Prairie du Chien, Wisconsin, not far from where I grew up. I always liked those familial connections to my stories. Jerry's cousin planned an open house for us so I'd meet some of the Oklahoma Kirkpatricks. We'd head to Oklahoma City and have time with a friend, Shilo Shaw, from Warm Springs, who worked on her doctorate in psychology at Oklahoma State.

But back to Rylee J.'s lion in the bedroom. The day before we were to leave for Oklahoma, Matt and Melissa came out to visit. We had seen them infrequently over the past year and a half.

That day, with the oats partway up, the wind blowing, and irrigation water still in the river and not on the field, after nearly two years of silence, Matt proposed working again on the ranch. Oh, so scary, that lion stretching in the corner.

What choice enables someone's bad habit, and what is the natural part of relationship risk? What is hanging on to something we once loved, and what is allowing what once was to change, to become the steppingstone to something better? I didn't know if wounds could be truly healed by time and distance. Some words might never get said, because while they may be true, the hearing of them would be too much to bear. Recalling Jane Sherar's words, I wondered if we'd choose to be happy rather than being right.

"If you always do what you've always done, you'll always get what you've always gotten." If you want something different in your life, you can't wait for someone else to change. You have to change yourself. If we wanted a different outcome, then we had to do something different.

We wondered aloud if we could do this "working together" differently enough to get a "different result." What could we change? That was the question we posed at a family meeting. Jerry recalled that when Matt was interested in ranching, he was the best at it of anyone who worked for us. Matt recalled wishing he had left here differently, that he'd found some way to say what he was thinking and feeling before it grew to a roar. Yet it is so much safer and less painful to simply let the relationship fade into what it has become, the wounds healed over, no longer tender to touch.

Best to not kick a sleeping lion.

Yet relationships are both nourishing and depleting, whether distant or close. It is in working through them, coming to accept the changes and create new avenues of connection, that we find life's meaning. No guarantees that the lions won't roar, only that to pretend the lion isn't there is to invite disaster. Family is always there, just not always in the way we'd like to see it. It's what living looks like, these family drains and strains.

We were "souls in progress," to quote a writer friend of mine, Harriet Rochlin. I suppose it was what I was saying in all of my stories of women coming to terms with themselves. It is a woman's journey, I think, to do the best she can for her family without losing herself in the process. We don't always get all the answers. Some things are chewed without the satisfaction of a swallow.

So we did a trial run. We flew to Oklahoma for research and a gathering at the hall of fame there. Matt's task: to get the irrigation up and running or show good progress toward that end. (Knowing the ranch's reputation for being a black hole at times, completing it could be just too much to ask.)

The event at the hall of fame included the presence of people like Kareem Abdul Jabbar (who raises horses and who worked with a basketball program on the Blackfoot reservation in Montana). I confess, I did not even *see* the seven-foot-tall basketball legend on Friday night. I took notes in the art wing, which housed a traveling exhibit featuring the Canadian First People, trapping, and western experience. Perfect timing for my research. Later, back at the hotel, Jerry and our graduate student friend Shilo commented on Kareem Abdul Jabbar being at the reception. "He was there? I didn't see him," I said.

"How could you miss him?" Jerry said. "He's seven feet tall."

"I was looking at art," I defended.

"He is art," Shilo said, and she smiled.

We met with the Iowa tribal historian—the only day she was scheduled to be in all week—and found a warm welcome in my research efforts, but what was happening at home was never far from our thoughts.

We were gone six days and arrived back to find the pump set, the suction lines in the river, the ditches dug, repairs made to the mainlines, and all nozzles ready and checked. Matt had put a search out for replacements for two dead fuses. By Monday, the day after we got back, the fuses were located. By Tuesday all the breaks in the lines had been found and fixed, and by Wednesday water in the big gun and the wheel line sprayed across the flat. On Thursday it rained. We'd take all the moisture we could get.

The next day, we held another family meeting, worked out a few more details, including ways to keep that lion sleeping while we made this change, tried one more time to involve Matt and Melissa and Mariah in our lives at this homestead. One small step taken again, with a prayer and a hand held for confidence, we walked toward that newly watered field. We risked again. The lion slept, but we promised ourselves we'd pay attention if it roared. And, of course, it soon did.

36

To Nourish and Transform

MY PENMANSHIP ELICITS COMMENT; it always has.

My stepdaughter can't read it; her husband can. My oldest friend in the world, living in Wisconsin, reads it fine; her husband can't. Unless I write the grocery list with one of the inexpensive calligraphy pens found at the grocery store, I can rarely read it myself. *What on earth is wucce? Oh, lettuce,* I discover, after we drive the fifty-two miles back home without it, and I vow to make looped *l*'s instead of what looks like a *w*. I've been accused of harboring latent desires to be misunderstood, but it isn't that. I just developed my own style of cursive and printing, and it usually works for me.

When I sent thank-you notes after our wedding, my mother said, "You didn't write them yourself, did you?"

"Of course," I said.

She looked aghast. "But no one will know what you said."

Still, there was an advantage, in case gifts and cards were separated. I could write *Thanks so much for the present of [illegible]* and then spend the rest of the note thanking them for the *real* gift, their *presence* at our time of celebration.

My secretary at the mental health program once typed a letter I'd written, as it looked to her, then slipped the copy into my box without comment. From the moment I read *Re: Transpesting horse petal pants,* I knew I was in trouble. It was a letter to the head of the state mental health division, about *transporting hospital patients*. It only got worse after that.

"You write so beautifully," a woman said as she stood watching me sign her book. I tried to accept the compliment without comment, though I remember Jerry's saying my handwriting "looks pretty—upside down." Perhaps the most personalized book I signed occurred at the Oregon History Center author signing, my very first one for *A Sweetness to the Soul,* where a young man bought the book and then used it to propose to his girlfriend, telling me word for word what to write, and making sure she could read it!

Last fall I sat next to an author who had an article called "How to Sign Your Book." Personalize it, the author said. Don't write something vapid like *Best wishes always* or *Happy reading to one fine reader.* Instead, find out something about the reader and incorporate it if you can. I don't think misspelling their name was what the author had in mind, but it would certainly personalize it. I try to get people to write their names, because there are so many new ways to spell Sharon, Charon, Sharin or Judi, Judy, Judee. I've stopped writing *Warm regards* after I once wrote *Warm Springs* instead.

Sign on the title and signature page and draw a line through your printed name, that author advised. That apparently tells anyone who looks at the book that the author personally signed it and thus their signature is of greater import than the printed name. I've only done that once. It felt like a knife slice, drawing a black line through my name, even if I signed just below it.

It is true, though, I do write what that author would call vapid things. For me, they're comments that arrive as I finish a book, a kind of one-liner about what I hope the reader will find inside that story. For *A Gathering of Finches,* I often wrote, *May you find nurture inside Cassie's journey through longing to light.* For *A Name of Her Own,* I may write *May this woman's journey inspire your own.* Even the Kinship and Courage series had its one-liners: *May you find the hearth of your heart.* I'll vary them some and am often surprised by letters that come later, telling me how much the comment meant to a person, seemingly just what they needed to read.

Not long ago, I received an e-mail from a woman that confirmed both my poor handwriting and the value of a one-line story. She told me that her mother-in-law was dying, that she was a wonderful woman who was ready for death, and that she was at home, surrounded by her sons. "Last fall, a friend bought *What Once We Loved* for her and asked you to sign it. You did, but we're not exactly sure what you wrote," she wrote. "We think you said, 'May all your memories nourish and transform.' I know my mother-in-law would be so pleased to know if we were correct in translating what you said, and if it wouldn't be too much trouble, might you call my mother-in-law who is your biggest fan." She went on to give me the phone number and tell me that while her mother-in-law would be unable to speak to me, her sons could facilitate if I might choose to make a personal connection.

Could I call a total stranger, someone I didn't know, as she lay dying? I could.

Her son spoke briefly to me, and then another son held the phone to her ear so I could tell her that she'd read it correctly, that I did so hope all her memories would be nurturing, that that was what I hoped grief did for the characters in the book she'd read. I told her how deeply touched I was that she would want to know what I'd written, especially now, at this transition time of her life. But instead of merely listening, she pulled the oxygen mask off and told me how much the stories had meant to her, "especially the Florida story," she said, which was all she could say before she needed help to breathe again.

Her son came back on the line: "My mother grew up in Florida, and after reading *Mystic Sweet Communion*, she wanted to tell you how that story took her back. She sat down to write you a letter. She wrote and wrote, of the bay where she grew up, of the manatees, of the foliage and water, the people and passions of her Florida life. But she never sent it," he said, "deciding it was too rambling a thing to post to an author she didn't even know."

"But did she keep it?" I asked her son. "Does she still have the letter?" He asked her and then told me she'd nodded yes.

"Then that's all that matters," I told him. "Because it inspired her to write her own story, and now you, her family, have that. After she's gone, her story will remind you of the woman she was and of what she knew first and how it touched her life, and by extension, yours. Her memories did nourish and transform, then," I said. He told her that, said she nodded yes.

I don't remember what, if anything, was said after that, but I remember being humbled by this woman's responsiveness to the stories I've been privileged to tell. And by a family who wanted to give so much to such a woman, who must have inspired and encouraged them through the years in remarkable ways, for them to want to meet even this small need she'd expressed.

If I hadn't written something vapid with my creative penmanship, I might never have been told this nurturing story. More important, I wouldn't have been reminded to tell others—of how important it is to write their stories down, regardless of what inspires them.

For me, those little comments written in books, just like the little stories I tell when I speak, find their way into a hundred different hearts in a hundred different ways. It is the power of story, I believe, and that's why I can't stop listening to the stories and writing them down.

Like this one: There was a research project that followed children for thirty years to see what enabled some to make it as adults despite terrible childhoods, when other children, equally challenged by life, fell apart. The project revealed that those people who overcame their difficult pasts could each name someone whom they knew would always be there for them. Often this was a parent or a teacher. But some children named people who had very little time to demonstrate their caring: a bus driver and a postman, for example.

After I had shared this research once, a woman came to me and said, "I have a gem for you." She spoke with a British accent, her white hair telling me she might call herself an elder. "During World War II, me mum was killed. Me father treated me badly, horribly. I had a terrible life as a child, but I won't go into that. Once when I was running in the rubble of London, I fell. I lay there, knees bloody, wondering why I should even get up. I was five years old.

"Then two women dressed in black suits and wearing black hats and carrying black purses came by. One scooped me up and held me in her arms. The other took a white hand-embroidered handkerchief and pressed it to my bloody knees. It was seventy-five years ago, but I remember it as though it just happened. Those two women were not in my life for longer than five minutes, but I made a decision that day. When I grow up, I told myself, I want to be like those women."

They didn't bring her mother back. They didn't rescue her from a bad family situation. But they did what they could do. They were present, and it changed that child's life forever.

I think sometimes that's what showing up to write has meant, what coming to this ranch has meant: giving what we could and, in so doing, touching other lives, the landscape, and changing our own.

"We're named by the choices we make," author Madeline L'Engle wrote.

I write, Jerry cooks and tends the ranch. Together, we chose to homestead in our way and brought a moment of joy to a loved woman breathing her last breaths. More important, that woman allowed the stories of her past to nurture and transform her family and mine. All from the hearth of this homestead.

37

Another Windmill

MARCH 2002

Turning off the highway from Moro onto Monkland Road, I drove past five old windmills before arriving home. I've driven past them for years. (Some still have the sucker rods in use, pulling up water, when once, wooden paddles turned in the wind.) At the turn of the century, cattle would have pushed around the troughs, drinking water pulled from the dips and crannies of the rolling, treeless hills. Now most of these mills lie still, or the rods have been replaced with electrical pumps, so water rises even without wind to pull it up from springs lying deep below the surface.

Those windmills must have once been controversial, breaking up familiar landscapes of tall grasses, windswept hills, wheat fields. Perhaps they caused frowns, the way fences first surprised sheep ranchers, or the way power poles and telephone lines, though welcomed, still rose as invaders to a westerner's eyes. Gradually, we became accustomed to the windmills' presence, appreciated the conveniences they brought. We barely noticed them in passing or when their paddles became silent. Landscapes change. It is a part of living.

Today, with Mount Adams as the backdrop, there are sixteen steel windmills spinning their hundred-foot-long steel arms out across the breaks above the John Day River. We can't see them from our homestead, but we can't escape them as we drive Monkland Road toward Starvation Point. They're churning out electricity, these wind farm machines, watched by tiny purple bird's-beaks, wildflowers growing in the quarter-mile spaces left between towers.

Because they're close to the Wasco airport (where fifteen years ago in March we crashed), bright red lights flash between the towers at night. Across the ridge, toward Condon, another twenty-five or so windmills spin—or will spin—not quite as large, but breaking up the landscape too, saying, *Things change.*

My dad would have loved seeing those new windmills. He'd ask a dozen questions about how they worked (a computer controls and pitches the props to catch the wind, sending power to where it needs to be), how much electricity they'd generate (1.5 million kilowatts each, enough for our whole county), at what wind speed the arms stop (fifty miles per hour), how much the ranchers receive for the use of their land (this answer will vary, depending on who you ask). I once asked an old coyote trapper in French Glen during a Thanksgiving dinner how many coyotes a year he trapped. Just curious, I was, that was all. "Well, ma'am," he said, "that's like asking a man how much money he has in the bank." He winked and went back to chewing his turkey.

But my dad won't get to see those windmills or ask those questions. He passed away this month. Hospice volunteers, staff at the assisted-living facility on the reservation, family and friends, all celebrated his life on a Sunday afternoon, and then the next morning, we buried him in a little Civil War–era graveyard near Sisters on a crystal clear day, with the sounds of birds in the Ponderosa pines and the presence of mule deer ripping at grass in the meadow beyond. Since Dad died on the reservation, a place he loved, we brought dirt from Warm Springs to toss onto the casket as we said our last good-byes. And we gave away dozens of flowers, a tradition too on the reservation, to give things away. Dad was a farmer, and planting and the weather were things he loved, so we also witnessed to his life by giving pansies and primroses and Minnesota Frisbees (my brother's family lives in Minnesota) and little toy loons and moose for the kids. The Reservation's Full Gospel Church ladies sang songs and played their tambourines, the Presbyterians sang and played a guitar, and Sherrie Gant, who helped us build the homestead, and friends from the Baptist community brought a keyboard and played original music my dad would have loved.

I was struck by the notes and cards we received from young men (my age now) who once worked for dad on the farm helping hay, working cows, and whatnot. Even my ex-husband wrote, reminding me that my parents had moved him and his wife from Oregon to Indiana in the 1980s in a horse trailer. My dad loved adventure, and once he loved a man like a son, he never withdrew that love. My dad was a model to these men, someone loving who stood up for what he believed was right, who gained wealth by giving money to food programs and children's services, who treated others with dignity and respect, and who "thought outside the box," as one man said, before people thought that way, when that person most needed it. Good stories were shared of his learning to fly when he was in his thirties, getting a motorcycle in his fifties, and welding a tractor seat onto the back of his cycle so my mom would have comfort. They moved west in his fifties, still learning, still asking questions. Many of those questions led him to a deeper faith.

He asked questions right up until a few days before he died.

We'd gathered, my brother and our family, for a dinner in February, and while we ate breakfast the next morning, we received a call about Dad's massive heart attack. Five days later we brought him home, with hospice help and the staff who had cared for him and my mom for the past year at High Lookee Lodge. During the time of his dying, I felt blessed that our lives at Starvation Point should be wrapped around my parents' lives through the wool blanket of comfort of the Warm Springs people.

I recalled that earlier that year, after walking down the hall, he told me his heart was tired.

"It's an old heart, Dad," I said. "It might be telling you that not long and you'll be going to join your family in heaven. They'll be waiting," I said.

"And I'm going to disappoint them, because I'm not going to heaven."

"You aren't?" I asked.

"No," he told me as he eased into his chair. "I got a letter from God not long ago, and he said I wasn't going to die." *Was this his goofy thinking?* "God said I was going to live forever."

I couldn't argue with that. Christians believe they will live forever in a better place.

Before he went into a coma, while agitated and hallucinating, he asked a question I will long remember. I pray I answered it with grace. He suddenly grabbed my hand and looked me in the eye and asked, "How will I know when to go?"

"They'll come for you, Dad," I said, swallowing. "The people you love, your parents and brothers and sister, your daughter, and Jesus will hold their arms out to you, and you'll know it's where you're supposed to be, and you will go and know exactly what to do."

He relaxed then. A perfectionist at heart, he always tried to do things right, sometimes worried aloud to me about looking foolish by making a mistake. Knowing he had nothing more to do here helped him lean back and fall into an easy sleep. Over the next few days, he made few coherent comments. Mostly, he allowed us to wait on him, change him, and bathe him, while his heart slowed down. I sang to him (poor soul!) and read to him and told him stories of what his life had meant to me. My mom and I shared stories of his life and reassured him that he could go to the place where he would be whole, that he'd left her well tended in the place they were living, surrounded by people who genuinely cared.

Then, on the morning before he died, I heard him say "Palma," his sister's name. "Palma," the woman who had tended him most in his young life, was the name I heard him say last; perhaps hers were the arms he laid back into. We played music for him later that night, and I held his toes and said,

"Do you remember when you and mom used to love to dance?" He smiled, I think. It seemed like it. The next day he died.

Surrounded by my mom, my brother, Dad's grandsons (one flew in from Florida, the other from Sisters), his great-grandchildren, his sons-in-law, and his friends, we celebrated his life. That next Easter—he would have called it Resurrection Day and insisted it happened on a Monday—held special meaning for us as we sang "He Lives!" We believe he does.

My father was German, so it's fitting to remember him with something the German poet, Rainer Maria Rilke, once wrote: "I would describe myself / like a landscape I've studied / at length, in detail; / like a word I'm coming to understand." As I considered this man of eighty-four years, remembered him and what his life meant in shaping mine, I considered that landscape of his life.

He was the last of his generation to die, the youngest of six children. His passing meant a change in the landscape of my life. If stories are the sparks that light an ancestor's life, the embers we blow on to illuminate our own, then I'll be blowing on these embers for years to come as I drive home to Starvation Point. Another windmill has shut down.

38

In His Time

FIRST OF ALL, WE'RE ALL RIGHT; the house though steaming is fine, and the shop survived. All the animals made it through (the mules and horse are now in residence in the yard), and we lost no equipment. Everything else is gone, though, black as the inside of cow's stomach, as my dad would say. Smoke damage is pretty bad. The vineyard is gone, all the fence posts burned, the plants fried, the old Rajneesh black plastic irrigation pipes melted. The metal gates are standing/leaning, as the posts are missing. There goes our gated community!

The flat where we'd tried once again to get alfalfa started did not burn, though the fire went on around the river, beneath the trees we'd planted years back. All the new trees and shrubs we planted this spring are toast.

We got to see some pretty fancy flying, with BLM planes dropping borate or whatever that pink stuff is that retards flames. When it drifts, it leaves little spots on your skin that look like chicken pox. It is a humbling thing to see (looking out from the porch swing deck) a six-foot wall of flames roar over the ridge with a sixty-mile-per-hour wind behind it and to realize how little stands between the flames and...you.

The firefighters were superb. They'd come down in the morning, telling us how they'd defend the house if the fire reached our ridge, what we could do until then to help. We cleared out any debris beneath the decks, started sprinklers to water the roof and soak beneath the wooden decks. Then about thirty minutes before the crest, after the planes had done their work, after the county's grader made a fire line around the corrals and behind the barn, we were told to "Get inside the house!" The firefighters backfired at the right moment. The fire jumped the line behind the barn, but we'd had the big irrigation gun on it for several hours, so it slowed the flames enough until we could get back to it to put them out. The flames burned up and around the house, slashing into the vineyard, taking posts and high tinsel wire, too. It melted the irrigation risers, bending them ninety degrees even with water inside them. The fire melted a hole in the PVC pipe, so we lost water pressure. But by then the fire had moved on and the smoke had cleared, and we could see how so much had been spared. Jerry's gunpowder supply hadn't caught fire and exploded in the barn. No one was hurt. Our dogs panted happily, and the mule and horse thought they'd died and gone to heaven, living in the yard with shade and green grass.

I had my latest manuscript and research material in the car, along with the deeds and papers. We were going to start loading Jerry's gun collection when the firefighters said nope, just get inside, close all doors and windows, and ride it out, which we did, smoke so thick outside we couldn't even see the pear tree off the porch-swing deck.

Trying to decide what to take and what must be left is a grievous task. Once again the women of the Oregon Trail entered my mind. Choices, loving, and losses write the story of our lives.

Our landscape offers no heavy timber to burn, just sage and grass, so the big fear was the rush of air sucked by the fire, a fear lessened by keeping windows closed so sparks couldn't be lured into the house. We'd been running irrigation water since early morning on the back walls of the house and the green space around the house and the trees we planted close.

The fire burned hot enough to curl the composition on the roof in places and melted the satellite dish. Where we were wetting the house down, it steamed. The green strip around the house was a big hit, and the lines buried in 1987, while we sat with our legs in casts after the plane crashed, worked as they should have. Jerry says we'll expand the green space in case we have a return engagement!

Matt, Melissa, and Mariah came out with a friend to help when they heard in town the words *fire* and *Kirkpatricks on the Point*. Matt positioned the big guns on the shop/barn and used an extra hose to keep the back of the house watered down. They stayed to put out spotty flames and even noticed in the dusk a tiny light coming from the horse trailer near the barn. Upon checking, Matt found a rubber mat on fire there. He easily put it out.

We were never alone.

Most of the cows were at Bob's old place upriver. The few we had here were all accounted for, except two, and they've been spotted alive. The fire didn't jump the river, so our view is still lovely.

This fire began as a lightning strike at MacDonald Crossing, where the Oregon Trail crosses the John Day River, about seven miles downriver. It began there Wednesday night, and it came around the point at our place on Friday the thirteenth, midday, and crested at the house at 6:00 p.m. Firefighters stopped the raging flames about a mile beyond us, and they backfired up on top about 10:30 p.m. to stop it from burning more BLM ground. So, all in all, we're very fortunate. We'd say we had divine intervention, and for this we are exceedingly grateful.

Jerry took a photograph from across the river looking back. The ridges are all black except for two small circles of green. The BLM man directing the planes drove down a week after the fire to tell us he'd been praying for us, fearful when we'd gotten back inside the house instead of heading for the river. "God saved this place," he told us. He looked at the photograph and the tiny circle of green amid the blackened soil. "It's really a matter of perspective, whether you focus on the small green circle or the larger black," he said.

We have terminal Pollyannaitis and still carry the belief that this is part of a larger plan. So of course we'd look at the green.

Our homestead didn't look very pretty after the fire. We had more than seven miles of fences to rebuild, some in rocky ravines and up the sides of ridges. It was work that would have made even my old fence builder throw up his hands in disgust, but we'd found a contractor who was willing. (Matt decided once again to look elsewhere for work. At least we didn't hear from him after the fire. That old lion crept away without saying a word.) If we're meant to stay here on this ranch, Jerry and I decided, someone will arrive seeking work. We have plenty of work. We intend to plant trees again, hundreds of trees, God willing. It's all in His timing.

In the following spring, the profusion of wildflowers overwhelmed us, and words from Ecclesiastes rang true: "He hath made every thing beautiful in his time." I thought of that verse each day when I left home for Warm Springs to work; I thanked God for its truth. His timing is what comforted me when I realized my time at Warm Springs was coming to a close.

Her eyes, brown as cobbled dirt, pooled in tears. She was only four, and we sang "Happy Birthday" to her at the reservation preschool, her little group of Early Intervention friends surrounding the table, sitting patiently, waiting for their piece of cake. But all the excitement proved too much for Julia. Instead of smiling and enjoying the attention, she slid off her chair to hide under the table.

While the adults tried to coax her out, the children did what was needed. They simply left their little chairs and joined her underneath the table.

That little girl went on to graduate from Madras High School, and her father, a tribal member, reminded me of the birthday incident fifteen years before. He'd sent me an invitation to her graduation and a note of thanks for helping him become a "better Mr. Mom" for his two girls. My call to thank him for her photograph promoted the memory of that day beneath the table.

And so this past week has been like that for me: so much attention, so many kindnesses, so many memories of times when the people at Warm Springs took me as I was. When I was embarrassed or chagrined by something I had said or done that showed my unfamiliarity with reservation life, they simply sat beside me underneath the table, a sign of mutual respect and the ability to wait.

This was my last week as a consultant to the Early Childhood Center at Warm Springs. After seventeen years, I'd found a way to walk a different path. The time of leaving was filled with tears and joy. Teachers created silk corsages for me, a different one to wear for every day this week. Daily someone walked into my office and left a card, a gift of his or her presence, a memory, a story. A hand-fringed shawl to warm me and to witness to my courage in pursuing a dream appeared on my desk. A plant arrived from the school district staff, with words meant for people more worthy than I. At the surprise party planned by Carolyn, the mom whom I served as a birthing partner, my friend Geneva, an elder who became my "cultural broker" through the years to tell me how to understand my errors and confusions, sang a traveling song. "Because Jane isn't leaving us. She's taking a different trail." It was a song she said she sang during her most troubling time, when her son served in Desert Storm. "And he came back home. Jane has been with us in troubled times, and this is a song I want to sing for her."

We ate and laughed after that, before I was shown how much planning and preparation went into their gifting. Someone had secured the nightgown I left at my bed-and-breakfast and used it for measurements for a reversible Pendleton vest. The staff had had it made of the colors of a morning sunrise, splashed against baby blue. It fit me with perfection. An inlaid turquoise dragonfly appeared, something I'd admired during an event last April at the Museum at Warm Springs. Earrings woven in the shape of huckleberry baskets, done in the colors of blueberries and bone, now adorn my ears. A stone with a butterfly on it to "remind me of my wings" will go into the walkway someday. A wooden cross with the word *Hope* on it came from a grandmother I've known for almost seventeen years, as she's raised two troubled children and been there for them always. Cards and kindnesses appeared like wildflowers coloring my days.

My brother, Craig, and his family sent a rosebush that we planted in the garden at the center. The little boy I'd worked with for four years helped Jerry and me dig the hole, fill it with water, tend the tiny leaves. He named the rose "Friend."

At nearly 5:00 p.m., with Jerry helping me decide what needed to be shredded from my office and what could be simply tossed away, I was called out. And there in the lobby of the center sat the children and their teachers. The children had created quilt squares of their hands and names, and these had been pieced into a quilt by one of the teachers. The pieces were signed. So many. Then, long-house style, each child and teacher came up to shake my hand or hug me as they chose, to say a word or two. There was no way to hold back the tears.

"Don't be ashamed or embarrassed by them," my friend Versa said as she let me cry into her shoulder. She cried too, and so we both sat beneath that table.

Even the little boy, my rose friend, leaned close, his arms tight around me. He hadn't said much about the changes I'd been preparing him for, but this time he whispered, "I'll miss you, Jane," before he walked shoulder-slumped away.

I almost changed my mind about leaving.

Jerry and I carried things to the car, and then the director asked if I could help her. She had a mom in her office, a woman aching inside because of an incident related to her daughter. And so I spent my last hour at the center doing what it was I believed I'd been asked to do there all along. I was present, and I listened, hopefully helping this mother see how strong she was to advocate for her child, to want for her daughter what had never been there when she had been a child, to see the strength that can come from even troubled times, transforming us inside the present.

At nearly 7:00 p.m. we drove up to see my mom for a bit. She'd known about the party and the presents. "People ask what I'll do now that you're leaving, and I tell them, 'She says she's still a part of this community. And this is my home now too.'" Both of those statements were true.

One last gift was given to me that day I left Warm Springs, a gift so precious in its thoughtfulness and craft. It told me that what I did all those years of walking beside Warm Springs people was received as a gift and not as a mere taking on my part. The Wewa sisters, a Head Start teacher and a tribal council member, gave me an exquisite necklace of ivory and purple stones. The pendant itself is a tiny beaded book, no larger than a book of matches. The women beaded the title in red, *Just the Rez,* and on the back, beaded, an eagle feather. A feather is attached to the necklace as well. But there is more: the tiny beaded pendant has a clasp, and it opens to reveal a leather-bound book of six pages, on which these two sisters wrote a story. "Struggling to keep the Spirit of all that is good alive through family, traditions, and cultural values...," they wrote, "in many of our hearts, we carry burdens unshared, tears unshed, and the strength that can only be found through our Creator, the one and only God of all things. Into our midst came a woman who had the gift to write.... Few people can see beyond the physical and weave stories like the magic you have." They wrote of how my vision will change because I walked there on the rez, just as my presence changed their vision. "Perhaps one day one of our people will pick up a pen and begin to share their special story. Perhaps they will remember a gifted woman who walked among us, and take the magic of that gift to weave into their own life—and also be a writer."

Their words demonstrated that such writers exist already on the Warm Springs reservation.

These women of "the rez," these children, have written words and made stories of their gifts that touch another's heart. They signed it with a blessing, that I might walk my journey bathed in prayer.

My eyes pooled in tears as, like Julia, I sat beneath the table. My life is full, all in God's timing.

39

Enough

So it's Monday morning, and the only other people in the grocery store look like us, middle-aged to old. Retired people, couples, pushing and pointing at products. Usually, I don't shop with Jerry because it's too stressing. Once, in Florida, while visiting his daughter's family, I left a store (rather than do him in before the eyes of the spuds) because he felt I failed to pick out the proper potatoes for dinner.

But now I'm "retired," sort of, and so we can do this together on a regular basis. Oh, joy. I'm still in a state of shock that the sales of the books, contracts for more, and the farm are sufficient for us to live on full time. It's been thirteen years since my first book was published. My brother in Minnesota called me one day to say that my books would sell more "if your characters had more sex."

"My characters do have sex," I told him. "Just not where you can see them. And there's a reason for that. I have an agreement with my characters: I will not reveal any of their sexual idiosyncrasies or proclivities. In return, *they* will not reveal any of *mine*."

I was grateful that I hadn't had to resort to gynecological descriptions to find readers for the books.

"Do we need soup?" Jerry says in the store.

I gaze at him as though he's spoken in Farsi.

"I don't eat it, so I don't know," I tell him. "But go ahead and get some. Cans keep."

"No, we can wait. Do we need bread?"

"Sure. Always need bread."

"There are two loaves in the freezer, so I don't think we need to buy more," he says then. "Should we get brats?"

This is a trick question. I'm not sure if he wants brats and is trying to find out if we have them so we don't need to buy them, or if he wants to truly know if I want brats. Sometimes I think he actually wants my opinion, but most of the time his questions are opinions in disguise.

"I'll get some. They'll freeze," I tell him, which I do.

"Not those," he says, when I put them in the cart. He takes them back.

"I'll buy bacon," I tell him as he gets the "right" brats, and when he sees what I've selected, he takes the bacon back too. How could I have ever managed a million-dollar mental-health budget when I make so many mistakes, even with such little things?

By now, I'm feeling pretty inadequate, and I'm afraid to pick out even his canned corn.

This is the story of our shopping, and I am learning that perhaps the reason why on July 31 we will celebrate twenty-six years of marriage is that I've been gone three days a week for more than half our marriage. Hmm. I may be looking for work away from home soon.

But I remind myself, as I sleep in until 5:00 a.m. or even 6:00 a.m., that I am not driving two hundred miles a week now. I'm able to schedule dental and eye appointments, put off for years because I couldn't figure out where to fit them in. And the dog, Brody, believes he's died and gone to heaven as I walk with him up the reptile road every morning. Even our newest dog, Calle Rose (better known as She Who Lives on Leather) likes having me around more. I remember to buy dog crackers when Jerry doesn't. And I'm convinced that familiarity breeds trust, so the longer we spend together, Jerry and me, the easier this shopping will be.

Or else I'll bring a book and stay in the car.

Retirement—if you can call it that—began with a grand trip to Amarillo, where the weather was cool and balmy and the people warm and welcoming. From that writer's conference, we flew to Minnesota and Wisconsin, for time with my brother and a family reunion. My English teacher from Mondovi High School (who does not look a day older than she did in 1964, when I graduated) arranged a gathering of a local writer's group and then a presentation and signing at the library.

The presence in that old brick library building of so many people, mostly women, whom I'd not seen for thirty-five years, brought unexpected emotion. Women who were neighbors to my parents. Women who fed calves beside their husbands, who taught Sunday school, who drove the school bus, who taught Vacation Bible School in the little Norwegian Lutheran church down the road from our farm. Aunts and cousins, and even my old high-school heartthrob—the only man present—showed up to spill out into the sidewalk of that little library, celebrating its one hundredth birthday.

On the day of the family gathering celebrating my dad's life, the bluegrass band warmed up, and we had the only day during the week that it didn't rain. So in perfect weather we wandered the little Waste Valley schoolhouse, where I attended first grade and which is now a museum (not because I attended there, thank goodness, but because so few schoolhouses remain from that era of gathering many children in many grades). My aunt Idella, who also writes, taught in one such school. It was how she met my uncle, since schoolmarms often stayed with families during the year. She met my dad and her husband while living with my dad's family.

My dad had four brothers and one sister. He was the last of the line, but the sisters-in-law were all at the family gathering.

My brother sang "Amazing Grace," and we told stories of my dad, showing how a simple, ordinary man can touch the lives of others.

With retirement from Warm Springs after seventeen years, I discovered this homestead anew. As when we first moved here, I took time to listen to the river gurgle its way to the sea, smell the sage, and pet the cat, who arched her back against my hand as she walked along the railing. All over again I heard "go to the land and write."

In August, as though to affirm once more the power of God's grace, I interrupted my writing to attend the wedding of our goddaughter, Anne Fredstrom. I'd been researching a little historical fact, that the first book published west of the Rocky Mountains was a Nez Percé primer. The second book, the gospel of Matthew, was printed in the Nez Percé language too. The printing press that produced them was sent by the natives of Hawaii to the Nez Percé. That fact intrigued me, and I wished I knew more, because it could fit in to the story *Every Fixed Star,* which I was nearly finished writing. I located that old press at the Oregon History Center in Portland (but not the story of how the Hawaiians happened to send it to the Nez Percé people). So I supposed it would be another detail of research I would have to leave out of my book.

Off we drove to the wedding. At the reception, we began talking to the parents of Anne's matron of honor.

"When did you come to Bend?" I asked. Fifteen years ago, the man told me, after Jerry and I had already moved to our homestead.

"But I originally came from Hawaii," he said. *Hawaii!* My ears perked up. "My people were printers there. In fact," he added, as the hair rose at the back of my neck, "my great-grandparents brought the first printing press—"

"From Hawaii to the Nez Percé," I said. "In 1839."

"How would you know that," he said, aghast.

"I've been looking for you," I said.

The Halls not only had a copy of the diary written by Sarah Hall as she and her husband traveled with the press from Hawaii to the Northwest, but he even knew where in their home they could find the copy!

I could not have been more amazed or affirmed, once again, that once one "makes a commitment to something, Providence moves."

We may be retired, but we are not alone on this homestead, and perhaps never will be.

If the work part of my life continued to amaze me, so did the ranching.

One morning, in the midst of change and managing upheaval, I shot a rattlesnake. I'd just come back from taking Mariah to school, stopped off to mail a letter to a fan, then visited a friend, Alice Archer, who in her eighties still works her garden and is an avid reader. She and her husband were the first people from Moro Presbyterian Church to wind their way down our road twenty years ago. Virgil told us then that they were newcomers too, having only been in Sherman County for twenty years. Now we've been here nearly that long ourselves.

Alice finds mistakes in my books even meticulous copyeditors miss, so she always gets a free book as soon as I have approved reader copies. Anyway, while driving home, I was listening to a CD of *Every Fixed Star* with the hope I could give the go-ahead to Oasis Audio for release when the print book would be launched. It's a strange sensation to hear someone else speaking words you've written. Stranger still that I don't remember writing some of those words. Once I even thought, *I need to write that down,* and then remembered that I already had.

So I sat in the car to finish listening to a scene I did remember writing, when Marie and her husband are trying to come to terms with a blended family, with issues related to how much is enough when it comes to children and stepchildren, how much we can give without giving ourselves away. It sounded as I'd wanted it to: the reader Barbara Rosenblat, giving just the right accent, just as I imagined Louie, the character in the book, would have sounded.

I left the car, transitioning to thoughts of Jerry's bad cold and increasingly aching back. I hiked up the wooden walk, waiting for Brody. We call this dog Mr. Pig for short, and he showed up in one of my series. Today I expected him to bound down the walk as he usually did, but instead he stood barking stiffly beyond the cement steppingstones made by our friends at Warm Springs. Calle Rose's tail wagged, and even Mariah's dog stood staring. I heard a trilling buzz and searched for the source.

The rattler coiled over the cougar-face steppingstone, evidently quite miffed that anyone dared to approach. A cat sat to the left, and all three dogs cocked their heads at the intruder. Dog three, Mariah's newest who came to us when she did, is a golden Lab named Rexamoondo. He'd spent the morning at the river helping Marc and Jerry with the irrigation system, or as Matt used to call it, the "irritation system."

After spying the snake, I had time enough to turn back, enter the house from the other deck, retrieve from the safe place the .38 Special revolver loaded with shot shells (foster families are not allowed to have unlocked guns in the house), let the dogs in, and stepped out on the other deck to see if the snake was still there or if he'd slithered off into the grass.

He was there. And the minute I stepped onto the deck, he began to buzz again, quite aggressively, since I was fifteen feet away and much too large for him to eat, and he had plenty of chance to disappear. I hoped I could hit him without breaking the steppingstone.

I did.

"Did you get it?" Jerry yelled from the river. He knew I'd only be shooting at a snake.

"Yes, but you'll have to come take it away!" I shouted back.

We haven't seen a rattler that close to the house for about five years. Perhaps it was lured here by the moist spring. I'd have thought that with the increased activity of more people and dogs, any smart snake would simply avoid us. Not so.

It's been an unusual month, so why not a rattler at the door?

I asked my niece Shorty to send postcards out as reminders of an event at a church in Eugene, but I gave her the wrong address! One night when the dogs barked to go out, I broke my fingernail. Seeing it lying on the floor, I picked it up, deciding I could glue it back on in the morning when I had my glasses on. In the morning, I discovered that instead of having a purple fingernail to glue, I had a dead fly. When I flew to Colorado Springs earlier in the month, I took my triple-A card and gas credit cards out of my wallet, and now I can't find where I put them. Last week I helped in the kitchen at the fine arts event (also a fund-raiser for Mariah's Spanish class). All I had to do was open bags of tortillas, put them into tinfoil, and warm them in the oven. I opened every single package with my teeth, thinking they ought to do something about the packaging, and only later, when another mom opened the zipper package, did I realize I'd opened every one from the bottom! "That's why you write," one mom said. And that's why Jerry cooks.

But then, it's been a time of stress. Retirement often is.

Last month, after learning that her parents had taken Mariah out of school and were homeschooling her now, I felt my stomach sink. Last year, after Matt once again decided to quit working by just never showing up, Jerry stopped talking to him. We kept paying for the phone in their house so Mariah could call out and we could sometimes contact her. I stopped by to see her parents, who sometimes invited me inside, more often didn't. Mariah looked tired but always answered cheerfully that she was fine. She was already fifteen.

When I learned of their plans to homeschool, though, I knew something must be very wrong. I think committed homeschool parents are terrific, but Matt and Melissa didn't have a history of following through on something as important as a child's high-school education. I asked to meet with them, and I shared my concerns that Mariah had such gifts that needed the nurture of regular school or formal education school. Neither parent wanted to hear me object to their decision; only Mariah said she was worried that I didn't think her homeschool education was a good idea.

I offered them money to send her to school; that's how fearful I was. They declined.

I left and drove to my Bible study. There four or five women heard me share my fears for this child, for her parents, for the brokenness of family. I pulled Kleenex tissues from the box all evening. But then we read Psalm 46.

I love those psalms! Surely the reading of them, all alone, could heal nations. The line that gave me peace was this: "Cease striving."

So simple, but to me it said we had done what we could, and now we had to let go and trust that God was still in control.

Exactly one week later, Mariah's parents were arrested. This time their charges included methamphetamine production and use, as well as child neglect. Once again the local sheriff allowed us to bring Mariah home. Then we began proceedings to care for her while her parents were incarcerated and while they'd go on, we hoped, to treatment.

Despite the chaos of the month, I learned things as we adjusted to Mariah being full time in our lives, proving that even during times of stress, we can still take in new information. Even old rats, they say, when given new mazes to learn, actually grow new brain cells. We counted on that.

Daria is a cute cartoon show, which is followed by a program called *Clueless,* where the only clueless people are the adults. Both have made me laugh aloud, and that's something, since I'm on overload with estrogen moments firing off like…well, like the buzzing of a rattler where you least expect it.

Parental units is a term that captures all the parenting souls in Mariah's life right now: her biological parents, the state, and us. Great term, one her friend used when checking in on her, as in "How are your parental units doing?"

The regional jail will not allow prisoners to have hardcover books, but inmates can have my paperbacks, and Matt and Melissa both asked for them. It's also very hard to find a journal without either a spiral or a hard cover. Both Matt and Melissa asked for journals to write in too.

Teenagers use a new towel every day. I'll be lifting one of the hotel cards about saving water to put in Mariah's bedroom (the former guest room, now covered in rock group posters) to remind her that it's all right to dry off with the same towel two days in a row if you don't leave it lying wet on the floor.

Thongs, as in teenage lingerie, are difficult to fold after laundering, and Mariah showed me that my laptop plays DVDs. I had no idea about either!

I see with new eyes, as Mariah says the lines coming *from* my eyes are "pigeon toes," and that little sag I call jowls, she refers to as "gills."

Every time I've gone into a store this month, it seems to have cost us a hundred dollars. Food? Shoes? Shampoo? How do parents of three, four, five do it? (This is a must-ask question for my nephew and Web site–managing niece who are the parents of five.

We moved the old clock that hadn't worked for fifteen years out of the guest room to make way for Mariah. A week later the clock started chiming as though it had never stopped. There is nothing we can do to stop the onward movement of time. Apparently there is nothing we can do to start time either. Old clocks pick their own time to tick.

We are blessed beyond measure with good friends willing to help out and hold us in their prayers, who supply resources enough to keep driving Mariah to school, make the doctor and dental appointments, and keep the connections necessary for her life to be as stable as it can be while her world changes, seemingly each minute, as the clock steadily ticks.

Prison ministries do amazing work, and this time might truly be the best time for Mariah's parents. As a gift, we learned that the woman who teaches a Bible class in the regional facility where Melissa is, is the wife of the lawyer we hired years ago to help us the first time Mariah came to live with us. Continuity. Details. God's grace. Enough.

God's timing is perfect. I retired from Warm Springs in order to write full time. Our homestead is able to survive off the farming activities and my writing and Jerry's retirement. One of the contractors who helped rebuild our fences after the fire called to say he heard we needed help. He's been working for us this past year. The vineyard teases us with new growth. As Ephesians 3:20 says, God "is able to do immeasurably more than all we ask or imagine."

During an activity at a retreat I led in May, I asked people to express to the person standing across from them in a circle something they hoped for that person in the coming months and weeks. Because our group was an uneven number, I had to participate too. The woman across from me looked thoughtful, then said, "Enough. May you be blessed with enough."

"Have you read *A Name of Her Own?*" I asked. "That's the theme of that book, that we are enough, will be enough to do the work we're set to do, our *métier,* as the French call it. What we lack, God will provide."

She hadn't read the book. "I just felt moved to tell you that you would be enough for what you have to do, that you'll have enough energy, enough patience, enough wisdom, enough to go around for all who need you."

I know God spoke through that woman's words, giving the gift of reassurance.

Enough.

My mom continues to improve, and I have enough energy to drive to Warm Springs to visit and spend some time with her. I had enough time to meet my deadlines. Another new book will include that little story of the printing press. We'll be visiting a variety of places in the Northwest; my brother and his family plan a visit; and Mariah and I will participate in Catherine's Legacy, a walk to honor a wonderful Wasco Indian woman who passed away just after my dad. I hope I have enough stamina to finish that walk and enjoy time with my brother.

"Have I turned yours and Grandpa's world upside down?" Mariah asked on the way to school one morning.

I thought about how to answer. "Our world is different, but you're not responsible for that," I said. "We made a choice when we agreed to have you live here. We decided what mattered was being there for you, giving you what you needed to carry on with your life, and having the courage to act on that. We're grateful God's provided a way for us to do that."

"I just didn't want to feel guilty for causing you and Grandpa's lives to be all mixed up because of me," she said.

"No need for you to feel guilty at all. We consider it a joy to have you here. You're not responsible for your parents' choices, either," I reminded her. "You have fewer choices, but you do have some: to make this time not just a time of grief and sorrow, but a time when you grew stronger, when you dealt with the unexpected and did what had to be done and did it well."

She did that. She studied, wrote papers, made more friends at school, read, shared her sadness with us, and her joys. She has a gift for art, a musical memory, and compassion and wonder in the way she sees the world.

"I ache for you, Matt," I told her father through the glass wall separating inmates from the outside world. "You're missing so much of her life, so much of her wonderful life."

"Look at me, Jane," he said, palms up, arms out. "You and dad are so much better able to parent her right now than either of us. We're just grateful you are there."

Will we be enough for the unexpected, for the demands of a child's life and our own? That's truly all we seek—to be enough. Well, maybe something more.

Our new gate sign (with thanks to poet mary ann radmacher) reads, *We seek neither convenience nor ease but to live at the edge of possibility.* We seek to live at the edge of what is possible for our son and his wife, for their child, for Jerry and me. We hope we are ready for the unexpected that lies there, be it a rattlesnake or the liveliness of a teenager gracing our days.

Being ready for the possibilities is, after all, what homesteading is truly all about.

40

Are You Ready?

"Are you ready?" the woman said.

The call came in at 6:00 a.m. to a motel in Idaho. Later in the morning I was scheduled to teach a writing class for the Idaho Writer's League, but the call woke me from a sound sleep. "Are you ready?"

It wasn't spoken with an "Are you ready? I've been waiting an hour for you" tone, sometimes expressed by Jerry.

It wasn't even that "Are you finished?" kind of "Are you ready?" said the way my mom asked it, when my sister and I prepared ourselves for Sunday school back in Wisconsin. Getting those old garter belts and heavy pink stockings situated on our schoolgirl frames took some "getting ready."

It wasn't asked with an editor's voice, waiting for me to attach my latest manuscript: "Are you ready?" As in, ready to send it?

"You must have the wrong number," I said.

She apologized and hung up.

But for two weeks afterward I couldn't get her voice or her question from my mind. Was I ready? And what was I ready for?

Maybe it was related to all the graduations that month. Was I ready to travel to them? Did I have all the presents? Hmm, no. Two special graduates were Lisa Tedder, the baby who was in utero during our airplane crash, and my sister-in-law and brother's son, Cohlman Rutschow.

Lisa arrived full term, is bright as the North Star, and will play volleyball in New York City's St. John's University next fall. Is she ready for how much her life will change from Coos Bay, Oregon, moving from one coastline to another, from the cradle of family and small town to the challenges of an urban life and extending and creating new family from the people she'll meet? Is she ready? I hope so. She's been given great gifts and wonderful intergenerational support through the years. But it'll be difficult to see her go, to know we'll have fewer and fewer opportunities to hug her fit, lean body, to hear her laughter. Are we ready to send her off? Maybe that's what the call meant.

My brother's son graduates from high school in Red Wing, Minnesota, and he'll pursue his interest in law enforcement and football. Cohlman is the kind of person who, as a citizen of this world, I want in law enforcement: kind, compassionate, a good listener, quick to respond, focused on solving problems rather than escalating them.

The military has talked with him, too, for positions in security or military police. Maybe someday he'll be asked to manage prisoners in a foreign place. I wonder if he's ready for the challenges that might face him there, challenges that can carve a person's character, the hero stories tell us, and challenges that require him to ask of himself, "Who are the families of these people I'm asked to interact with?" Or, "How did these prisoners (or people about to be arrested, or teenagers violating curfews, or drug dealers) arrive here, and am I ready for what I might be asked to do, ready to sort right from wrong, good from bad?" Is he ready to give orders that might save lives if obeyed or be described later as dereliction of duty? It's a hard world he faces. He's so young, so gentle, so sure that life has good things waiting. Am I ready to see him become a man, perhaps give up his life, or even more difficult, agree to kill another in order to protect my way of life? "Are you ready?"

Was it a graduation question, the readiness the woman spoke of? Maybe.

Or maybe it was the voice of Christmas past. She had a happy lilt to her voice, as though whatever I was to be ready for was going to be…pleasant, as memories often are. My sister has been on my mind this month. Her two oldest grandchildren won writing awards in Florida, and I know that if she'd lived, she'd have been there celebrating. She came to my graduation at the University of Wisconsin, and I could hear her shouting out my name from a high bleacher in the field house, above the seven thousand voices of the graduates. Three letters from readers this week made a connection that Judy Hurtley was my sister (the book set in Coos Bay, *A Gathering of Finches,* is dedicated to her), and they had stories to tell of her joy and compassion. I've been asked to participate in an anthology about sisters. Am I ready to write about Judy? I'm now older than my older sister was at the time of her death, so the question asks if I am ready to explore mortality and aging. Am I ready for the end? I'd like to think I am.

"Are you ready?" The woman held such promise in her question. Yet it haunts me, I think, because it says I must prepare.

Prepare for letting go. Mariah will be going back to her family at the end of the month, and I can't say that I am ready. I'm not ready to trust that this time it will be different, that the lion will go back to sleep. I'm not ready to do the work we'll have to do to grieve her going. She is excited about the growth of her parents, their jobs, their sobriety. She's ready to be back home, without the long drive to school, though she tells the stories now about her wintering on the ranch and having to ride in the baby Humphie (our golf cartlike six-wheel ranch vehicle) through the snow to meet her carpool kids. She talks like old veterans talk of their campaigns. She wasn't ready to arrive at our home fourteen months ago, and we weren't ready to have her, but we adapted. We got ready. And it changed our lives.

Are we ready for the empty places in the house, for getting our guest room back, for the return of the bathroom, which will smell of old people's powder now instead of tanning lotion and piña colada lip gloss? Am I ready? No, but it will happen anyway, and our greatest prayer is that we do this well, in ways that support and sustain her and her family and ourselves. Thank God we do not do this alone.

My appreciation has risen (and it was pretty high before!) for the gifts that foster parents give by providing all they do, knowing that a call will come one day, asking if they're ready to release a child to their biological family fold. They must always be ready: to accept a child, to give a child love and shelter and hope, and then, when that call comes, asking "Are you ready?" to let them go, when that means packing up the child's bags and saying good-bye. There's love in receiving and love in being ready to let go.

Kids are ready to try again, and as community, it's in our interest to support those transitions, knowing that children always do best when they are with parents who love them and meet their needs. Lots of parents love their kids; it's meeting their needs, putting a child's needs before their own, that they need to be ready to do. Lots of people believe Mariah's parents are ready, and we've also seen things to hold tight to. So she is going home.

Am I ready for the work that it will take to make this relationship keep growing? This child whom everyone around says has blossomed; this child who brought *Daria* and Netflix and the rock group Yes into our vocabulary is going home. We'll still see her, and she's even spending ten days with us at a family reunion and my nephew's graduation party—we're taking my mom to Minnesota with us too. The relationship isn't lost, but it is changing, and I don't know if I am ready.

I do know that with some things, it does not matter if I am ready or not. That childhood game, when we hid our eyes and counted, then said, "Ready or not!" prepared us for the way the world works. It will happen. There will be disappointment. We will grieve. We will change, even while protesting, "Wait, wait! I'm not ready!"

But it is the mark of our character how we come to terms with life-as-we-know-it having ended, how we allow others to help us find new direction in our wilderness places.

I'll cling to that verse in Isaiah that says "You will keep him in perfect peace, whose mind is stayed on You, because he trusts in You." Perfect peace.

Am I ready for that, or will I fill the space with duty, work, and worry? It is my choice, how ready I will be.

I take comfort in the memory that the woman who called sounded excited, as though she knew something that I didn't know, and it was pleasing. Maybe my fantasy when the Kinship and Courage Trilogy was chosen as a Doubleday Book Club selection would come true and that woman knew it! On that cherished book-club catalog page, an Anne Tyler novel took the top position. My three books came next, and at the bottom of the page was Charles Frazier's National Book Award–winner *Cold Mountain*. I was on the same page as best-selling authors Anne Tyler and Charles Frazier. Imagine that. And I'd just read that Charles Frazier had garnered an eight-million-dollar advance for his next book. Inspired, I copied the catalog page and faxed it to my publisher, WaterBrook Press, with a note that said: *I'll bet this is as close to an eight-million-dollar advance as I'm ever going to get.*

I'm ready for that.

I write this as we're traveling down I-84 toward Pendleton for a signing at Armchair Books on Dorion Street. I think of peace and the word *shalom,* a word that in Hebrew means "nothing missing, nothing broken." I don't know how that fits, but I think it means that if I trust God to be in control—of the future of young graduates, of young award-winning writers, of Mom's pacemaker working at top speed, or of a granddaughter moving forward with new skills—then I'm accepting that there is nothing missing in my life, nothing broken on this homestead, despite the ups and downs of more than the reptile road. Perhaps our coming to this homestead years ago was wrapped up in learning to be ready, to lean back and trust despite the struggles.

"Are you ready to put it all in God's peaceful hands?" That's my challenge, not only to get ready, but to *be* ready. Anticipation. Connection. Nothing broken despite what past memories step into the present to teach us, despite what future risks and realities bring.

41

When He Was Running

THE FIRST CHILD OF JERRY'S I met was his oldest son, Kevin. With a runner's lean body topped by tight, dark curls cut into the army's requirement, he arrived in Bend on leave. He walked with a limp. While serving with high security clearance in the DMZ, he and his friend had been struck by a drunk driver as they walked the streets of South Korea on a sunny afternoon. His buddy died at the scene. Jerry received a call in the night, saying his son was unconscious and wasn't expected to live. But Kevin did, and at Christmastime 1975 he came to be with his dad.

When I met him, we were visiting Jerry's parents' home in Prineville, Oregon. We'd barely begun dating, and I often wondered what Kevin thought of this almost-third-wife of his father. Kevin had kind, blue eyes like his dad, this son. And his face held a charming smile and a wistful look to it, as though life had already presented him with more challenges than it should for a young man who had recently turned twenty-one.

"He's cheated death twice now," Jerry told me as he described Kevin's earlier close call. As a high-school senior in Lake Havasu City, Arizona, Kevin missed his first-baseman spot in the school game due to the flu. In what everyone said was a freak event, the young man who took his place was struck by lightning and died.

Kevin was very much alive on this treasured Christmas day in 1975. I watched as he and his father talked together over my future mother-in-law's famous twenty-course holiday meal. They reminisced about hunting. Kevin said he used to hate hearing his father get ready for the opening of deer season, banging around downstairs, digging up sleeping bags and pack boxes. It wasn't something Kevin looked forward to. "Until we got out there in the wild," Kevin said. "I loved being in the mountains, riding horseback with my dad." They spoke of missed shots, of Kevin's allergy to rabbit brush that often cut their trips short, and I could see by the mutual respect and spark in their eyes that father and son were friends. I imagined that Jerry might have looked like Kevin when he was a young man. Jerry was four inches taller than his son, even with the inches he'd lost in his fall from a scaffolding two years before, breaking four vertebrae in his back.

When it came time to open presents, Kevin presented me, his father's latest girlfriend, with books and music. I hadn't written anything for publication at that point in my life. The idea wasn't even in my dreams, yet Kevin couldn't have presented me with more attentive gifts to feed the spirit and soothe the soul.

The next year, after Jerry and I married, Kevin was discharged from the army, and he returned to Bend to go to school. We were building a house then, and renting a mobile home whose owner frowned on our having a third resident, so we helped Kevin purchase a mobile home in town, close to the college, where he began classes, hoping someday to become a physician. We saw him off and on, but he was a busy student, and our lives, too, had taken on a frenzy. Matt arrived to spend the summer with us, and over the 1977 Fourth of July weekend, Kathleen, Jerry's daughter, traveled from Idaho with her kindergarten-age son. While Kathleen's husband of six months visited his family in Bend, she joined us for a traditional western roast of half a steer over a deep pit, an event where all three of Jerry's children were together for the last time.

We'd been out of telephone contact on our dentist friend's ranch while we watched the steer turn a crusty red at the pit. We shared wine and sodas with friends, returning to our Tumalo home after 8:00 p.m., the sun just starting to set over the mountains. We'd been away longer than planned but had enjoyed the family time together.

The phone rang. It was Kathleen's husband. They'd married earlier that year after just a few dates, and we'd discovered a volatile man. Over Mother's Day a few months before, his temper had sent Kathleen to the emergency room and him to the local jail. This time he was jealous and furious that Kathleen had not been back at our home when she had said she'd be. He'd been trying to reach her all afternoon, and by the time he did, his outrage reached a dangerous height.

Jerry took the phone in defense of why Kathleen had been unreachable. "They have no phone at that old ranch," Jerry told him. "She was with us the whole time. No, it was our fault she wasn't near a phone." Nothing Jerry said seemed to appease him, and then suddenly Jerry handed the phone to Kathleen and went into the back room. She listened, but her husband had apparently hung up. Her father came back into the room carrying a pistol. "He's coming over here to shoot me," my husband said. "Told me I wouldn't again interfere with him and his wife."

"Call the police," I said.

"He'll get here first," Jerry said, securing his weapon.

Kevin, too, prepared to defend her, us. Matt paced, chewed at the side of his nails. Kathleen's five-year-old son, blessedly, played outside with the dogs. My heart pounded. How could this be happening, this totally unacceptable way of resolving a problem, here in our home, in the shadow of our new marriage? Was this what blending families was all about? Was this how my husband handled family problems?

"Can't you see what will happen?" I asked my stepdaughter. "Your husband is on his way over here to shoot your father, you, maybe all of us. What do you want in this marriage? You've got to get clear. This is your turning point."

She wanted out. The marriage had been impulsive. She'd been abused by him, and she worried over her son's safety too. She was sure her husband wasn't happy either.

"Then call him back. Tell him that you know he doesn't want to hurt anyone and that this is between the two of you and that perhaps it really is time to call it quits. Give him an out with some honor. Let him know he doesn't have to escalate this to make a change."

She called him back, caught him before he rushed out the door, and told him that, and thankfully, he agreed. He spoke to Jerry briefly on the phone to reassure him that he'd taken back his threat. He and Kathleen began that afternoon the nonviolent dissolution of their marriage.

But the memory of the heat of that moment never left me, seeing family defenders splayed out like she-wolves with pups at their side, recognizing that my husband's absolute willingness to do whatever was necessary to protect his child had a power far beyond my own meek words.

Jerry drove back to Idaho that weekend to help Kathleen move her things to Bend while her five-year-old son spent the long weekend with me. After a significant negotiation to get him to wear unmatched pajama bottoms and tops, he begged to be allowed to sleep with me, afraid to be alone on his mat. He kicked through the night, a restless sleeper, but then he was only five years old and had witnessed too much already, I suspected. Now he'd been left alone with a woman he'd spent little time with, a "grandmother" whose name he might not even know, while his grandfather and mother disappeared. He could only hope they'd return.

Later that summer Kevin told us he had a chance to earn good money that he could put aside for school. A friend had worked the Trans-Alaska Pipeline and made a "fortune." Another friend had told him of a job in the South that promised equal riches. If he went to Tucson for the interview, there was a good chance he'd be hired.

The day before he left, he sat at the kitchen counter, talking about his year away from school. That's all it was meant to be, just enough to pay for the next year. He'd let his hair grow out into a bushy Afro style that made him look slightly unbalanced, with his frame as slender as a cigarette. He'd tried to run again, something he'd done in high-school track with success, but the bad leg just hadn't held up. He cajoled himself about gaining height, someday, sharing research he'd read that people didn't stop growing at sixteen. His younger brother, Matt, had four inches on him already. He was hopeful, he said, and grinned. He spoke with anticipation about the job interview and seeing his friend of the same name, where he planned to stay a few extra days in Lake Havasu City.

"Call your mother," I told him. The two had been estranged since his parents' divorce, and he rarely called her or wrote. I'd yet to meet his mother. "She'll want to know about your change of plans, to drop out of school for a year."

He sat at our kitchen counter, his narrow shoulders leaned back against the wall, as he talked to her. He was vague about the job, said he'd know more once he got there, and didn't commit to any time he'd be calling her again. He was vague with us, too, about when the interview was, when he'd be back, and all the details. "One of these days you're going to slide off the side of the road and be stuck in your car, and no one will even come to look for you, because they won't have any reason for alarm," I told him. "You've got to be more definite, and remember to call if you're going to be late."

He grinned that charming smile. Spontaneity was one of his virtues; offering information up wasn't.

His girlfriend called us first. She had a worried tone to her voice, but not a panic, exactly. It was after Labor Day weekend, and she'd gotten a call from Kevin the Friday before, saying he was leaving Tucson, heading for Las Vegas, where he'd catch a flight to Portland. He asked her to drive to that city, stay with friends there, and he'd be calling from Las Vegas when he knew his flight number and arrival time. She'd driven the three hours to Portland and waited. He hadn't called or shown up, and she'd cursed him through Labor Day and then all the way back to Bend to attend classes. She said that there'd been one strange phone call in the wee hours of Sunday morning, with a voice, not Kevin's, saying Kevin would be delayed. That was all. The digital clock said 1:26 a.m.

"He's always behind schedule," Jerry said when she drove out to talk further. "He was a week overdue when he came home from the army."

"This is different," she said. "He wouldn't ask me to drive all that way and then not contact me. It's just not like him. He got the job. He was coming home to get his stuff and go back."

"So what do you think?" Jerry asked.

She shrugged her shoulders, the hoop earrings she wore swinging.

"Maybe he plans to go to work from there and come back next weekend for his things," Jerry said.

"Maybe," Kevin's girlfriend said.

The following week, Kevin's high-school friend called, his voice strident, asking where Kevin was, saying he was supposed to show up in Virginia for this job and he hadn't appeared, and he was in a world of trouble, since he'd recommended Kevin. He'd been with his friend in Lake Havasu, and as far as his friend knew, Kevin had left for Portland.

"You contact the Lake Havasu police department and report him missing," Jerry said. "We'll list him missing from here."

There are two ways to leave Lake Havasu and arrive in Las Vegas: through Kingman, Arizona, or Needles, California. Jerry asked the local sheriff deputy to send a missing-person's report to all four states: Arizona, Nevada, California, and Oregon, assuming that he'd made it that far. Jerry gave a physical description, but not knowing whom Kevin had gotten a ride with to the Las Vegas airport, or what he was wearing, or when he'd supposedly left, Jerry couldn't be very specific. We could only hope that if something showed up, they might make a linkage.

The next weeks we went on about our business in the shadow of the mountains and the uncertainty. Jerry let Kevin's mother know, so if she heard from him, she'd please let us know. Matt flew back to Florida to start school, frustrated that he hadn't had a chance to tell his brother good-bye, a frustration that defined his life, I think now, looking back.

I hoped that it was one of Kevin's lapses, his not realizing how others worried. I imagined what we'd say to him when he walked through the door, looking fit, and wondering with those deep blue eyes and his engaging smile what all the fuss was about.

His grandmother sent prayer requests around the country. She'd served as an evangelist for years and knew hundreds of people who would pray for Kevin's safe return. One day she called us with joy in her voice, saying that her friend from California told her she'd been praying for Kevin. "God told me that while 'Kevin was running, he called My name and that everything will be all right.'" Jerry's mother was cheered by this news, and I wanted to hang on to its hopefulness too, especially for Jerry and for Kevin's mother and their children.

Kevin's twenty-third birthday passed without a word from him.

I knew my husband to be a caring father. In fact, the day I met him, while he recovered from his back injury at my sister's ranch, I was most impressed that he knew the birth dates of his children, all three of them, and that he spoke of their mother with kindness and respect. There are sides to another human being one can't know about, though, until someone is challenged, like that day in July when I wondered if violence would be the way to solve a marriage problem. I'd seen my husband rise to his daughter's defense in a volatile way, calm down in an instant, then assist her to make a new life. I had no idea how he'd respond to bad news of his son, to the unthinkable.

One evening, while we changed the irrigation on our five acres, long before we even thought of a homestead far away, I broached the subject. "It's possible that Kevin might not come back," I told Jerry.

Jerry stared at the Cascade Mountains, which were sporting a new dusting of white. "He climbed all Three Sisters in one day; did I ever tell you that?" Jerry asked.

"Kevin did? All three mountains?"

Jerry staked a sprinkler, to keep it from falling over and gouging a ditch with the persistent flow of water gone awry.

"What if he doesn't—"

"I can't talk about 'what if,'" Jerry said. "We'll cross that bridge if we come to it."

In late September we came to that bridge.

I don't remember now which came first, the call telling us to contact the sheriff in Arizona or the arrival of the Deschutes County sheriff's deputy at our doorstep. It seems strange to me to be confused about that part of the sequence. Perhaps the neighbors called us at Jerry's parents' house, where we were spending a Sunday afternoon in late September 1977. Maybe they told us that a sheriff's car had been out at the house but left. That might have been it. I remember being anxious on the way back from his parents'. I remember the brown officer's uniform standing at the door later, then Jerry's turning to me, eyes already pooling, saying that Kevin was dead.

My husband left then and walked out into the night.

My first phone call reached my parents, who lived just a few minutes away on my sister's ranch. My sister and my brother-in-law came with them, and we sat and waited for Jerry to come back in from the dark, my heart eclipsed with pain for him, a pain I couldn't know as he did, the loss of a child. My pain wrapped itself in my own selfish wonderings about how such a grief might change a person, a family, a future; and I grieved my inability to ease Jerry's sorrow. No one ever prepares for the death of child. There's no way to do it.

Jerry did come in, and then a call came from the Southwest, asking us to gather Kevin's girlfriend and any other friends for a phone call the following evening. The detective hoped to collect information about time lines, learn where Kevin had been, get some sense of his whereabouts. They felt sure, though, that it was Kevin's body they'd found, and they asked that dental records be sent to verify.

The next evening, we answered the questions as best we could, and when the detective finished with us, he chastised us. "Why didn't you people put out a missing-person's report?"

"We did," I told him. "Kevin's friend put one out there, and we put one out to three states through our county."

"Well, none of them ever showed up," the detective said. "I've had people scanning for missing persons for weeks."

"For weeks?"

"Yeah, and that means a cold trail," the detective said. "We've been trying to figure out who he is, when I should have been trailing who did it."

"When did Kevin die?" I asked, thinking it had just happened, thinking it was a car wreck or something, where he'd been pinned, and they'd just found the wreckage.

"Labor Day weekend. He had no identification on him."

Nearly a month before. "But how did you find us, then?"

"I figured his age and started going door to door with a photo of him, a pretty bad one, given the 110-degree heat on that shooting range the night we found him. But I finally got to a door of someone who knew him and who said he had his suitcase. We went through it and found his address book—and you."

"Shooting range? How did he die?" I asked.

"He was murdered."

Jerry and I left the next morning for Arizona. I hadn't seen Jerry cry, hadn't felt him reach for me to salve a broken heart. He'd called Kevin's mother, who made arrangements to fly to Oregon, and, along with Matt, to stay with Jerry's parents until we returned. Jerry called Kathleen and Miles, Kevin's best boyhood friend from Ohio, and with each call, his voice was firm, certain. "Kevin's been killed. We don't know the details. We're heading south to bring his body home."

I wondered if Jerry would rail at God for the loss of this son. Or at me for not making room in our home for Kevin to live in. Maybe we could have mortgaged the house to pay for his college so he wouldn't have had to go south to work. Maybe we could have invited Kevin to live with us, to make his future easier. I imagined Jerry sinking into despair, going someplace deep and dark, a place I might never share. His silence hinted at a separation as wide as the Three Sisters Mountains are high.

We spent the first night on the way to Arizona in a small sleepy town in the Nevada Mountains, in a motel with paper-thin walls. The black-and-white television flickered *Lavern and Shirley,* and something those two characters did, some antic too ridiculous to ever happen, began my laughing. I laughed at those women until the gasps and laughing tears turned into sobs, deep wrenching sobs I couldn't stop. Jerry held me, and then he, too, began to weep, to cry for all the things Kevin would never know again: the touch of a woman's skin, the scent of a mountain morning, the feel of a horse beneath him, the wind on his face, laughter and life so filling that a man's heart could burst with the joy of it.

Nevermore.

We held each other grieving through the night, and I remembered then that when Native American healers come to heal a person, they ask three questions: when was the last time you laughed; when was the last time you danced; when was the last time you told your story?

We reached Lake Havasu City midday. It was early October, hot, with the leaves of the cottonwood trees brushed yellow. We drove directly to the police station. We'd brought with us letters we'd found in Kevin's home when we'd gone there the night we'd learned of his death. They were from friends in Korea and other places, and they spoke of transporting "things." Kevin didn't live like someone who'd made fast or illegal money. He was a poor college student planning to work for a year to raise funds; but with his charming ways, we could see him agreeing to traffic, to "help a friend out." We had no idea if it had anything to do with his death, but it was information, and it was all we had left to share, vague information of a loved, lost son.

They showed us Kevin's jewelry, a unique necklace he'd worn and a ring. But the designs were black and pitted, and I objected. "These can't be his. He always kept them shined," I said. "He was neat and tidy."

"He was wearing them, ma'am. When we found him," the detective said. "In that heat, the metal would begin to be affected by the body's decomposition almost immediately. That's what caused the pitting."

"Oh," I said, details of a death I found I didn't really want to know.

But Jerry wanted every detail. He wanted to know if Kevin had been armed, or where his pistol might be. He wanted to know what they knew, every shred of evidence they'd gathered up. He wanted to visit Kevin's friend, the one who hadn't gone to the police station; but then he learned that our own county had failed to put out the missing-person's report because it was "too vague and covered too many states to make any sense." People were being interviewed, the detective said. It would be best if we didn't try to talk to any of Kevin's friends.

We ate dinner with the officer that evening, and he told us he rarely gave these kinds of specifics to a family, but that Jerry had seemed both willing and capable of hearing what they knew. They believed Kevin had gotten into a car, either with someone he knew or someone a trusted friend had told him would be a safe ride to Las Vegas. Instead, he'd been driven to a shooting range, where the sound of a weapon's discharge wouldn't be noticed. Since his body had not been moved after his death, the police assumed his ID had been taken from him in the car, so that Kevin would have known that something bad was going down. They found tire tracks in the hard sand that showed where the car stopped. Two sets of footprints, one in front of the other, and the leading footprints bolting and running.

I could almost see Kevin running through arroyos and toward mesquite bushes. He lost his sandals. He zigged and zagged and almost made it to the cover of the brush.

The second set of footsteps stopped, set firm. It's from there the shot was made. One shot, at a moving target, at the back of his head, felling Kevin.

"Was it… Did he feel any pain?" I asked.

"Instant," the detective said, his eyes looking at Jerry, then away. "He would have died instantly. He just had a little time to run and pray."

We had the body cremated. The heat of the desert eliminated any kind of funeral showing. While we worked through the paper details to take custody of his remains, Jerry and I savored our fondest memories of Kevin; mine with him sitting at the kitchen counter talking to his mom; Jerry's on a hunting trip in Steen's Mountain where the two had camped together for a week.

After some confusion about the release of his body, since an investigation still pended, we drove to the coroner to bring Kevin home. I waited out in the car, my dress sticky with heat against the car seat, eyes swollen from tears. When Jerry came out carrying a small metal box, I opened the car trunk. He stood there a moment and then he wept. The small metal box harboring Kevin's ashes was the color of the mountains. "He weighs about what he did when he was born and I brought him home from the hospital."

I met Lelah, Kevin's mother, the day after we returned from Arizona. She stayed with us those four nights or so, leaning on the father of her son through the memorial, the burial at the Tumalo Cemetery, with a view of the Cascade Mountains Kevin loved. I came to like this woman and later, yes, to love her and to grieve with her as we struggled with Matt's addictions. Still later, as she dealt with an aggressive cancer that took her life, she said the kindest words to me: "You're a good friend. I leave my children in good hands."

That fall of 1977, after the memorial service, she and Matt returned to Florida. We never learned who killed Kevin or why. The detective thought that some day some professional killer would confess to a string of crimes committed in the Southwest desert, and maybe Kevin's death would be explained by one of those. It appeared to be a professional killing, and since Kevin hadn't been in the area but a few days when it happened, it might have been a mistaken identity. Or perhaps he had taken money for transporting drugs and stepped into a pit he'd had no time to crawl out of. Neither his identification nor the sandals the killer retrieved from the desert sand ever showed up.

In 2004 I had a dream while attending the Festival of Faith and Writing at Calvin College in Michigan. Robert Redford, in my dream, told me to write about my family. When I awoke, I told my friend and roommate that I'd been doing that for years, trying to find myself inside these stories of enduring women, family connections, and despair, landscapes, spirituality, and the healing nature of work. Most of my stories are about wilderness places, living with ambivalence, unanswered questions, seeking new ways, and letting others help us in our vulnerability.

They are about running, too, I realized as I thought about that dream to write about family.

Sometimes I think we've all been running from the grief and loss of Kevin's life. Maybe his death spoke to Jerry about the fleetingness of life, showing him that if one is to live fully, one must live now, aware of God's guidance, trusting in that presence, and taking risks that might to some seem foolish. Maybe we are on this homestead still because we wanted to celebrate what Kevin couldn't, to live at the edge of possibility, even at the risk that we might fail.

Perhaps we "enabled" Matt and Melissa when we should have let our children stumble and fall. I often told families in counseling who said such things that we all do the best we can; no one ever starts out saying, "I think I'll mess up in raising my kids." We could remind ourselves of that as well.

The homestead gave a place for work to offer healing to Jerry's youngest son. Once, during the first custody hearing related to Matt and Melissa's drug addiction, Jerry told Matt, "I've lost one son. I don't want to lose another." Matt responded, "And I suppose that's my fault too," telling me that we all carried unrequited grief, the separation between us all as distant as the mountains are tall.

Perhaps we harbor guilt—for somehow not preventing such a grievous loss as that of a child's life, and later, for not being able to help Matt and Melissa or to protect Mariah from the chaos of her parents' troubled choices. Living looks like this, though, the wrinkles of decision mixed with the smoothness of attentive moments that thrill us. Losing someone young, someone you love, has a way of crystallizing life, making us either hard and firm or open to the sweetness. I've been forever grateful that Jerry chose the sweetness.

As I write this, Mariah is back home with her parents. She lived with us for more than a year, bringing us joy and taking some with her, we hope. Her parents hit bottom, as they say in the recovery world. It's been over two years since their initial arrest, and now they've been out, employed, keeping treatment connections. They have a church family. Their lives know the presence of prayer. With them and with Jerry's daughter and family, we've begun the dialogue of saying good-bye to Kevin in healthy ways, letting his life and now death bring us together again, prevent us from running away from the loss or each other and running toward the abundance of life.

Maybe all the stories I find to tell, the abundant resources God has provided so that we can stay here on this homestead, are a part of our running too. Not running from the loss of Kevin's life, but running *toward* the life Kevin never had the chance to know. We run to find meaning, knowing life is short yet beautiful, running to let tragedy transform instead of holding us hostage.

Kevin's childhood friend called us on the twenty-fifth anniversary of Kevin's death and unsolved murder, one of the few such homicides in that county in Arizona. He'd been trying to get them to consider reopening the case after all these years. "Maybe he's in the witness protection program," Kevin's friend said. "He had a top security clearance. Maybe they moved him, and he's living somewhere warm, and dancing and having a good life with his wife and kids."

Tragedies happen, I thought, remembering a William Stafford poem I'd come to love. "People get hurt or die; / and you suffer and get old." What get us through are the threads we weave through our trials. There's an old German saying: "Begin to weave; God provides the thread." That's the thread we've come to count on.

"Don't you ever wonder if it might be so?" Kevin's friend said. The longing in his voice made me ache.

"The dental records matched. He'd dead, Miles. I'm sorry."

"How do you live with it? How does Jerry?" he said.

"Something his grandmother's friend told her when we were all praying for Kevin, hoping he'd return alive, gives us comfort." I didn't know if he'd remember it, but her words have reminded us through the years during troubled and turbulent times. " 'When he was running, he called My name,' she said God told her in her prayers. 'And everything will be all right.'"

It's the thread we hang on to, running toward something while calling God's name. It's that hope that carries us each day to the edge of possibility.

Epilogue

The Dance

WE HAVE NO IDEA how much longer we'll be allowed to stay here on this homestead. We tire. This January while Jerry fed the cows, I pulled the hose to fill their water tank. After I opened the gate for Jerry, I walked back with the puppy, a wirehaired pointing griffon who looks like *Star Wars'* Chewbacca but who we named Fritz. As I approached the tank, I could see that the hose had pulled out and was stuck in the fence. But the arc of the water was still perfect. The tank hadn't overflowed, and water hadn't sprayed everywhere to form hazardous ice for the cows. I was so grateful for this little gift that I said to the dog, "This is my lucky day!" Then I promptly tripped and broke my arm.

I knew it was broken as I lay there, praying it wasn't. I had a book to write, work to do. But I could see the bone out where it didn't belong. It was the same arm I'd broken in the airplane crash seventeen years before. I slowly got to my feet. With one hand I got the gate open, turned off the water, then signaled to Jerry. He got out of the tractor, and I yelled, "I think I broke my arm."

"Oh no," he said, all filled with compassion.

I expected him to come down toward the tank and whisk me into his arms, then rush me to the emergency room. Instead he calmly got back into the tractor and finished feeding. When he finally came to where I waited, I said, "I don't believe you did that." He told me he knew we'd be spending the day at the hospital and he really wanted to get the cows fed first. "If we were newlyweds, you'd have been down here in a minute," I said. He just smiled and drove me the fifty-two miles to the same doctor who fixed my arm the last time.

Later when I mentioned my newlywed comment to a friend, she said, "If you were newlyweds, you wouldn't have been out there feeding those cows in below zero-weather." But I think we would have been. It's what homesteading is really all about, dealing with things together.

In March 2005 my mother had a stroke and later passed away. A week later Jerry was diagnosed with bladder cancer. We've learned new vocabulary where the rocks on our trail have new names. After two surgeries to remove his malignant tumor, we prepared for the next step, BCG treatments known as "acid washes," which sounds like something from a macabre novel. Live (attenuated) bovine tuberculosis virus is injected into Jerry's bladder through the urethra. It's supposed to kill the cancer. One wonders how that discovery was made, that such a virus could help treat bladder cancer. (I could imagine a researcher coming home to tell his wife of such a discovery.) Anyway, before the weekly treatments began, Jerry signed many waivers related to possible side effects of using this virus. We were given strict in-structions about how to handle voiding following the treatments. Jerry was told to be very careful not to "splash." And after voiding, we were to pour two cups of bleach into the toilet bowl and allow it sit for twenty minutes before flushing it down. "What if I used a urinal?" Jerry asked. We were staying at Ellis's home during the treatments and wanted to avoid any contamination. The nurse agreed that was a great idea.

So after the first treatment, we did as we were told. In his brother's bathroom, Jerry used the urinal. I added lemon bleach, and he put the cap on the plastic urinal so nothing escaped into the air. He turned to say something when out of the urinal soared an explosion of foam! Lemon bleach foam and acid sailed up to the ceiling, attacked the windows, and slithered down the mirrors, the sink, and the floor. We hacked and coughed from the bleach, and Jerry scolded, "It was the lemon! You shouldn't have bought lemon bleach."

All I could think was we were inhaling a virus, exposing his brother's household to contamination, and we'd need a HazMat team to come in and make it safe.

We scrubbed and cleaned and tossed the rags in special garbage bags. I called my nurse friend who assured us we very likely wouldn't die. We'd created a bathroom bomb (terrorists take note!) by not having a proper concentration of water. We'd poured bleach into acid. I was never good at chemistry. It was Lucy and Ricky having a very bad day.

The attenuated virus is used to inoculate people against tuberculosis, we learned. It actually tells the immune system to wake up and resist the cancerous intruder. It certainly woke us up and reminded us that laughter, love, and the kindness of family and friends have been our constant companions on this homesteading journey.

That and adapting.

The winters have been dramatic for their ice and snow. The dike is likely to need rebuilding once again this spring. We have Dexter cows now, Irish house cows they're called. We sell the meat as range-fed beef, low fat and flavorful. Last winter we fed them across the river, putting hay in the boat, until the river froze over. This fall the road softened while Jerry took calves to market, and the trailer sank into a switchback ravine, tearing up the side of the truck but leaving the calves free, a reprieve from their trip to the butcher. The cows still trouble our days, but Matt's back working for us full time and, with good cheer and sobriety, moves them back in when they break through the fences.

Jerry wistfully thinks about getting another plane. I tell him when a book is optioned for a movie, we can consider it, figuring I'm safe. We have alfalfa to harvest again. The grapes are growing back, and perhaps this year we'll put the energy into them they need.

Or not.

The fruits of words have become our yield for both Jerry and me, researching, writing, talking to people about the power of story in their lives; reminding ourselves that our lives are the stories other people read first. Going to the land to write has taken us to states and places across the ocean, entwined our remote homestead with cultures different from our own. Amazingly, I've just finished penning my twelfth novel, fourteenth book; I have contracts now to write four more. The books have been selections of the Literary Guild, Book of the Month, Doubleday Book clubs and Crossings International, so I hear on my Web site from people in New Zealand, Germany, South Africa, and France. The very first novel, the one written as an act of commitment and trust was named by the Oregon Heritage Commission as one of Oregon's 100 Best Books published about Oregon in the past two hundred years. *Awards.* I doubt that I'd have written a thing for others to read if we hadn't driven down that reptile road to make a home here, followed our hearts.

Once at a signing, a man pushed up toward the front, holding the first edition of *Homestead.* He had long hair, kind of wild eyes, and he spoke loud enough for everyone to hear. "This book changed my life! I sold my home in Portland. I bought 220 acres on the other side of Prineville. I'm off the grid. I'm living in a tipi. I'm chopping wood. I'm so happy!"

My first thought was a hope that he wasn't married. But my second thought was how wonderful that he had found a place of nurture, received courage through our story.

Jerry and I loved to dance. We've square-danced and danced across ballrooms; at weddings we close down the band. But after the airplane accident, the one time we tried to go dancing—aside from the day our casts came off—we realized this was an activity we'd have to give up. Jerry's hip hurt too much; my right foot just can't stand the pain. Not much residue from a major plane accident. It could have been so much worse.

One day, not long ago, though, while I dusted with lemon Pledge and listened to Linda Ronstadt and Aaron Neville sing "I Don't Know Much but I Know I Love You," Jerry said, "When you finish dusting that table, I might like to dance to this song." He sat in the big chair with his blue coveralls on, a section of his white hair brushing his forehead.

"If I finish dusting this thing, the song will be over," I said.

"I was afraid you'd say that."

That day Jerry stood, took the furniture polish from my hand, set it down, and took me in his arms. We began to dance. The dogs, splayed about the living-room floor, stared up at us, stunned.

It was awkward at first. He had to adjust to my shifted position; I had to lean a little to his right, change where I held my hands. But we did it! We found a position through trial and error, found a way to hold each other tight as we moved across the oak floor. And isn't that what life is about, that adjusting and holding each other, moving to rhythms that may not last forever but are worthy of witness and treasure?

I looked out through the window at the ribbon of river, the rocks, the vineyard—such as it is. Cows munched on the flat; Henry, the last of our mules, ripped at grass. Cows with long horns dotted the rimrocks in the distance. Dogs panted at our feet. As Jerry swung me around, I realized I'd never been happier in my life than I was at that moment. I told Jerry so. He pulled me closer. "And I almost missed it," I whispered. "I almost passed this up."

I almost let my fears hold me hostage, let my dreams become clouded and gray with the strings of perfection, the need to be orderly, to never look foolish, hemming me in while God promised, oh, so much more.

The Hebrew word for "salvation" translates as "to make wide" and "to heal." When people come to visit, they say our homestead is a healing place, and so it's been for us and for our family, too, we believe. Jerry still has a bad back, gotten worse through the years; my foot can tell the weather days before the forecast can. I tell people who read the earlier version of *Homestead* that it is not a how-to-do-it book. We made many mistakes, many tracks, as writer Wendell Berry notes about the fox, some in the wrong direction. But perhaps it is a how-to book after all. Through the words, we've "made wide" that healing, which has not come from my writing so much as from the willingness to follow a dream, however strange it looked to many, including myself, nearly twenty-five years ago, when we first drove down that reptile road.

Because of the writing, I was privileged to travel to Europe to speak with teachers around the world, telling stories. I'm writing my thirteenth novel. Matt, Melissa, and Mariah will join us for Christmas this year. Matt and his dad fish together. And when the people from France ordered flowers to thank me for participating in their conference, Melissa, working in Condon at Country Flowers and Gifts, took the order and hand-delivered the arrangement down the reptile road. With his daughter and family, we plan a gathering around Jerry's seventy-fifth birthday, to create memories without the pain of death and destruction. We'll gather together for the first time since Kevin's death. We hope there'll be laughing and dancing and storytelling.

"Nothing but good things came from all this, Grandma," Mariah told me one day as she looked back on her time of living on the homestead.

On this land we have known a life rich beyond measure, and we share our story as an invitation to all who read it to trust in the faithfulness of God's promise, the one from Jeremiah: "I know the thoughts that I think toward you, says the LORD, thoughts of peace and not of evil, to give you a future and a hope."

Not all has gone well as we've danced on this land. Accidents, arrests, illness have plagued us. But such visits come to all lives, to all families. We have chosen to keep dreaming and to remain here for as long as we're allowed, because, as the poet W. H. Auden wrote, "I know nothing but what everyone knows: / If there when Grace dances, I should dance."

We have truly danced with grace, and wish such music for each of you. Thank you for sharing our journey.

Jane Kirkpatrick
www.jkbooks.com